New Dimensions in Supervision

STANLEY W. WILLIAMS

California State University, Long Beach

INTEXT EDUCATIONAL PUBLISHERS
College Division of **Intext**
Scranton / San Francisco / Toronto / London

U-QN-RC

ISBN 0–7002–2397–5

Library of Congress Catalog Card Number: 70–183722

Copyright ©, 1972, International Textbook Company

To my mother
LAURA WHITE WILLIAMS

whose interest and encouragement over the years made the production of this book possible

Preface

American schools are currently engaged in one of the most comprehensive considerations of the manner in which educational planning and development can take place and who or what agencies are responsible for this task. In the process of making essential changes in the educational program, the decade of the seventies has opened new vistas as to how and in what ways this important mission shall be accomplished. In view of the broad nature of the educational enterprise, the very real task of getting people to work together, the societal barriers that confront the progressive movement of the organization, and the need for a work-oriented approach to the evolvement of the teaching-learning function, it becomes apparent that the educational task force must characterize its activities in terms of maximum cooperation with a minimum of conflict. How to do this in an intelligent, thoughtful, and collegial fashion is what this discussion concerns itself with.

Recent research indicates that not just one or even a very few persons are responsible for instructional leadership, but that many individuals contribute to the total improvement of the educational program found in any outstanding school district or school building. Many persons share in this effort: faculty members, supervisors, principals, consultants, counselors, department heads, student and community leaders, district administrators, and many others. There no longer exists a simple leader-and-follower relationship in which there is inferred a superior-inferior stance. Under these circumstances supervision became a simple "telling" process—a technique that went out of vogue twenty-five years ago. Today status leaders direct their attention and effort to the cooperative nature of the task of improving the curriculum and the instructional program. They help the faculty to identify problems, establish priorities for attacking them, recognize the parameters that must govern their activities and attention, provide the guidelines for action that should lead to their solution, and specify the options that may have to be taken. Basic to this approach is the establishment of a common desire on the part of the educational community that improved changes in behavior should be expected by all participants.

Each affirmative action by the organization, if it is to increase its capacity to meet its mission, requires a commitment. Some of these commitments are found in a determination to promote long-range planning, balance research with practice, promote the extension of communication opportunities, seek the improvement of measurement of the success or failure of the educational venture, and effectively release the talents of members of the organization to pursue excellence in improving the teaching-learning act. The tempo of increased dialogue should be encouraged between the individual and his organization so that creativity is not stifled and, in fact, a reasonable amount of divergence and dissent should be expected. Open communication channels are essential to the movement upward of suggestions, ideas, and concepts from the members of the organization within the hierarchical structure, as well as the downward sharing of information, knowledge, and facts essential to the welfare of the institution. In effect, communication on fundamental issues must flow on a unilateral basis from one group to another as teachers, administrators, and others become participants in strong organizational movements within the educational, economic, or political sphere.

In any organization there has to be a driving force that assumes the responsibility for certain phases of task accomplishment. Much as the teacher assumes the responsibility of energizing the productivity of the pupil's learning experiences in the classroom, supervisory personnel must be held accountable for capturing the imagination of the teaching staff as to the many professional potentialities that can and should be satisfied. Supervision implies purpose which, in turn, requires fulfillment if the well-being and health of the organization is to be maintained and improved. Purpose is not or should not be a static element; it must be accomplished through a time-line procedure in which the status leaders are concerned with cycles and strategies of time required to accomplish rational purposes set before them. Supervision must be a visible affair; its accomplishments in helping the faculty with goal achievement should be known and respected, yet its attainment of agreement and consensus among professional educators as to mode and direction is better down-staged than otherwise. In other words, the skill of relating people to a variety of situations, interpreting causal and reaction patterns that perplex organizations, and having the vision to garner the educational forces in the community to work cooperatively toward the solution of common problems, represent basic functions that must be performed through supervision.

No thesis is advocated that supervision is inviolate—that this function of status leaders in educational planning and development may not some day in the future be replaced by a more perfect collegial authority in which accountability and responsibility for goal accomplishment and assessment is a task uniformly shared by all educators. This would be the ultimate development in promoting educational change and reform.

However, even greater task allocation and specificity in tomorrow's schools would demand that someone assume this responsibility for the group, and the supervision function, in another form, would still exist. Group purpose requires action and decision and that is what supervision is all about.

The author wishes to express appreciation to Dr. Harry L. Tennyson, former Superintendent of Schools, Lehighton, Pennsylvania, for his professional advice on the manuscript in its final stages. To his wife, Patricia, and their daughters, Anne, Katherine, Marilyn, and Laurie, he offers his gratitude for their patience and understanding while he spent long hours in travel, research, and writing related to this work.

Stanley W. Williams

Anaheim, California
January 1972

Contents

Leadership and Change

Part One discusses the creative, shared leadership role to be assumed by persons involved in curriculum planning and development programs in the elementary and secondary schools. In fulfilling the supervisory task, great emphasis is placed on the process of changing educational programs and how the strategy of change is developed. There is recognition throughout Part One of the high priorities that the instructional leader establishes for himself; these will determine, in large measure, the essential shifts being made during the decade of the seventies in the areas of educational exploration, experimentation, and research. However, the occasional serious and disastrous results of conflicts between status leaders and teachers, as an organized group and as individuals, cannot be overlooked. Many factors related to sociological influence are considered and viewed as to the manner in which they affect the change process, as well as new dimensions for status leadership.

The developing of a set of major commitments to education and the constant task of redesigning educational programs recognize the criticial role that the supervisor plays in furthering the quality of the educational program. Great strides have been taken in the preparation of supervisors as shown by the movement in a number of states to set up special certificates with a particular set of requirements for preparation. New internship type programs or special programs for supervisors have provided appropriate bodies of field experience, as well as the use of simulated materials and other means being introduced for the preparation of supervisors.

The validity of the high professional status of the teaching force in working with supervisors illustrates the fundamental concept that status leaders must work with teachers in all aspects of their professional relationships on a dyad basis that recognizes equal competence and skill in their respective fields. The relationship of the supervisory task to various aspects of the instructional and administrative program of the school, and the factors involved in varied instructional staffing patterns should be reviewed as they relate to the matter of improving the quality of education.

One of the most important issues in education hinges on the manner in which pupil inquiry and deliberation can best be fostered. This issue offers a sound argument for curriculum change through the shared development, expansion, and implementation of supervisory services. Added to this is the spectrum of imposing evidence that there exists a need for greater emphasis on individualized instruction for youth at all age levels.

CHAPTER 1

Change:

Its Perspectives and Dimensions

The emergence of the decade of the seventies has underscored the necessity for designing new dimensions for the supervisory role. Within this purview the status leader's task will necessitate far more definitive functions of supervisory leadership than has been the case in recent years. The teaching force in this country is now and will continue to be increasingly concerned with the instructional role that will be performed by supervisory personnel as it relates to the free academic pursuit of knowledge in and out of the classroom. Supervisors, who have long been in quasi-administrative roles in the public schools, also are being confronted with new controls by teachers as to what or what not shall be their function in the hierarchical structure of the public school system. In effect, an atmosphere of tenseness is evidenced as a reasonable number of faculty personnel view the supervisor as a person who performs a less "helpful" task than that demanded by his teaching colleagues.

Every effort shall be made in the ensuing discussions to point out and clarify means by which the supervisory task does indeed evolve around conceptual skills and follows modular patterns that will result in upgrading instructional programs throughout the entire organizational structure. In effect, all status leaders who provide a supervisory function do need a strong commitment toward the development of innovative methods for stimulating behavioral changes in teachers. Such changes should increase the teachers' understanding of their unique role as dynamic human beings in an institution devoted to the improvement of the educational enterprise. As a result, teachers will require more than protection from interference and autocratic supervi-

3

sion; they will need an unlimited but reasonable opportunity to carry out their instructional plans and aspirations on a cooperative basis. This will require taking command of the situational environment in which they can best project their unique teaching skills and accomplishments.

A NEW FOCUS ON SUPERVISION

The American public has long expressed concern for the supposed inability of the educational system to respond to the demands of the theoretical as well as the practical realities of a new technological age. This is not surprising in view of the fact that many of these individuals were born in the 1920's or before. These persons, in effect, have already lived through four ages: the machine age, the jet age, the atomic age, and the space age. As a result, many of these public-spirited citizens view education as a gigantic enterprise that appears to be, on occasion, both inept and sluggish as it attempts to focus its energies on new directions and dynamic programs.

Review, revision, and reform are needed in many quarters of the educational organization. Further, many of these efforts are often fractured and fragmented as they rest on small-scale individual bases. Frequently, these ventures have been successful in building level or pilot program situations but they generally lack that coordinated effort by many educational agencies that permits a sizeable reform movement to take place. What apparently is necessary in educational circles is a larger view to be taken of many critical problem areas that represent a large or national concern in education and to develop communicative networks that can harness leadership forces to solve them. Our concern, of course, is limited primarily to the areas of instruction and curriculum but even within these confines there lie many foci. Some of these, for example, relate to the challenge of the urban schools, cultural deprivation, school integration, teacher militancy, political pressures, student activism, and militant parents. All of these pressures represent vigorous components in combatting the tendency for educational organizations to remain inert in the face of volatile and often uncompromising demands from these groups. If the supervisory process is indeed regarded as a resource base for the improvement of the curriculum and the teaching process, supervisors do have a highly challenging and perplexing task facing them.

There is ample evidence that change does not always result in improvement, although improvement necessitates the involvement of the change process. It becomes highly essential for status leaders in education to be able to differentiate between those demands for change that are legitimate and constructive and those proposals that are ill-conceived and are spurious in their claims to provide needed reform. Throughout the whole network of democratic human-relations-oriented undertakings of status leaders, the main thrust to the solution of educational problems must be based on a reformist-type leadership that is both uncoercive and wholly committed to improving the social process at all educational levels.

All educators have great interest in what underlies the factors involved in the teaching and learning acts. As the role of the status leader and the teacher are currently undergoing monumental revision and upheaval, supervisors and administrators are becoming far less authoritarian in their approach and much more responsive to the desires and demands of their colleagues. Teaching and learning are no longer considered to be objects to be appraised on a superior-inferior basis; the whole concept of accountability for what happens in the classroom has to be shared by the faculty member and the status leader alike. In this fashion teaching and learning relate closely to the development of goals, to motivation and problem solving, and to the coordination and evaluation of classroom activities. All this requires a close look at the behavioral expectations of both the classroom teacher and the supervisor as together they are involved in the teaching-administrative process.

Decision-making in a democratic society, if education is to attain its goals at all levels, must be broadly shared by faculty and administration alike. A broad spectrum and apportionment of professional and community groups also must be concerned with the improvement of the teaching and learning act if the credibility of the educational enterprise is to continue. The time has arrived when status leaders and teachers should view their efforts on a totally coordinate basis and derive a new sense of fulfillment from becoming partners in improving and stimulating the learning process.

THE STRATEGY OF CHANGE

In considering the effectiveness of the role of the supervisor, it would be impossible to overlook the basis for much of the strategy so successfully utilized by persons who serve this function. That strategy is *change*, not change for change's sake but change as a means of improving the climate for teaching and learning in the school. Fortunately, the foundation for permitting a much more rapid acceleration of change in today's schools is the result of spectacular improvements in several educational areas.

Perhaps the most spectacular success in the foundation area for change has been the phenomenal rise in the last 20 to 30 years in the requirements for *certification of teachers*. Many states now insist that teacher candidates meet one or more of these minimum requirements: a postgraduate year beyond the baccalaureate degree in a program leading toward a teaching certificate; a Master's degree; a teaching major (36 units) and a teaching minor (24 units) or a diversified major-minor program especially designed for elementary-school teaching; a minimum program in education course work; and a minimum of one semester of supervised student-teaching experience. Supervisors can be assured that such well-qualified professionals should be able, with proper leadership, to embrace change on a high level of aspiration as well as expectation.

The emergence of *new instructional systems* has laid the foundation for change. Technological advances have made possible the introduction into the classroom of many new types of media: educational television, teaching machines and programmed learning, magnetic-tape equipment, opaque projectors, and the like, have assisted the teacher in enriching the intellectual climate of the classroom. The modern school plant coordinates these many communications devices so that they are available to large numbers of students. Merely by dialing for a certain record or tape, the student can instantaneously have at his disposal a large variety of instructional aids. All of this, in an age when instructional technology is emerging in an explosive fashion, lends great support to the whole aspect of change.

Pervading the attitude of parents and students is the insistent demand for *quality education and an extension of educational opportunity*. Citizens' committees have been formed in many districts to study school building needs, wrestle with the problem of teachers' salaries, assist the board of education in solving some of its more pressing problems, and constantly seek ways of improving the educational opportunities of youth in the community. Parent-teacher associations have shown much interest in the revitalization of the curriculum, in the quality of classroom teaching, in the out-of-school educational and recreational opportunities of youth, and in the extension of the school day and the school year. Labor unions, service clubs, educational associations, patriotic organizations, and various governmental agencies are only a few of the groups that are pressuring the schools to improve and to extend their educational programs. Little wonder, then, that the supervisor has "an ear" from the majority of the staff when he cites and demonstrates the need for change.

Some Changing Directions in American Education

Few problems are more persistent or persuasive in American education than those of means and ends—that ends are not dominated and determined by means. Particularly in an accelerated technological society, means must be fashioned so that they serve clear and forceful purposes and support viable ends.[1]

Society cannot live simply by conservation and perpetuation of the past, says Sterling McMurrin; it must be critical and creative. If the school, then, is to be a chief agent of progress, it must advance knowledge, improve the arts, technology, and social conscience, and attain large visions of the future. Unfortunately, out of the dialectic of conservation and creation issue many of the basic tensions that develop between the schools and the community.

Much attention in the past has been given to educational methods and too little to the substance of education and the purposes it is to serve. With technology holding out much promise for education, the schools need to refine their goals and prepare for new directions in which learning will take place. In view of this, three functions of instruction should be recognized:

(1) The *cognitive* that is directed toward the achievement and communication of knowledge and involves the immediate grasp of sensory objects as well as the abstractive process;

(2) The *affective* that concerns itself with practical matters (emotions, motives, morals, esthetics, appreciation, and the like); and

(3) The *conative* that reflects overt behavior (striving, commitment, decision, and so forth).

Too much of the school's attention has been devoted to the cognitive function of instruction and it has only begun to move in the areas of the affective and conative functions. A preoccupation with knowledge, reason, and abstraction has placed a high priority on the communication of ideas and complex conceptualized structures through a mastery of language skills. Such emphasis should not be depreciated, but certainly new concerns must be directed toward the expressions of various facets of personality and life.

Countless divergent and conflicting forces are to be reckoned with if the schools are to change from their traditionally conceived tasks to undertake greater custodial care of children, become community centers, and to embark as instruments of social policy. As society comes to

[1] Adapted from Sterling M. McMurrin, "What Tasks for the Schools?" *Saturday Review*, January 14, 1967, pp. 40–43.

accept and expect these changes, it should be willing to recognize proper limits in the school's ability to carry out these tasks. Future purposes and goals of the schools will consider such practical considerations as individual aspirations for autonomy and freedom, national security, demands of the economy, and social justice. Such demands as these require a full commitment on the part of the schools to exceed past accomplishments in mastering their intellectual, moral, and spiritual resources to bring future greatness to education and society.

Change—A Force in Supervision

The student of supervision knows that pressures for change come from many directions: the courts, business and industry, government, and even from private individuals. Such pressures should be received, analyzed, and evaluated in terms of their validity and reasonableness. Some futuristic administrators and supervisors foresee the forecasting of change through the assistance of electronic computers that can with amazing speed assort, analyze, and interpret the data given to them. Others recognize that the elements which indicate a need for change are found all around us in such sectors as professional literature, neighboring schools and school systems, workshops, and in the pronouncements of professional associations. In any event, the supervisor must be sensitive to the possibility of and the need for change if he is to succeed as an educational leader.

Change has a greater chance of success when those persons who will be affected by the change are involved in its planning and implementation. Curriculum improvement, for example, can result only when the teacher recognizes that his role is important. He should realize that he cannot be satisfied with the status quo, and must be convinced of the need for the change; he should be permitted to participate in all stages of the plan, be challenged by the possible gains to be derived, be inspired by the supervisors and administrators with whom he is working, and share in the success of the venture or, if a failure, be convinced that the scientific spirit of inquiry represents the will and the desire to tackle the problem again on the basis of another hypothesis. Throughout the process supervisors need to assist the individual or the group to state or restate their objectives, to obtain the data or materials they need as they proceed toward the fulfillment of their task, and to provide the leadership necessary to lead to the conclusion and implementation of the projected change. As an agent of change, the supervisor should exploit his shared leadership role to the fullest so that educational practice will not seriously lag behind modern educational theory.

Needs and Purpose

The strengthening of the desire to bring about change evolves around individual or group need to improve the task function. As the rationale for change becomes apparent, an increasing number of persons are likely to become more interested in the exciting educational possibilities that present themselves. Research evidence, accompanied by field tests,that an innovation or idea is workable is a first step toward its ultimate acceptance. Recent discussion has indicated that specialists in educational design and implementation should be available on a regional or state basis to aid in the encouragement of new experimentation. As a vendor of educational ideas to certificated personnel at the local level, such an individual could do much to assist teachers in exploring and utilizing the innovations that would improve their classroom instruction.

Educational ferment, accompanied by technological advances and rapid growth patterns, has brought new dimensions to the present educational climate. The term change has become a byword in our time and all but the extreme conservatives are willing to support reasonable change efforts. Recognizing that the change phenomenon is a common educational occurrence, undoubtedly the basic question to which educators must address themselves is "What kind of change is needed?" and "For what purpose?" The answers to these questions are fundamental in all educational endeavor.

Current Change Characteristics

The problem of change is that its process has been haphazard and, so far as knowledge about change is concerned, virtually noncumulative. There has been, however, an impressive cluster of ideas and concepts pertaining to the changes taking place in schools. As a result, there are several characteristics that represent today's educational programs.[2] These are: 1) clear statements of institutional objectives, stated in behavioral terms; 2) instructional emphasis on learning how to learn, and on long-term structural elements of subject matter rather than isolated pieces; 3) multi-media learning packages in every classroom, designed with concern for the integrity of content as well as intrinsic appeal for students; 4) extensive instructional recognition of individual differences, reflected in evaluation procedures, assignments, and expectations for students; 5) considerable use of basic principles of group dynamics, human interaction, and democratic classroom leadership; 6) use of sound principles of learning pertaining to motivation, reinforcement, transfer of training, and so on; 7) little attention to age and grade

[2]John I. Goodlad, *Educational Change: A Strategy for Study and Action* (Melbourne, Florida: IDEA Reprint Series, 1969), pp. 1–2.

as criteria for what to teach as in nongraded, continuous progress plans; 8) flexible use of personnel resources as in team teaching; and 9) clear evidence that this is a period of real advancement in instructional materials. This represents the flavor of America's schools and the pursuit of the educational reform movement as they appear during the decade of the seventies.

Change Tactics

The change process, as previously indicated, is a highly complex affair. A multitude of impacts upon the school within the last few decades have done much to change the nature and the condition of education. Shortages of highly trained personnel in a variety of professional fields have accentuated the need for teachers, mathematicians, physicists, and other individuals in similar categories. The explosion of knowledge has re-emphasized the fact that education is a continuous, life-long process and many individuals need to be retrained several times during the course of their vocational careers. Advancement in communication techniques most certainly will revolutionize the structure of the school and, indeed, the educational process itself in terms of greater reliance on automated equipment and less emphasis on the human (teacher-to-pupil) contacts. The increasing efforts of the federal government through its Elementary and Secondary Education Act have added new stimulus to the expansion and enrichment of programs for disadvantaged children and others who can benefit from the improved school facilities at their disposal. Conditions such as these have notably accelerated the pace of change and increased the role that the educational leader plays in capitalizing on new ideas and fostering programs of planned change.

In any change process, however, there always have been some inhibitors to change and innovation. An awareness of the sources of resistance to change is necessary to overcome their insidious effects. A few basic factors related to a resistance to change are these: an unwillingness to recognize one's shortcomings; a refusal to experiment with a new idea because of an imagined risk that may be involved; the rapidity with which the need for change became apparent and the inability of the individual to readily adjust to the situation; and a lack of strong administrative and financial support that seems likely to doom the change venture in its initial stages. Although some educators may have little reluctance to accept the idea of change or the procedures that must be followed, there can be some real resistance to the way it was presented to them. Assurances must be given to individuals that the change will not interfere with their position nor its basic roles and responsibilities. Whenever individuals or groups of persons decide to resist change, it generally has been the result of an urgent desire to protect themselves in the socio-economic role that they have held in the organization. It then becomes necessary to demonstrate to the individuals concerned that the contemplated change is one that will bring greater satisfaction and reward by its acceptance and implementation.

Although the need for change may not be readily apparent, an axiom representative of the attitude of business and industry as it retools for change is that "we may be behind already." Education, too, should periodically inventory its own position in relation to the change process as it looks to the immediate years ahead and the situation that will confront its young people after they leave its doors to step out into the world. Projection studies and assessment programs might involve a careful review of current educational efforts to ascertain that coordinating, planning, and evaluation accompany the development of projection for innovations so that a realistic approach to the situation will result.

Several tactics need to be followed if the change process is to be a success: there should be a total involvement of the people who are to be affected by the change itself; priorities must be established on the basis of determining needs as they relate to the goals of the organization; decisions should be formulated on those areas of change that show the greatest growth potential for the organization; the involvement of people must be stressed at the very beginning of any projected change proposal; recognition needs to be given to the area where change is most readily apparent—the market-place; and modern facilities and the latest techniques of learning should be available for those who would move into an area of accelerated innovation. Too few schools have attempted in the past to follow their youthful products into their new environment after they leave school. Educational services and technical know-how should be available to both the former student and the receiving employer or institution to insure greater success for proper adjustment than is now the case. Educators could move out frequently into the field to contact people in the community who are making notable changes in the socio-economic lives of its citizens.

One of the primary reasons for the school's inability to cope with obsolescence has been the lack of new techniques and tools such as the computer and other automated machines. Training, too, is an important factor in approaching the acceleration of change. There will be many instances when personnel should consider returning to institutions of learning to become better acquainted with new ideas and skills that are becoming identified with their particular field. Greater reliance could be placed on the many professional publications that are found in professional libraries and these made readily available to school person-nel. Finally, the creation of an atmosphere which is acceptable to change and the support of individuals in their efforts to improve the educational program should be promoted. The categories of social influ-ence to recognize are compliance with the overall goals of the organiza-tion, identification of the needs of individuals, recognition of persons who are important to the change process, and the internalization of change so that its tempo and growth can be experienced readily by those involved in the constructive movements of the organization.

Agents of Change

To what extent do elementary school principals initiate change in school systems? Under what circumstances are they more likely to initiate change or to support it? Daniel Griffiths and Daniel Davies reported recently on two studies that concerned themselves with these questions.[3] In one study the subjects were 232 principals who were put into a simulated administrative situation called the Whitman School. Although none of the 232 principals were definitely "change agents" or "innovators," an analysis of the data showed that some characteristics of the principals were more related to the tendency to produce change than others. These characteristics were: (1) mental ability—there is a general tendency for bright people to be more productive, to write more, and to attempt more; (2) sensitivity to the needs and wishes of others—asks, informs and discusses with subordinates; communicates face-to-face; informs, follows, and is courteous to outsiders; recognizes good work and is informal; (3) practices making final decisions—takes leading actions, directs, relates to other material, decides on procedure, and makes concluding decisions; (4) instructional awareness—sensitive to teacher personality, pupil interest, curriculum, and student partici-pation; and (5) permissiveness and flexibility as an innovator. Change in school systems, it appears, comes from the central office, but once that change is sanctioned by superiors, the principal will work to effect that change at the building level.

The second study found that staff inventiveness is highly correlated with the staff belief that the principal supports creative teaching and that the rest of the staff does too. Principals with innovative staffs were highly concerned with professional matters like improving classroom procedures, encouraging teacher growth, and continually evaluating pupil learning.

[3]Daniel E. Griffiths and Daniel R. Davies, "Elementary School Principals as Agents of Change," *Executive Action Letter*, Croft Educational Services, vol. 3, no. 8 (March 1964), 4 pp. See also Lanore A. Netzer, *et al.*, *Education, Administration, and Change: The Redeployment of Resources* (New York: Harper and Row, 1970), 207 pp.

As a result of the two studies, several suggestions were made as to how to encourage principals to be change agents: (1) pick highly intelligent persons to be principals; (2) find principals who are sensitive to the needs and wishes of staff members and outsiders; (3) encourage principals to learn the difference between "taking terminal action" (making unilateral decisions) and "preparing for decisioning" through adequate discussions, data gathering, and good problem-solving procedures; (4) make the principal the "captain of his ship"; (5) place high priority on the educational outcomes from the school, rather than upon administrative processes; (6) encourage principals to create a climate in their schools which supports innovation; and (7) encourage principals to study the social and time pressures upon their teachers (rearrangement of time schedules through released time, use of substitute teachers, and the like can aid teachers in feeling freer to plan for innovations).

Planned Changes and Organizational Health

The Center for the Advanced Study of Educational Administration at the University of Oregon recently turned its attention to the enhancement of school officials' understanding of the planned change process and of their skills in carrying out planned change.[4] Any review of today's applied behavioral sciences would note a remarkable professional interest in the entire problem of planned change and scientists and practitioners alike are concerned with how the change process can be managed in a meaningful sense of the word. Inasmuch as organizations have careers in much the same sense that individuals have careers, a number of changes can be detected, even among the most stable organizations.

There are six possible approaches for the induction of organizational health and change. First, *self-study* rejects the technocratic change model involving the recommendations of a detached expert and, instead, involves the system itself in organizational introspection. Group self-study by various teams in the organization, personal introspection, and re-examination by role occupants are examples. Second, *rational emphasis* does not conceive of the organization as a collection of jobs with isolated persons in them, but a network of groups and role relationships, the functioning of which calls for examination and self-operated, experimental alteration. The aim, for example, is not to change the "attitude" of the principal, but to focus on the relationships and group settings in which the principal's attitudes are evoked. Third, *increased data flow* involves the heightening or intensification of com-

[4]Richard O. Carlson, *et al.*, *Change Processes in the Public Schools* (Eugene, Ore.: Center for the Advanced Study of Educational Administration, 1965), pp. 30–32.

munication, especially vertically, but also diagonally and horizontally. The use of status-equalizing devices such as intensive residential meetings also encourages fuller and freer flow of information through channels which may have been blocked or have always carried distorted messages. Fourth, *norms as a change target* by focusing on groups and relationships have the effect of altering existing norms that regulate interpersonal transactions in the organization. For example, if a group that does not "disagree with the boss" engages in a training session, it is likely that norms such as "be open about your feelings whether or not they tally with the boss's wishes" will develop. Such approaches have a strong cultural-changing component, based on intensive, data-based interaction with others. Fifth, the *temporary-system approach* involves the use of residential meetings; this constitutes a detached "cultural island" approach to organizational introspection and self-correction. New norms can develop there and, given the suspension of the usual pressures, meaningful changes can be made in the structure and functioning of the permanent system. Last, *expert facilitation* includes the presence of a semi-detached consultant figure, whose main functions are to facilitate, provoke, and support the efforts of the system to understand itself, expand communication, and engage in more adequate problem-solving behavior. The outside role is impermanent and is associated with the system during the actual period of intervention itself. If the intervention is successful, the organization continues the self-corrective processes which have been begun by the intervention.

The supervisor or administrator, then, acts as an advocate for change as well as a mediator for the same purpose. He is expected to see the possibilities for change, the means of overcoming the resistance, and the important role that he plays in a political sense as he seeks to facilitate the change of operational structure.

The Teacher and Change

As was indicated earlier, one of the prime movers of change at the classroom level is the teacher. His insights into the need for change will have a great effect upon his attitude toward change—whether or not he feels that he should innovate, experiment, or reach out for new ideas and methods. In too many instances the teacher may decide to wait until change patterns have become accepted and even stereotyped and then adopt these concepts in the classroom learning situation. Fortunately, due to the increased pre-service training that many teachers have experienced, they will be anxious to avoid pedagogical obsolescence and be willing to seek help for new and better teaching tools and techniques.

Due to rapid change and the explosion of knowledge, much more in-service training of teachers will be necessary. To maintain a high level of in-service training in tomorrow's technological age will call for much greater expenditure on the part of local school districts to promote these in-service activities. Industry currently makes these provisions for key personnel and public schools should expect to attain a similarly high level of support for in-service training. The offerings of outstanding workshops and institutes, the payment of tuition and books, the granting of sabbatical leaves of absence for the continuance of professional growth, and the instituting of research projects (with compensating released time) will do much to provide the incentive to "keep up" with an ever changing professional world.

Beyond this, some consideration needs to be given to the identification of those teachers who will be the most likely to be responsive to change and to be the most desirous of becoming involved personally in change. Research has shown that younger teachers are more apt to fall in this category, that they often receive professional evaluations that are considerably higher than the average, that they portray keener insights into the soundness or deficiency of any new proposal, and that their professional contacts with other educators are on a much wider geographical and administration level than those of their non-innovative peers. Attention to such characteristics as these, when recruiting teachers, does much to assure supervisors and administrators that they can screen and recruit persons who are innovation prone and who will do much to meet the demands of new tasks and challenges.

Some school systems, however, have relied on inexperienced personnel to launch innovative programs where experimentation is occurring with bold new conceptions of education.[5] Often these systems have hired teachers without experience on the premise that it would be easier to train these individuals in new approaches then it would be to take experienced teachers and retrain them. It should be apparent that experience can sensitize the teacher to the linkages and connectives between the part of the system being changed and other parts as well as to the problems that may be created when there is a disturbance in the various linkages. Experience, then, can be helpful in these ways: it can alert the individual to the myriad complexities of a social system that may remain hidden to an individual unfamiliar with the particular social scene; it cannot only anticipate problems, but it can be valuable in coping with problems that develop; and it permits implementers to improvise and engineer intermediate actions that will move the innova-

[5]Edwin M. Bridges and Larry B. Reynolds, "Teacher Receptivity to Change," *Administrator's Notebook*, vol. XVI, no. 6 (February 1968), pp. 1–4.

tive project forward satisfactorily when the unproved educational practices may not be operating as intended and may not be producing the desired outcomes. The experienced teacher offers great potential for reshaping education in an era that is placing great stress on change and the change process.

Overcoming the Obstacles

One of the basic problems that faces the schools of today is the gap in education between what "is" and what "should be." As school leaders consider the changes that need to be made in the curriculum, they recognize that there must be bold and dramatic new ideas introduced into the mainstream of program development that will positively affect the lives of young people. Curriculum change should not be the outgrowth of mere dissatisfaction of the community with the task that the school is accomplishing. It should represent an awareness of the necessity for constantly reviewing and improving any or all segments of the curriculum at such a periodic rate that the slightest indication of any needed reform or change will be recognized and compensated for at the earliest possible moment. In the event that curriculum progress is both slow and diffused, dissatisfactions that do occur should be recognized and identified as a means of promoting change. If, for example, the school administrator can provide the in-service training climate that will make his teachers unhappy or dissatisfied with the results of their teaching product, he will have come a long way in fostering a new awareness for the need for curriculum change in his school.

What are some of the obstacles that may be encountered as educational leaders contemplate change and reform in the curriculum? Several factors should be considered. Any curriculum change may require additional funds to provide the facilities and personnel required to expedite it; thus, resistance to increased budgetary costs and possible new tax increases may become an issue. Change in itself represents an attack on the status quo of any organization and such a move constitutes a threat to those who have led themselves to rationalize or others to believe that they are maintaining a position of excellence by continuing indefinitely their former practices and techniques. Increased qualification requirements for many personnel may result from the acceptance of new curriculum task levels that will demand a better educated individual to assume the new responsibility. Curriculum organization, too, may be affected by the contemplated changes and other segments of the curriculum may have to be adjusted to compensate for the innovations projected in a particular area of the curriculum. Finally, the implementation of new ideas and practices may arouse the distrust of those who do not understand or who may not be fully informed of the reasoning behind the innovation. These persons may consider the change a fearsome thing that could adversely affect what is thought to be an otherwise acceptable program.

Curriculum change, then, must be judged in the light of its possible assets and accomplishments. If there is to be an additional expenditure of funds and personal effort, it must be made clear that the venture is necessary and that it will have a positive effect upon the program being offered. The change itself must add perceptibly, either directly or indirectly, to the understanding or the application of knowledge that is to be used by the learner. In each instance, there should be an assurance that there will be a gain in the advancement of the total spectrum of knowledge that will result from the initiation of the innovation. Both a clear purpose and a sound value base are essential elements to the development of a strong agreement for the acceptance and furtherance of any curriculum change pattern. The message that is given to the people concerned must carefully indicate that the integrity of the program will be judiciously maintained, that there will be proper balance and stability in the total dimension of the curriculum, that all information related to the change and its future implications is being furnished the professionals and the public, that the human as well as the materialistic involvement is being considered, and that reasonable curriculum change is an absolute necessity if the community is to remain in a position where a strong educational program is maintained.

The Wisconsin Study

Perhaps one of the most important developments in the area of change is found at the University of Wisconsin in The Wisconsin Improvement Program—Teacher Education and Local School Systems. The program is a statewide effort to assist instructional leaders in helping people change, drawing together university staff members, schoolteachers, and officials to break new ground in education. This collaboration represents a trend toward change and experimentation in the nation's schools by enabling prospective teachers to grasp the pattern of the future while in training and to contribute to educational improvements at the same time. One of the chief methods of creating change is through *team teaching,* a division of labor long practiced by other professions. Improved instruction is provided by pooling the knowledge and talent of a group of teachers to a larger number of pupils than any single teacher would normally handle. *Non-professionals* are used to assist in the harrowing mass of detail and routine (attendance, grade and health records, supply purchases, and the like). Time for creativity in the teaching function is available through such help. *Flexibility in scheduling* provides more individual attention through smaller groups, varying sizes of classes, and differing lengths of time to suit a variety of classes and subjects. The *adaptation of technology to instruction and learning* has given impetus to change through the use of televised instruction, films, tape recorders, overhead projectors, radio, language laboratories and programmed instruction. *Differentiated assignments* for outstanding teachers, based on special skills and levels of competence, have freed these gifted persons from less important chores by allowing them to spend more time in the classroom. The effectiveness of the Wisconsin program has been demonstrated by its careful application of innovations to educational goals and realities. Instructional leaders can profit in their attempts to promote change in certificated persons by fostering ideas similar to the Wisconsin program.

Research and Development

The Wisconsin Research and Development Center for cognitive learning has combined team teaching and the ungraded curriculum with a heavy emphasis on student self-directed learning. Non-graded organization and team teaching are developed in a unique manner. At the head of each team is a unit leader who takes the major responsibility for team coordination and planning. An instructional committee, with decision-making responsibilities, integrates the wide spectrum of the school's curriculum. Various unit leaders and the principal compose this committee. The principal has much emphasis placed on his role as an instructional leader as opposed to the conventional concept of the practical administrator of the school. Non-graded organization, team teaching, unit leaders, and para-professionals (classroom teacher aides) are all important segments of this plan that is aimed at giving strength to the educational program in the 1970's.

AUTOMATION AND CHANGE

The term "automation" has become a well-known word in educational circles. With the rapid expansion of automatic data processing equipment as a basic tool for educational programs, many changes have occurred in the traditional disciplines and methodologies as they relate to the school. Educators have been impressed with the fact that there must be better ways of providing for the dissemination of highly technical information and for the encouragement of deep, intellectual thought on the part of students as they attempt to amass and digest complex educational material. As the use of automated equipment increases in the school and in the classroom, a delicate balance needs to be maintained that will protect the basic integrity of the human practitioner as well as provide for the satisfactory utilization of the machine system. At whatever level the machines are accepted as an aid to educational practice in any school district will largely depend upon the attitude and support of the district's teaching staff.

Educational technology has moved into some challenging research and development areas as it relates to automation. The Educational Testing Service (ETS), for example, is conducting studies in these areas: investigating the possibility of using computers to assist in test administration by having the computer select succeeding questions on the basis of students' answers to previous questions; and seeking to find ways of using computers to improve the reporting and interpretation of test scores for guidance purposes.

In some respects computers operate at a rather distant and impersonal level in relation to students as they are used to assist in schedule preparation, to take attendance, to record grades, and to make class lists. In other ways the computer is much more closely allied to the student's day-to-day activities as it helps him more directly in his study activities: in learning centers that are equipped with automated machines to retrieve desired information, in his personal contact with programmed teaching machines in the classroom, and in simulated situations in which he participates in decision-making roles by use of the computer.

It would be unrealistic to think that the introduction of new automated devices in the school system have not been upsetting to many faculty members. These professionals have spent much time and effort in producing their own classroom materials and developing highly personalized teaching techniques. In view of the rapid explosion of knowledge and the advancement of technology, however, it becomes imperative that educational leaders undertake the responsibility for establishing new attitudes and concepts regarding automation as it affects the teacher, the student, and the classroom.

The education profession plays a responsible role in placing the science and art of automation at the service of education. There is now rather widespread acceptance of the fact that there are broadening influences affecting education even to the extent that organized educational activities are being accepted outside the formalized school situation at the elementary and secondary levels. With several million citizens enrolled in adult education programs, with an increasing spread of educational television programming, and with increased extension course activities, the base of the traditional school offering has been greatly extended. Factors such as these lead to the possibility of a greatly extended market for research and development activities that are oriented toward a technological base in education. The pervasive impact of technology at all levels of education must be recognized by educators as they prepare pupils to accept revolutionary changes that will accompany our continued progress in an automated age.

Man-Machine Systems Aid Individuality

The Continuous Progress Plan (CPP) for individualizing instruction and other similar projects illustrate that man-machine systems in education are no longer a development for the future. What, then, will be the behavior-shaping powers of the educator? Also, with the implication of man-machine systems for instructional content, what will be its potential impact on the development and freedom of choice of individuals?

To answer these questions a scholarly investigation was made of the nature and application of computers, media technology, and systems technology as they pertain to the instructional, administrative, and supervisory services in terms of society today and tomorrow.[6]

Four basic assumptions can be stated: 1) that growth and implementation of man-machine systems in education is inevitable, 2) that they will develop at an extremely rapid pace, 3) that the development and implementation of such systems will involve much conflict, and 4) that resistance to these innovations will be made by the older generation but accepted by the young. In addition there are several problems of implementation of man-machine systems: information regarding these systems must be disseminated to several different audiences at various levels of sophistication and with varying emphasis; in addition to the development of information to be communicated, there is a problem of helping the recipient to understand it; man-machine systems are expensive and their development will have to share attention and financial support with other developments; and aggressive resistance and apathy in the educational establishment must be overcome so that educational programs can be redesigned.

In devising a communications model or guide for man-machine systems, the following factors can be considered: *monitoring systems development* to keep track of the status of the art, thus helping in the assignment of research and development priorities; *documentation*, although expensive and time consuming, must include specific evaluation data as well as descriptions of the populations involved; *safeguarding individuals* involves the concept that information is power and

---

[6]John W. Longhary, *Man-Machine Systems in Education* (New York: Harper and Row, 1966), pp. 223–235. See also Virgil M. Howes, *Individualization of Instruction: A Teaching Strategy* (New York: Macmillan, 1970), 256 pp.

there needs to be a determination of the kind of power that is available as well as how much any one agency or individual can use for a particular purpose at a particular time; and *social control* implies that man-machine systems in education must be built with the full realization of changing social concepts, such as the changing functions of work in society and their implication for functions in education.

If education is the final remaining hope for achieving a peaceful world, supervisors and administrators are in a good position to see to it that man-machine systems in education are deployed for a useful purpose. Perhaps the greatest problem will be to utilize the systems to maximum advantage as a tool for learning while at the same time protecting the stubborn individuality of each child.

Some Advantages of Automation

As teaching machines free teachers to do more creative work, their role in programmed learning will be that of a planner of educational experiences. Educators will be able to meet increased demands, such as motivating and guiding youth toward particular careers (almost untouched now), as they have additional time to devote to many new creative tasks.

Supervisors and administrators will find a real challenge in automation. Broadened curricular and school services will require an enlarged budget. There will be a need to improve offerings in mathematics and science, to strengthen guidance services, and to reassess courses in business, the trades, and industry. During periods of rapid social change, supervisors and administrators will have the leadership task of identifying changing goals for the school but they must devise and maintain the patterns by which resources are found, organized, and applied to accomplish educational purposes agreed upon cooperatively. Access to data and expert advice on social and economic trends will be essential. Specific provisions, made in the organization and budgetary plans, will help guarantee adequate research services and effective means to transmit essential information to the teaching staff and the community as it relates to the accountability potential of the school system in its program planning designs.

SUMMARY

Instructional leaders today are faced with four challenging aspects in the whole area of influence and change: 1) the confrontation of pressures on the school system, 2) the need for positive assistance to help instructional personnel change, 3) the awesome but dynamic specter of automation in the classroom, and 4) the task of providing individualized instruction to children as a basic key to learning. Relative to the wide range of pressures on the instructional program that face the supervisor or administrator, positive measures can be taken through commitment to excellence in education, making cogent decisions as to what knowledge should be taught, permitting decisions to be made by those affected by them, and providing the means for problems to be solved on a scientific basis. The urban school crisis requires that the supervisor or administrator recognize the situation as both multi-racial and multi-cultural. Cultural deprivation demands a major effort on his part as he strives to help teachers overcome or prevent early deficiencies in these individuals, while the racial situation bids that he maintain a continuous dialogue between the school and the home to provide the social encouragement so necessary for these children. Teacher prestige, collective bargaining, and student militancy are all new aspects of pressures on the school and require both professional training and skill in meeting the demands from these sources.

Unquestionably the central problem facing instructional leaders is how to help people change. In providing this assistance, several factors are important: any proposed change should be charted carefully with those to be affected, faculty articulation is essential at all levels for any major change, research should be utilized to prevent unnecessary failures, and the health of the organization is a primary consideration in designing a "planned change" program.

Automation in the classroom has added a new task for the supervisor or administrator as he provides certificated personnel with an adequate understanding of the new media and their fascinating capabilities. Beyond this he can make available educational specialists at the professional level and technical specialists at the operational level to insure maximum assistance to staff as public demands become greater for automated aids and facilities.

The challenge of individualized instruction fosters the development of new concepts of learning that involve student interaction, intellectual stimulation, self-control, and gratification of basic interests and needs. Man-machine systems in education promise to grow overwhelmingly in the future and supervisors and administrators must strive diligently to assist teachers in understanding the possibilities as well as the advantages to be gained from the new media.

SELECTED REFERENCES

Becker, Wesley. *An Empirical Basis for Change in Education.* Palo Alto: Science Research Associates, 1971.

Brickman, William W., and Stanley Lehrer. *Automation, Education, and Hu-*

man Values. New York: School and Society Books, 1966.

Campbell, Roald, *et al. Introduction to Educational Administration.* Boston: Allyn and Bacon, 1971.

Center for the Study of Instruction (A.W. Foshay). *Curriculum for the Seventies: An Agenda for Invention.* Washington, D.C.: National Education Association, 1970.

Cordasco, Francesco, Maurie Hillson, and Henry A. Bullock. *The School in the Social Order: A Sociological Introduction to Educational Understanding.* Scranton: Intext, 1970.

Educational Research Service. *Decentralization and Community Involvement: A Status Report.* Washington, D.C.: National Education Association, 1969.

Hurwitz, Emanuel, Jr., and Robert Maidment. *Criticism, Conflict, and Change: Readings in American Education.* New York: Dodd, Mead, 1970.

MacDonald, W. Scott. *Battle in The Classroom: Innovations in Classroom Techniques.* Scranton: Intext, 1971.

National Association of Secondary School Principals. *The Computer in Education.* Washington, D.C.: National Education Association, 1970.

Searles, John E. *A System for Instruction.* Scranton: Intext, 1967.

CHAPTER 2

Characteristics

of Helpful Supervision

Democratic supervision, by definition, represents the fulfillment of any task that leads to the shared development of an improved instructional program. No one person nor any group of individuals can claim that they alone have the sole responsibility for carrying forth this function. Many persons in both a supervisory and/or administrative capacity have varying degrees of responsibility in providing for the supervision of instruction. In fact, many educators who might be classified as line administrators may spend as much as thirty to forty percent or more of their time offering services to the instructional staff so that they may facilitate better their function of teaching in the classroom. Expressed in another fashion, democratic supervision may be characterized as a type of activity in which functional assistance and encouragement are key characteristics.

Under no circumstance is supervision a mere telling or directing activity in which the teacher is placed in an inferior or subordinate position. Partnership of ideas, planning, and creativity are essential between those who would supervise instructional programs and their colleagues who will be the beneficiaries of a planned program of supervisory help.

Flexibility and adaptiveness are essential elements to aid in the promotion of an improved teaching-learning process. Staff members recognize that anyone who undertakes to fulfill the responsibility of a supervisory role must demonstrate an attitude of helpfulness and consideration for those who would seek his assistance. Many opportunities should be provided for individuals to work together; the problem-solving process must be used continually; adequate supplies, services, and other resource materials must be made available; and periodic evaluations should relate to the previously formulated goals and purposes that have been stated by the individual and the organization.

Democratic supervision recognizes that an organizational framework can be devised in which classroom teachers will be given every opportunity to modify their behavior to meet individual and organizational needs. In as many instances as possible, supervisory-teaching models must be created at the local level to provide the means for teachers to move in ever widening areas of social influence and change as their work encompasses increasingly critical levels of task relationships. The ability to design and periodically renew functional plans of organization will permit the status leader to make the kinds of instructional decisions that he will need to formulate under stressful and often frustrating situations. His sequential models for democratic supervision will open new vistas for perfection of the teaching-learning act for both new and experienced faculty personnel.

The supervisory role cannot be wasted on spurious or pernicious tactics that have little relationship to the sociological, psychological, or philosophical roles that are so important to the development of systems plans or functional models. Instead, it requires a broad analytical approach to the theoretical, clinical, and interdisciplinary areas that represent the functional bases on which behavioral expectations can be prognosticated. Commitment, dialog, and action are features essential to such a model for democratic supervision.

COMMITMENT

As the educator considers the enormity of the pressures and influences that will confront him, he first may wish to analyze his personal commitments on which he will base his actions and his pronouncements. Forces that are symptomatic of the socio-economic atmosphere that is represented by opinions, attitudes, and beliefs of society at any given time could be examined carefully by the supervisor or administrator. These should be considered in the light of the ideological framework that he is willing to promote as well as to defend. Fortunately, it is generally recognized that basic values will change or assume different priorities from time to time. As a result, commitments to which the educator subscribes will also be subject to re-evaluation and review in the light of new data and increasingly valid information. Values related to such philosophical concepts as the role of the individual, the function of a democratic society, the proper use of administrative power, the function of groups, and utilization of the decision-making process, are all related inherently to the final determination as to the direction that the educational leader will take in meeting educational needs and aspirations in an uncertain world.

Considered from another vantage point, the value and commitment base determined by educational leaders on an individual basis will have much bearing on the eventual total value and commitment structure of the school. The proper extension of such values and commitments on a system-wide basis will depend also upon the timely release of the creative energy of the district administrative and supervisory staff in working toward the attainment of concomitant personal and group priorities. These priorities should represent a sound philosophical base for later action and implementation.

All persons within the community need to understand and appreciate the urgency in developing a school-community coordinated approach in the assignment of proper educational values and commitments to the school. If the school is to exert a meaningful influence upon the student body and the future growth of students, it has to be given an opportunity to be constructively evaluated by the community that it seeks to serve. If the challenges of today's pressures and influences are to be met, the educational enterprise should be permitted to exert a salutary influence upon the social order in which it finds itself. This can be done by the school's continuing to make a sound commitment to the furtherance of the democratic values that it holds inviolable.

Relationships

Interpersonal relationships that supervisors experience need not be faulted by inadequate inclusion or exclusion of appropriate behavior patterns that are designed to assist others on a helping relationship basis. Basic to any relationship is the development of a proper communications base that is central to the professional interaction process. The fewer the intermediaries in any communications system, the better the communications procedure works. The ultimate, of course, in any interpersonal interaction is the maximum use of the person-to-person technique. Contained in any hierarchy of behavior techniques is the necessity of personal involvement which can be equated with others in the helping process. Personal involvement can and does lead to a greater understanding of the needs of others as the helping person attempts to operate from the other person's frame of reference. It should be noted that such an empathic approach does not mean that there has to be a one-to-one relationship in terms of intellectual ability on the part of the two or more persons involved in the helping relationship. Personal feelings, of course, must be communicated with a genuineness of expression that does not lead to distortion of the intent of the message. Irritations and exasperated concerns should be dealt with on an honest, open basis by the individuals involved so that frustrating situations can be squarely faced by both parties wrestling with the problem. Whatever is said should be in concrete and direct terms so that the vagueness so often encountered in many conversations that supervisors have with others can be overcome.

Anxiety and Relevance

Instructional leaders have the opportunity to make a commitment to the development of a stable, inflexible educational program that represents the past or to move toward the evolvement of an uncharted and unknown program that will meet the challenges of the future. They face greatest danger if the past is sought only on the basis of complacency, while the future is looked upon with timidity and apprehension. The choice should be made between the continuance of a resistive school and a dynamic school; between following a safe, unimaginative professional career and a dangerous foray into the world of the unknown whenever called upon to do so. The educator, however, cannot afford to overlook the important values and performances that have emanated from the past as he seeks new ground and ever increasing horizons leading to new knowledge and understanding. As he broadens the areas for enriching human effort and achievement, he must attempt to assign to their proper places the values of the past, the achievement of the present, and the promised fulfillment of the future. Only then can he commit himself to the task of encouraging others to dream of the future that lies ahead.

There is general agreement among psychologists that the best learning climate for persons of any age is one that is in the low-mild anxiety range. Anxiety of this magnitude gives clear evidence that an individual is interested in having change take place, either in himself or in the organizational framework in which he experiences involvement. Teaching and learning are subject to this anxiety state, and the supervisor is presented with an excellent opportunity to foster a "change oriented" program that will challenge teachers and administrators alike. When anxiety levels are increased to intermediate or high, the individual is likely to become disorganized with little new learning taking place. On the other hand, very little or no anxiety for the individual is apt to make him passive and strongly motivated toward maintaining the situation "as is." This low-mild anxiety range for the teacher is often reflected in a dissatisfaction with the classroom performance, a recognition that goals are not being met or that methods might be improved, or a realization that the entire teaching-learning process needs to be reconstructed so that new ideas and concepts can be tested for improvement purposes. To bring this anxiety level into focus will require the cooperative sharing of responsibility between the supervisor and teacher to determine what can be done to find a better way of raising instructional standards. Only through a cooperative teacher-supervisor approach to the problem can there be an establishment of goals, the designing of significant experiences, and the evaluation or assessment of meaningful patterns of behavioral change. Both the supervisor and the teacher must feel reasonably uncomfortable at a low-mild level of anxiety to the extent that a *status quo* equilibrium situation does not exist which will tend to stifle the urge that both will have toward continuous change and improvement. This is the kind of relationship that ideally exists, in some form, between the teacher and the supervisor. Only in this manner can the supervisory process assure itself of the will and the energy to meet the demands of the monumental tasks that confront it.

Relevance of the educational task represents another large area of concern for the educational leader. Students, in particular, are raising questions about education as to the course structures that are being followed and their germaneness to their daily and future lives. Too often students ask, "How meaningful is this course or program to me now, and will I ever have any use for these subjects in the future?" This is a pressing problem for teachers and supervisors alike and students are becoming impatient in their search for answers. Many perplexing sociological problems confront the youth of today and presently there are few areas of the curriculum that offer much, if any, help. Although there is a polarization of young people on the right or the left who are quite vocal about this situation, there are many youths in the "silent middle" who have said little, but if aroused will voice strong and articulate feelings about their frustrations. Unfortunately, the number of rebellious students is on the increase and few teachers or administrators are paying much heed to their demands. Whole faculties, therefore, must involve themselves in an agonizing and meaningful reappraisal of the learning experiences being provided by the school. This does not mean that education is to be diluted or that some pertinent areas of educational mastery should be overlooked. Instead, a new excitement on the part of both teachers and students should take place and the learning task should be both relevant and energetic. With change occurring in many sectors of society, students find it difficult to believe that some aspects of the school's program can be so disengaged in this effort. No previous society has experienced the enormous and immediate effects that our communication system has wrought and this episode in modern times has made the student population even more sensitive to the need for relevant study in the school. Educational institutions every-

where must relate to the demands of a modern age to foster the evolvement of a significant and relevant educational experience.

SUPERVISORY LEADERSHIP

Instructional leadership at both the district and the school level is
a shared responsibility as well as an educational commitment. It is based
upon the belief that there is a cooperative relationship between those
in supervisory positions and the certificated staff. All partners in this
association should be willing to communicate their thoughts to one
another and to energize their deliberations into action. Many persons
will be involved in instructional leadership tasks, namely: superintendents, assistant superintendents, building administrators, supervisors,
and counseling personnel. Each of these individuals will be working
closely with teachers in the identification, clarification, and support of
any worthwhile instructional venture.

Supervisory leadership has the responsibility of focusing on the
broadening of educational vision of certificated personnel as they center their activities on goals and objectives. Total program planning
includes the mutual assistance of teachers who are working with administrative and supervisory personnel in raising the level of the professional talents of the teaching staff. Faith in the responsible attitude of
teachers to fulfill their professional obligations, the sharing of recognition of the contributions of all those involved in the improvement of any
instructional program, the taking of a positive position in relation to the
encouragement of creative activities on the part of professional personnel, and the constant encouragement of self-evaluation of the teaching
and learning process are essential elements.

The supervisory leader will recognize that he has to foster a sense
of well-being among the members of the teaching faculty through improving the school's psychological environment in order that their
behavior can be changed. So much discussion of what needs to be
accomplished in instructional improvement remains at the verbal level
and does not extend into the level of overt action. Supervisors, as a part
of this psychological enclosure, can provide for faculty members a number of alternative directions in which they might wish to move on a
behavioral basis. In a sense, reasonable permissiveness to determine
their behavioral direction is provided the staff members so they can feel
a sense of responsibility for their actions and a desire to be fully accountable for them. All of this requires a fervent regard for matters related
to faith in the professional attitudes and actions of each other—teacher
and supervisor. How much permissiveness and how much faith the
supervisor will place in the teacher is largely optional with the person

in such a position. However, in the era of the seventies with the gradual elimination of a superior-inferior relationship among teachers and administrators, such permissiveness and faith will be large indeed.

Much of the environment of the classroom needs to be reoriented so that new and more meaningful learning experiences can be developed. After significant learning begins to take place, then relevant meaning can occur on a personal basis as a result of providing more experiences that assist young people in gaining new individual perspectives. Interestingly enough, in some school situations supervisors may find that it is the administration that is less likely to desire this reorientation of learning experiences due to the possibility of disturbing the peaceful "status quo" situation that may exist. Teachers should welcome the opportunity to make learning more than an information or fact presenting condition and be desirous of help in restructuring the learning process to make this possible.

Learning must be designed so that it is not only continuous, but is infectious as well. Pupils should be assisted in recognizing that learning never ends, that it is a life-long process in which the love of learning never ceases. Teachers will become secure and knowledgeable in the fact that they are receiving support from the supervisory staff in taking the steps necessary to foster a love for learning by youth. Supervisor's supportive attitudes toward this kind of change has to be perceived by teachers if they are going to risk the changes that must be made in the classroom to improve learning.

The role of the supervisor, then, is one in which there is a continual planning procedure for dynamic growth in the areas of learning and instruction. This function consists of a highly organized attempt to establish as succinctly as possible the short-range and long-range instructional objectives of the institution that is providing these services. These objectives may be translated into precise curricular requirements and organized in concrete form so that, together with teachers and administrators, they can be utilized on a realistic basis both in the classroom and on the school level. The supervisor is not to function simply as a catalytic agent with teachers; his position is to make major creative contributions based upon his broad experience and on his ability to weld together the multiplicity of disciplines that will be brought to bear on the problem by members of the school faculty. In addition to this, he will focus the entire resources of a district supervisory organization as well as augment these services with those of consultants in specific areas of the curriculum where specialists are needed.

In many respects, the supervisory organization permits the school district to possess a vital organizational tool that will allow relevant information concerning the program of instruction to be presented to the institution at the appropriate time. As this leadership procedure unfolds, a continuing series of decision situations must be encountered and, if the organization is adequately prepared, these interrelated decisions can be made in logical sequence and in relation to the adjustment needs of the program. As the planning process moves ahead, the supervisor will undertake the responsibility to see that each decision is considered or made in its proper order. The information upon which each decision has been based should be available to the institution at the appropriate time. Although each supervisory experience contains many elements that are not duplicated elsewhere, there is a general process of planning and programming that calls for orderly progression in each instance. From the exploration of the nature of the problem to its final accomplishment, the process calls for the pursuance of several carefully defined steps that can lead to a solution. Fundamental to each of the steps that are to be taken is the establishment of a searching and constructive dialogue between the supervisor and the parties involved. At the appropriate time, others in the institutional circle and even outside this circle may become a party to the dialog and planning structure.

Confrontation

The educational world is in dynamic state of movement at the present time—flashing action taking place at unprecedented speed and many new developments that tend to leave the educator exasperated and bewildered. Supervisors are discovering that their long-standing influence as members of the administrative structure is beginning to dissipate and they are confronted by faculty power and drives that have long been dormant. Many peremptory demands are being made on the present day instructional leader that would have been unthinkable a decade ago, but they are now here in the era of the seventies. Some of these confrontations and demands are so startling in their impingement on curriculum and supervision that the role of educational management as we now know it could be destroyed before our very eyes.

Conflicts in some quarters have brought forth deep anxieties, strong tensions, and a state of confusion as to the kind of posture the program of instructional leadership should take in the face of faculty hostility. Such a condition—schools without guidance and leadership in the area of curriculum—can only bring a chaotic state in which school personnel will no longer be pulling together to educate the children in a community. One factor that must be recognized is that teachers and status leaders cannot be detached or isolated from each other and at the same time expect the educational process as we know it to survive or even grow. Although chief school administrators expect supervisors and building administrators to keep teachers content with their classroom work and under control, teachers are moving at loggerheads with these propositions and are making demands of their own concerning what represents their rights and privileges in these sensitive areas. In working with faculty groups the supervisor must be able to demonstrate his own prowess in the teaching-learning fields so that he can gain the cooperation of the faculty in demonstrating an impelling need for his services.

Prediction

Perhaps the ability to predict represents one of the most important tasks of the supervisors of instruction. The supervisor will be expected not only to work vigorously toward short-range objectives that are important to the district for attainment, but also to be able to operate on a high attainment level so that he has a clear vision of the long-range plans that should be followed. His predictive ability need not be a solitary one. He must be skillful in his working relations with influential and knowledgeable educators who can provide him with the supporting data that he needs. These persons, too, should have rather reliable forecasting talents. In most instances he will build system models that will design a course of action and indicate the kinds of alternatives that can be followed in reaching satisfactory goals. On the basis of these prediction models, the supervisor is in a strong position in his working relationships with his clientele as he has, through the development of his predicted plan, indicated what action he plans to take and the direction that he feels the organization must take. In any predictive situation values and concerns are given a high priority in developing the schematic model. Values and concerns change over any time sequence and the supervisor must be prepared to compensate for these changes so that the risk of predictive error will not be too great. Over and over again the practitioner in instructional supervision should allude to the fact that there is no such thing as a "certain" prediction. Acceptable alternatives, in any event, will be required if previously planned contingencies do not occur.

Role Expectations

Not everyone will agree upon the major functions and responsibilities of the supervisory leaders. Because of this, the administrator should provide periodic opportunities for the groups with which he is in frequent contact to discuss with him what they feel are the expectations for his leadership role.[1] These discussions should result in a better un-

---

[1]Stanley W. Williams, "Leadership Functions," unpublished paper, California State College at Long Beach, 1970.

derstanding as well as agreement concerning the manner in which the role is played and its final results. Much stress should be given to the findings and conclusions of research studies in this area as they relate to role analysis. Even matters concerned with supervisory attitudes and behavior should receive major emphasis in this context.

As the educational setting gradually shifts toward a new base of operations, the supervisory leader will require greater assistance from members of the faculty in aligning the school with the social forces that increasingly impinge upon it. He must weigh any opportunity to improve the school with its capabilities, both human and material, and be able to synthesize the development of the school's total program with that of other formal and informal groups in the community. His vision and foresight should be his only limitations for accomplishing the task that he sets out to do.

THE PURSUIT OF EDUCATIONAL POLICY

The supervisor or administrator of any school or district should expect to operate under a secure framework that makes possible broad policies and procedures that facilitate the proper functioning of the educational program. In fact, the development of sound educational policy represents one of the most important actions undertaken by educational leaders as they strive to make provisions for continued program improvement. Although the local board of education establishes basic policies that govern teaching and its supervision, it must be provided information that is impartial and factual by the supervisory staff that will assist it in reaching and making effective decisions. Beyond this the persons in supervisory positions should consult with the individuals who are to be involved in any policy decision before it is made at the district or school level.

The supervisor or administrator has a responsibility to see that the agreed upon policy statements become written. This means that all instructional policy regulations and procedures affecting the faculty should be in written form and made available to all concerned with them.

Instructional policies are fashioned from a multiplicity of sources. Certain aspects of instructional policy are predetermined by legal diction, and most states publish state educational codes that categorize the many policies that refer to instruction. At times the state board of education will issue its own set of rules and regulations that govern certain policies affecting the instructional program not already prescribed by state educational codes. Instructional matters that have been tried by the courts often influence the direction that is taken by supervisory personnel in working with groups (the current emphasis on bargaining agents for classroom teachers represents a new approach in providing leadership in the highly sensitive area of instructional improvement). Legal determining bodies at the intermediate or county level often give opinions about policy matters and local boards of education have the responsibility for preparing policy statements as they relate to curriculum and instruction.

When these policies and regulations have been considered, the supervisory staff and faculty can begin to clarify how they will attain their instructional objectives by human means. The supervisor or administrator has the responsibility now of determining that these policies are respected and, if not, why this is the case and what, if anything, needs to be done to correct the situation.

In almost every instance instructional policies are being made through staff-administrator or staff-supervisor discussion and decision. Modern school systems recognize the tremendous educational and professional resources that faculty members can bring to the many policy decisions that must be made. On most occasions the supervisor or administrator and the staff will strive for a consensus of agreement before arriving at any final decision. It is obvious that the staff will support more wholeheartedly the policies that they have helped develop, for people respond better to an idea or a policy when they have been active in its development.

Human Concerns

The central theme of educational management centers upon public policy decisions and supervisors must be aware that the public interest in education extends from the broadest dimensions of the cultural environment through social processes to each individual. Therefore, an educational system must consider the total range of human concerns that are operative in public-policy decision making. Supervisors will discover that there is need for clearer exposition and dialog on both the means and the ends of education. The roles and the purposes of education will be determined by the character of existing social institutions and by the values of the culture. Demands for change in educational practices appear to arise primarily out of three evidence-producing processes: evaluation of the effective productivity of the schools in performing currently assigned functions; evolution of the culture and the creation of societal demands for change in educational functions; and a realization that new alternatives exist for the performance of educational functions.

The supervisor will undoubtedly accept the assumption that the basic purpose of education is to prepare each individual for effective participation in society. As a result, he must be willing to accept the consequence that evaluation of the educational process must be in terms of the degree to which each individual is judged to be effective. Unfortunately, decisions regarding effective productivity and performance contributions are made by individual environmental judges who possess differing points of view. Each judge's point of view will reflect his unique pattern of values and expectations. Supervisors should note that two common criteria are generally used by each judge in relation to performance and productivity regardless of his point of view. These criteria are the individual's ability to exhibit behavior in conformance with the social group to which he elects to attach himself and to demonstrate economic independence. In each instance, these criteria are applied by different publics whose respective memberships share different perceptions as to what constitutes performance effectiveness in society. As an instructional leader, the supervisor may solicit societal involvement in the identification and definition of acceptable performance indicators and productivity patterns. He should realize that establishing and maintaining value sensitivity must be made a continuous concern of instructional improvement. In the last analysis, the success of programs of planned change will depend upon human judgmental decisions that programs are effective and that the educational enterprise is moving forward at a reasonable pace.

Some Typical Policy Statements

As the supervisor or administrator, with the faculty, strives to provide the finest possible educational experiences and opportunities to pupils, several illustrative statements might be written as they relate to his task:

—He should base differentiation of educational experiences on the differing needs and abilities of pupils, refraining from any discriminating decisions.

—He has the obligation to inform the board and the community of any deficiencies in the educational program or its services.

—He resists all attempts by vested-interest groups or individuals to infringe upon the educational program to promote such interests.

—He seeks teaching candidates, regardless of race or creed, solely on the basis of their professional qualifications for the position.

—He recognizes that provision of equal educational opportunities for all children may require a great variety of resources for differing groups.

—He has the professional obligation to be a positive instructional leader in the community by defining the role of the school and giving directions as to the manner in which it can fulfill its purposes.

New York: An Example

The public schools of the city of New York have, by board of education policy, given the Division of Curriculum Development the supervision of all activities in these related areas: curriculum development, and educational and vocational guidance; the preparation of courses of study, syllabi, and other curricular publications; and the selection of teaching materials—textbooks, library books, audio-visual and objective aids. It has direct supervision of the Bureau of Curriculum Research, School Library Service, Audio-Visual Instruction, Educational and Vocational Guidance, the office of Textbooks and Supplies, and the office of the Coordinator of Curriculum Periodicals. It also supervises other directors in relation to curriculum development.

The New York Division of Curriculum Development has a fantastic responsibility for furthering the development and coordination of curriculum policy for the city's schools. Most districts, on a much smaller scale, however, are confronted with the same basic tasks as they become associated with policy development.

PREPARATION FOR INSTRUCTIONAL LEADERSHIP

Institutions of higher education increasingly have been working together on a cooperative basis to improve the preparation programs for those who would become supervisory leaders as indicated in the University Council for Educational Administration (UCEA) and similar reports. Numerous inter-institutional organizations have encouraged various types of joint endeavors as a relatively new phenomenon in regard to preparation programs. At present fewer institutions are directing major efforts toward change and improvement in administrator-supervisor preparation as they have found much strength in utilizing inter-institutional cooperative tactics. Career development seminars or institutes, the development of new internship programs, the inclusion of social science personnel with education faculties, the development and assessment of simulated materials for classroom use, and the establishment of college-related centers for educational research are but a few of the latest inter-institutional cooperative efforts.

Redoubled attempts are being made to attract the finest candidates possible to enter programs leading to an administrative and/or supervisory credential. Professors of educational administration are seeking ways to assess better the latest research information as well as attempting to upgrade the instructional media that can be used to enrich the classroom experience. Exploratory work and new research have been initiated in regard to the development of a taxonomy as it relates to educational leadership and an emphasis on the behavioral sciences as a means of improving the preparation program. Urban communities have been studied in relationship to such unique factors as formal and informal power groups, socio-economic class unrest, the relationship of the community to the school's functional design, and the peculiar sensitivities that exist in such a setting. Attempts are being made to attract candidates from the area of social science as well as education to enter supervisory preparation programs.

Much interest has been shown in the relationship of the work of supervisory and administrative personnel in business and industry as well as those individuals working in the private educational sector. Areas such as those that fall in the matrix patterns of non-school organizations are being studied for their relationship to the development of new strategy and thrust. The complexities of exchange and feedback are being reviewed for more desirable arrangements to improve public school organizational and instructional patterns. The management of computer systems for educational administration is being investigated so that candidates in training will acquire the necessary knowledge concerning the processing of automated information and restructuring its results as a means of upgrading the educational program. Models and other prototypes that will be used in decision-making processes are receiving expert attention so that they may assist in the improvement of future teacher on-the-job plans and strategies.

In effect, ongoing and projected activities that will change radically the preparation programs for educational leaders are currently under way. Outstanding scholars from many disciplines and institutional settings are working together diligently to enhance the probability that new and innovative programs of preparation will pervade the campuses where challenging and exciting opportunities for future administrative and supervisory assignments will exist.

Preparation for Tomorrow

Training programs for supervisors should not cause them to become cogs in a static educational system that retreats only within itself to stay where it feels undisturbed and unafraid. Instead, the preparation program should be relevant and functional to the extent that it assists the trainee to search for new challenges to face in the social, economic, and political arenas. It should spur him to be aware that the social institutions of our time represent an infinite amount of diversity and challenge as he attempts to cope with their problems. As the schools are being requested to take on new tasks and make new commitments, trainees must learn not to be exercised over the appearance of new factors that confront the school and challenge the authenticity of its educational program. Some of these societal occurrences are: the rapidity in the pace of change, the increased demand for more education for everyone, the population explosion and the growth of the cities, the rapid development of a sophisticated and affluent society, the fantastic increase in our sectors of knowledge, and the rise of secular and pragmatic attitudes on the part of the citizenry. These environmental factors are ones that will cause a reasonable amount of control over the educational program. The supervisor should learn how to react to these phenomena with sophistication and directness in developing an instructional program that can synsthesize these forces. Obviously he cannot become detached from such significant social developments. He must come to close grips with these and other issues and be able to predict the extent to which the staff and district can cope with them as they impinge upon the educational programs.

There is a growing awareness that supervisors are becoming more sensitive to and involved in community life. With increasing demands made by the public for greater participation in the affairs of the school, candidates must be given real-life experiences in their training programs. These experiences will provide an opportunity for them to discern how to give the public an active, rather than a passive, role in assisting the schools in developing modern, relevant education programs. The supervisor, too, requires knowledge of how to develop plans and maneuvers that will enable him to satisfy the needs of the populace as they become immersed in the philosophical discussions leading to the formation of school goals and objectives. In many large urban areas, for example, supervisors should have a trained ability to do more than merely become familiar with the causes of urban problems. Instead, their training should develop the ability to generate the necessary behavioral patterns that will lead to the establishment of a cooperative environment in which the school and urban community can work together closely.

There are many social forces that have a bearing upon the life of the school and the supervisor-in-training needs exposure to these. In the future it may be that the supervisor's main functions will be analyzing the community and determining how it can aid or adversely affect the educational program. More attention must be given in the seventies to the interpretation of the metamorphosis occurring in many communities that will affect the school and the direction in which it moves if the school is to remain a pervasive force as a power structure. To do this, candidates will be taught ways in which they can analyze and interpret these transpositions for their future teaching and administrative staffs. In effect, this stance represents a "look from within" by all parties in the educational establishment as a basis of meeting the deep societal needs that lie without.

Training programs should develop a new series of communications links or patterns for their candidates. In today's world students and their families often exhibit an entirely different type communication model than that of the staff within the school. A lack of understanding or appreciation of this sometimes raw and rough communication model by educators has caused frustration and breakdown in the development of a cycle of understanding between these two forces. Further, overwhelming personality differences may exist between the educators and the community groups and these must be allowed for and appreciated by the staff before a reconciliation can take place that will lead to a basic understanding of each group by the other. Recent requests by minority groups to have supervisors and administrators chosen from their own minority culture is an example of the demand by some inner-city elements to strengthen the communication and race bond between the school and the community.

The most functional phase of the training program comes through actual participation as an instructional consultant at the district level. Inasmuch as many training functions lend themselves to this kind of direct participation, this task becomes the cornerstone of any training program. In fact, being given responsibility and commensurate authority will permit the trainee to become acquainted with some of the awesome demands that he will face in the future. The promotion of interpersonal understanding and the role of human relations are substantial areas of participation that can be encouraged, not threatened during the training process. Every effort should be made to make these functions a focal point of all that follows during the training experience.

An Interdisciplinary Approach to Preparation

Strong evidence has been given that supervisors and administrators should not only be highly knowledgeable in terms of their own value systems, but they must also be well aware of other important value systems in the fields of economics, sociology, political science, and the like. Beyond the usual strong concentration in the fields of supervision and administration, as much as one-third of the preparation program should be spent in interdisciplinary fields, particularly those of the social sciences and related areas. Both formalized courses and discussion-type seminars should be taken as a means of insuring wide exposure of trainees to the value systems of those disciplines that are closely related to the central role of the public school—the ability of the learner to engage in rational thought in solving the many problems he will encounter in his lifetime. Ohio State University and Teachers College, Columbia University, have successfully used interdisciplinary advisory committees from the university faculty to advise the staff in educational administration concerning its program. The Department of Education at the University of Chicago is a part of the Division of Social Sciences, and sociology, psychology, political science, and other disciplines are integrated into the supervisor-administrator preparation program. The University of Oregon operates on the basic premise that the preparation of school administrators and supervisors is a responsibility of the total university and requires interdisciplinary cooperation.

The Mott Program for interns at Michigan State University provides a high interdisciplinary and academic approach to the preparation of future supervisors and administrators. This program focuses on the exercise of leadership, rather than on the theories about leadership. Students from various classes read widely from the discipline fields, even more than from publications that are in education. They engage in a dialog with a renowned scholar once a month and, prior to the lecture, students read voraciously in the lecturer's discipline field. During the other three weekly meetings during the month, lecturers are selected from universities within the state. Once a week students listen to presentations from staff members in many fields at the university and, in addition, students carry on a prolonged dialog with another staff member at a noon-day luncheon. In addition, the director of the interns conducts a seminar session one day a week. The experience is promoted to help students evaluate their intern work, to discuss implications that relate to educational needs in the field, and to present some of the director's concepts about relevant educational theory and practice.

A southern university has developed a training program that has: provided day-long seminars that are based on the concept of helping trainees prepare supervisory programs; organized internship experiences in which supervisors at the district level work with interns; offered summer session academic programs that are devoted to the preparation of educational supervisors; and scheduled regular semester classes for interns to assist them in pursuing their supervisory training program while enrolled as full-time graduate students at the university.

Discovering Talent

There is reasonable evidence that written tests do not effectively appraise human-relations qualities, that rating scales do not identify the most capable applicants, and that the oral interview does not provide sufficient information in depth to objectively select the best applicants. To overcome these singular deficiencies, several types of additional techniques should be utilized by a district seeking outstanding supervisory or administrative candidates to fill an important post.

Job analyses should be provided for each position opening so that the candidates are fully aware of the requirements of the position. Training programs might be offered each year so that the candidate will have some insight into the many types of experiences that will be expected of him as he prepares for a possible opening, and an appraisal made each year of the candidate's potential for such a position. In addition, a new set of experiences should be provided so that he will have an opportunity to improve his performance as well as broaden his perceptual understanding of how to fulfill his role as a supervisor or administrator. Peer ratings should be included in the candidate's cumulative file that should be housed in the district office. Finally, utilize a selection committee at the district level that will be expert in the matter of evaluation of candidates and their qualifications. This committee can make valid recommendations to the central office as a basis for the selection of new personnel who will become instructional leaders in the district.

An Internship Program for Supervisors and Administrators

The Riverside (California) Unified School District has recently embarked on a program for interns who are interested in demonstrating their effectiveness in a supervisory-administrative capacity.

Recently fifteen experienced teachers in the district who hold administrative certificates were chosen to take part in this program. Active participation, involvement, and reaction are developed in the series of meetings which are held each year for these interns.

Riverside is looking for individuals with courage, vision, intelligence, an eagerness to work, a desire and an ability to seek new horizons, and possessed with the dynamic leadership qualifications of internship candidates. In providing for these interns, several techniques are used to produce an outstanding in-service program for these individuals. Approximately fifteen meetings (4:00–8:30 P.M.) are scheduled during the year. Provocative problems and topics are discussed with key administrative and supervisory personnel in the district taking part. Interestingly enough, the superintendent and associate superintendent of the district attend every meeting of the intern group and also serve as district leaders to the program. In addition to this, a two-day retreat in the mountains is scheduled for the entire group. Before meetings are held, the intern leaders place materials of importance in the hands of the group (instructional guides, pertinent literature, policy handbooks, etc.) so that they will have had an opportunity to prepare themselves for the afternoon and evening sessions and to be in a position to raise pertinent questions concerning the material as it is presented. Beyond this, visitation studies are made by the intern representatives. Arrangements are made for interns to spend a few days in such places as these: the district central office investigating the development of the instructional program, the structure and functioning of the pupil personnel program, and so forth; the administrative office of some school wherein, for example, a journal might be kept on a selected principal, supervisor, and others; the central district office or school within another district other than one's own; the campus of a college or university where research and training programs could be reviewed; the offices of pertinent industries and commercial houses where a close view could be gained of the relationship of these ventures to the school; and in a variety of other places that offer the intern an invaluable experience in the development of an understanding of the vast sociological and technical changes that are closely related to the exercise of good leadership functions by the prospective supervisor and administrator. Resource people in the program are recruited from district staff personnel, university and college staffs, the press, and from other related groups. Analyses are made of newer methods of presenting data, ideas, and information, and an assignment is made which concerns a major problem or problems of the district as a group study. Included in this study is an analysis of the problem or problems, a review of the research, a consideration of new studies which must be made, and a proposal of solutions in terms of the needs and capabilities of the district. Reading materials in several provocative areas are suggested for the increased edification of the intern.

Obviously the school district that undertakes the initiative to sponsor and develop such a program will do much to assure itself of the availability of outstanding certificated persons who have thoroughly demonstrated their capacity for filling a position of leadership when the opportunity presents itself. One of the most serious shortages of manpower in our society is at the executive level and, unless there is a willingness in our school systems to budget for this type of internship experience, the entire program of supervisory and administrative personnel replacement will greatly suffer through haphazard recruitment and selection procedures.

SUMMARY

The basic characteristics of good supervision require a keen insight into these basic areas: goals, organization, changing attitudes and behavior, democratic processes, experimentation and the flow of ideas, self-improvement, decentralization of authority, staff and budget requirements, accreditation, change, educational research, and staff morale. In working with each of these phases the supervisor or administrator should know how to provide the intellectual and emotional climate to implement each of them. His penchant toward supervisory leadership will be founded in his belief that the teacher is a partner in the instructional endeavor and that his function is largely that of a resource or service person.

In any situation where judgment is necessary, the supervisor must know where he plans to go and what he wishes to do and this calls for policy development. The early establishment of instructional policies will provide the routines for personnel and the procedures to follow that will insure judicious use of supervisory time, effort, and intelligence.

Facing up to the issues in supervision requires that the program should be organized and operated so that human relations are fully utilized and encouraged. In recognizing the basic issues that supervisors or administrators will face, adequate programs of preparation should identify good prospects early, recognize the need for an interdisciplinary approach, give heavy emphasis to scholarly research, and provide a challenging internship program experience.

SELECTED REFERENCES

Association for Supervision and Curriculum Development. *To Nurture Humaneness: Commitment for the '70's.* Washington, D.C.: National Education Association, Yearbook, 1970.

Foley, W. I. *et al. Educational Decision Making Through Operations Research.* Rockleigh, N.J.: Allyn and Bacon, 1971.

Granger, Robert L. *Educational Leadership: An Interdisciplinary Perspective.* Scranton: Intext, 1971.

Hough, John B., and James K. Duncan. *Teaching: Description and Analysis.* Reading, Mass.: Addison-Wesley, 1970.

Johansen, J. H. *American Education: The Task and the Teacher.* Dubuque: William C. Brown, 1971.

Joyce, Bruce R., and Berj Harootunian. *The Structure of Teaching.* Palo Alto: Science Research Associates, 1967.

McClosky, M. *Teaching Strategies and Classroom Realities.* Englewood Cliffs: Prentice-Hall, 1971.

Rubin, Louis S. *Frontiers in School Leadership.* Chicago: Rand McNally, 1970.

Van Til, William. *Curriculum: Quest for Relevance.* New York: Houghton Mifflin, 1971.

CHAPTER 3

Supporting the Educational Enterprise

With the impact of research on the educational structure, the entire concept of supervision has undergone a dramatic change within the past decade. Today the pressure for innovation comes from both internal and external forces as the teaching faculty and status leaders direct the educational enterprise. To accommodate this, both theoretical and practical means of supporting the existence of change agents are fostered and encouraged. Management study, increased data flow, expert facilitation, and new organizational designs are but a few of the methods that are utilized as means of creating a climate leading to change and improvement. The educational structure is able to improve itself by basing its efforts on a continuum that repeatedly energizes change agents at every level of operational input and output.

If the educational enterprise is to succeed in its effort to meet environmental changes, it has a responsibility to gauge its effectiveness in terms of the willingness of professional personnel to support educational movement and change. Desire to engage in experimental activities, working closely with teachers in building a team spirit, providing sufficient supervisory support services, and recognizing fundamental tenets of responsibility and function are important areas of concern in aiding the improvement of the educational process.

EXPERIMENTAL ACTIVITIES

The availability of supervisory leaders to teachers and other personnel needing instructional assistance is an important aspect of the supervisory task. Conferences with teachers, instructional meetings, and a variety of committee functions concerned with instructional improvement all relate to the necessity for administrators and supervisors to be available to help solve problems of this nature. The matter of quality control of instruction in the classroom is essential if curriculum development is to be a successful joint undertaking, and administrative-faculty personnel must work as a team to provide for needed improvement. As resource persons, supervisors and administrators must actively promote better understanding of the teaching-learning process to assist teachers in the continued development of professional skills and techniques. Probably far too little has been accomplished in terms of disseminating information on an individualized basis. The relevance of such information to teaching practices will promote a high level of instructional improvement. Many community groups and agencies must be contacted as a means of involving them as resource bodies that can offer to the teacher information that cannot be obtained elsewhere. Assisting faculty members in the development of experimental or pilot programs in their own classrooms is a further aspect of the role of good supervision. Only recently has the school classroom been viewed as an ideal laboratory situation in which supervisory personnel can play an important part in fostering the growth of new and exciting ideas and concepts.

Trained and skilled supervisory personnel have the necessary knowledge and procedural understanding that makes it possible to help teachers embark on a constructive program for improved teaching. Few enterprises can match public education as a huge community-professional endeavor; and educational leaders must be competent practitioners in assisting teachers to understand the school's role in the community as well as interpreting the educational program and its functions in that community. Both presentation and analysis are common elements in a coordinated involvement of teachers when they utilize their classrooms as learning laboratories.

As experimental activities in the school become known to the public, supervisory leaders can expect themselves to become involved with and under pressures from political activities. Professional associations, such as the National Education Association (NEA), have gone on record proclaiming the need for educators to become political activists and to take an active part in politics in their community. Such involvement certainly includes supervisory personnel who, with the faculty, are on the leading edge of the development and improvement of the instructional program.

Instructional leadership, then, involves the structuring and redesigning of many of the older and outmoded phases of the curriculum. Frontal attacks on these sacred segments or areas of many portions of the curriculum will demand that administrators and supervisors take strong stands as educational leaders in the defense and promotion of innovative practices.

BUILDING TEAM SPIRIT

Recent developments in supervisory practice indicate that supervisors are working closely with teachers and administrators as builders of a team spirit. These are the individuals who seek to assist the team in solving mutual problems that affect the instructional program. Every attempt should be made by supervisors to devise activities that are mutually satisfying and to involve all those to whom they are responsible in working toward common goals. One of the supervisor's primary thrusts is to organize a satisfying and stimulating intellectual climate that will permit the faculty to acquire an emerging attitude toward the development of personal and professional goals. His views of the educational system are directed toward the elimination of hurried, unstructured procedures and the furthering of long-range plans that permit professional growth and increased academic involvement in the educational evolution of the school. As a colleague to faculty and administrators alike, the supervisor portrays the image of an individual who is attentive, understanding, and responsive to the needs and desires of all those with whom he works. His collegial stance in the community of educators is one in which he works as a fellow master teacher, not that of a demigod who considers his role and person to be above that of the teaching faculty. His humanity must be as wide as the profession itself and he must give daily evidence of this cooperative stance.

In the past the role of the teacher has been downgraded because of the numerous routine tasks that have been assigned to him. Too many clerical functions have been allotted to the teacher with little regard to the challenging role that he wishes to play by concentrating primarily on classroom teaching. It is difficult to visualize how teachers can improvise and innovate in any meaningful way under the intolerable circumstances that exist in some schools today. So saddled down are some teachers with secondary-level functions that many of them will have to be taught new techniques and procedures when these routine jobs are taken from them. In some respects, supervisors may, in the seventies, be performing an almost incredible task if they are able to convince boards of education and administrators that teachers do indeed need paraprofessional assistance to enable them to concentrate on teaching. Extraneous requests from school officials must be brought to their attention and ways devised to permit them to utilize their energies as directors of learning as opposed to "office clerk" managerial efforts. Many tasks are commonly expected to be performed by teachers *in addition to* classroom teaching and the supervisor must intelligently plan to promote ways in which these frustrating burdens can be lifted. In effect, this will require a reallocation of the work week in which teachers will spend only one-third of their time teaching classes, one-third in devising strategies that will lead toward effective teaching-learning situations, and the remaining one-third in working with students on a one-to-one basis.

In the profession one hears occasional discussion as to the means by which the teacher's role can become broadened and thereby more significant and challenging. There is, of course, nothing wrong with extending the teaching task and its influence, assuming that this is a meaningful commission that leads towards the increase of teacher effectiveness. How can this be done and at the same time not create a gargantuan problem by overburdening an already weary instructor? Such a move would necessitate the development of new and more meaningful tasks to replace the older stereotyped images that have beset the traditional teacher for decades. With the advent of negotiations, teachers' roles can be expanded by giving them, through their department or other organizational structure, a far more authoritative voice in the affairs of the school by granting them reasonable autonomy as a recommending body in such matters as the recruitment, hiring, and promotion of teachers. Committees that have both advisory and coordinate-administrative functions could provide much of this thrust. Even the matter of cooperative evaluation of teachers (to be discussed in detail later) by selected groups of teachers should be weighed by teaching faculties as a coordinate function with the evaluation by the school's administrative staff.

Almost constantly during the day teachers must make decisions that affect the success or failure of their classes. What they do is largely determined by the way in which their behavioral responses are arranged or linked with one another. The teacher's range of actions will vary from those that are habitual or intuitive to those that are deliberate and carefully weighed. Supervisors should provide a system of models that can serve as a basis for understanding and improving these variables in teacher behavior. Such models should assist teachers in recognizing ways in which their behavioral characteristics can be upgraded and can result in an improvement of their teaching skills in the classroom. Seminar-type in-service programs devoted to a searching study of teacher behavior and how it relates to learning are illustrative of the numerous types of unifying experiences on a close, informal basis that can be made available to the teaching faculty.

In conclusion, there are several concepts related to strengthening the work that supervisors accomplish with their teaching colleagues. These are that: good supervisors see their major responsibilities inextricably interwoven with the process of teaching and learning; the relationships that supervisors have with teachers and students be based on dignifying and enhancing these individuals as they work together; successful curriculum revision can take place only if there is a real consideration for the ideas, thoughts, and feelings of the teaching faculty; the dual process of rejection and acceptance of change can be controlled and channeled effectively; and the supervisor understand the rejector and the kind of rejection that is taking place and work patiently with him so that he can take part in the vital process of change.

STAFFING FOR SUPERVISION

The current trend in educational administration is for individual schools to become more autonomous and more functional as basic units of administrative structure. As programs are defined and assistance provided to develop the educational thrust at each local school level, the supervisor should view each of these units as having certain distinctive characteristics that need to be embellished and supported. No longer should the homogeneous, unified plan for each school be expected to further the singleness of purpose and function of all schools throughout the district. Instead, differentiated patterns of learning and productivity should produce reasonably independent programs that are related to and dependent upon the district office only insofar as the situation demands this at the central administrative level. Various school faculties will be engaged in deciding what will be their short-range and long-range goals and the processes necessary to bring these into existence. These faculties will look closely at the composition of their student bodies and will take a measured assessment of the cultural surroundings in which they find themselves as a means of determining the functions that they must fulfill. Schools will take cognizance of the fact that several phenomena will occur in the future: there will be a vastly improved system of communication, and information storage and retrieval; dramatic breakthroughs will be made in the biological sciences and in the areas of ethical and moral concepts; greater psychological and political tensions will be found among the general populace; urbanization will increase and with it will come accelerated problems in the areas of transportation, housing, and waste disposal; and the populace will have shorter work weeks and more leisure time as the result of increased automation that will require greater technical competence and educational exposure for the work force. School faculties must be prepared to identify new educational purposes that will meet these new and demanding requirements.

The progress that students make in school will depend more and more on the individual initiative and creative demands made by the school faculty and less upon the forceful tactics of the central office administrative staff. Supervisors will be held accountable for providing supportive services that broaden the inventive efforts made by individual faculty members as they exploit their own knowledge and professional skills in raising student learning opportunities. They must be in a position to assist faculty personnel in assessing and rationalizing their educational performance to the community at large and the central office administration in particular. The amount of assistance that supervisors can provide teachers in this instance will, in large measure, determine the kind of support that teachers demand as well as reject from the supervisory force.

Suvervisory Staff Practices

The Chicago management consultant firm of Booz, Allen, and Hamilton, Inc. recently conducted a national survey of 741 school systems to determine central office staffing practices, particularly in terms of the broad classification of curriculum, instruction, and special services as one category. The findings of the survey can be used as guidelines, but they should be used cautiously.[1] It is interesting to note that districts in excess of 75,000 enrollment had the lowest ratios of general administrators and curriculum, instruction, and special service personnel and the highest ratio of data processing, clerical, and secretarial personnel. These statistics suggest that districts with more than 75,000 enrollment probably make more use of support resources (data processing, clerical, and secretarial personnel) and thus reduce the need for additional administrative and supervisory personnel.

The average number of curriculum, instruction, and special services personnel per 1,000 students in varying-sized districts is indicated as follows: more than 75,000—.583; 50,001 - 75,000—.634; 25,001 - 50,000—.659; 12,001 - 25,000—.754; 6,001 - 12,000—.602; 3,001 - 6,000 —.901; 1,201 - 3,000—1.138; 1,200 or less—2.182.

School officials might ask these questions that relate to the value of their staffing practices: (1) What responsibilities are assigned to the central office staff? (2) What performance standards are to be met? (3) What tasks can be grouped to maximize skills at the lowest required cost? (4) What are reasonable work loads for personnel? (5) What special skills and knowledge are required by the central office staff? These and

[1]Clyde N. Carter, "How Many School Administrators are Enough?" *Nation's Schools*, vol. 82, no. 3 (September 1968), pp. 51–57.

many other questions need to be answered before staffing can be accomplished.

A Strategy for Curriculum Development

Pressures for innovation, for change, and for improvement have been coming from society as a whole and from pressure groups within the community. How then, can schools move with greater efficiency and with more definite planning into procedures of curriculum development? In developing a model that will accomplish this, there are three aspects to consider: research, demonstration, and dissemination.[2]

The first responsibility of the central office staff is the collection of existing research and the second is its evaluation. In being relieved of much of this frustration, the Educational Research Information Center (ERIC) will make it possible in the future to feed a question (for example, grouping) to ERIC and get all the research that has been done on that problem. Some university research centers which will also assist are: Oregon, on educational administration; Pittsburgh, on individual differences; Georgia, on stimulation of the intellect in children from two to thirteen. New regional educational laboratories under Title IV will add another dimension to the possibilities for curriculum experimentation and dissemination. These centers can help the central office evaluate models that are or are not appropriate to a particular local school population.

A third function of the central office is carrying on significant activities in curriculum planning within the system. Each school in the system might become an experimental center (one with nongraded organization, another with team teaching, a third with individual study, and the like). Some teachers may wish to work on the exploration of a given hypothesis in their particular school. Each central office consultant might wish to be associated with at least one experiment. Certain teachers, too, could serve in a demonstration and in-service clinic while others might be associated with basic research.

A fourth central office responsibility is to provide for the participation of teachers and local schools in the initiation and formation of policy. A curriculum council is needed where ideas are initiated, studies proposed, problems identified, and procedures recommended that should be tested for system-wide adoption.

[2]Kimball Wiles, "Strategy for Curriculum Development: Some Aspects of a Comprehensive Plan," *Curriculum Exchange*, vol. 8, no. 7 (April, 1966), pp. 1–2 and 4. See also Marcella R. Lawler, editor, *Strategies for Planned Curricular Innovation* (New York: Teachers College Press, 1970).

In-service education efforts should support largely those teachers carrying on experimentation, and clinics focusing on particular demonstrations. Special seminars, too, could be part of in-service education and be built around the study of research on a given topic. Finally, a research staff should collect evidence in demonstrations that are not controlled experiments and help to identify areas where the evidence is not sufficient to justify a demonstration, therefore setting up the procedure to get the research done.

Team-Principal Design

The major premise of the team-principal concept is that cooperative teaching has some viable lessons for the supervisor and administrator. Considering that the "self-contained" school may be open to some criticism, the Harvard plan is an attempt to prevent the comparative isolation of the school unit as it now exists.[3] The plan uses three categories for the team-principal design.

First, the *team-leader type.* This refers to a team with a hierarchical authority structure involving a designated leader. It possibly would be a principal with experience in a given area to assume the role of the administrative team leader and two other principals or senior administrators. In this model, supervisors would be under the jurisdiction of the principals as well as the central office. The administrative team leadership might be rotated among the principals depending on the administrative task. In this model it would be mandatory that there exist a vertical authority structure with one designated leader for specific task areas who would act as the final decision maker.

Second, the *associate-type team.* In this type of structure all team members have equal status with no designated leader. This provides for a pooling of talent and a group of final decision-makers as opposed to one decision-maker. This plan possibly would not make the principals involved feel so threatened. It would seem also to permit the emergence of special competencies as specific tasks arose.

Third, the type of team that comprises an *experienced administrator and a beginning administrator.* Many times new, inexperienced administrators have not had the opportunity of working with more than one man while learning the job. This type of team provides for the new principal the opportunity to work with all members of the team for a given period of time in order to gain insights into different leadership

[3]James Grieg and Robert R. Lee, "Cooperative Administration," *The National Elementary Principal,* vol. XLIV, no. 3 (January 1965), pp. 71–76. See also Alvin C. Eurich, Editor, *High School 1980: The Shape of The Future in American Secondary Education* (New York: Pitman, 1970), pp. 214–217.

styles. It is felt that valuable time is wasted by administrators casting off alternatives or not being able to perceive a number of good alternatives in the decision-making process. Through this experience the intern-administrator would be able to make quicker and better decisions.

Organizing for Improvement

To increase the capacity for instructional leadership for secondary-school principals, a western school district has deployed its administrative staff so that 60 to 70 percent of each principal's time may be invested in this area of activity. In addition to assistant principals in each school who have basic responsibilities in the areas of counseling and guidance, curriculum development, and student activities, fulltime subject-matter coordinators are assigned. Generally there are three or four of these coordinators who exhibit expertise in a number of fields and their assignment is determined accordingly. Each of these faculty coordinators gives leadership to teachers through orientation meetings, classroom visitation, demonstration teaching, and evaluation of the total classroom program. Much of the coordinators' work occurs during the summer months when they are responsible for in-service workshops and activities. The faculty coordinators are hired on a twelve-month contract so that a uniform plan of curriculum improvement develops on a meaningful basis at the school and that it coordinates with over-all district purposes and plans.

The Center for Planned Change in Los Angeles has intiated a project in which a mid-city Planning Team has provided additional pilot activities directly affecting pupils in the classroom.[4] The Planning Team, consisting of four members, has gone directly to: people in the community, teachers in the classroom, pupils enrolled in the schools, and supportive personnel in the operational and instructional service areas of the school district. The Planning Team has been an important adjunct to the supervisory staff in that it has helped: establish a closer relationship and a continuing dialog between the school and the community; school personnel to become better acquainted with the community in which they serve; school personnel to learn the social and native heritage of pupils as a basis for adapting their teaching methods; and teachers to innovate and broaden the educational programs through greater implementation of the district's Research and Development services. Educational complex targets are designated by the Planning Team as a basis for identifying and developing new methods of instruction and increasing community awareness and participation in the evolvement of the total school program.

[4]Center for Planned Change, *Progress Report*, May 1969, pp. 33–36.

RESPONSIBILITY AND FUNCTIONS

Recently some crucial questions have been raised by educators in regard to appropriate supervisory theory and practice. In reviewing some of these searching questions, the author has attempted to come to grips with several important aspects of supervision as they relate to the basic task of supporting the educational enterprise.

What educational units (state, intermediate, school district, or individual school) should become responsible for supervision? Although there is general agreement that the strong local school district should be basically responsible for providing adequate supervisory services, the state should be encouraged to expand its leadership position. With the ever-expanding requirements for programs "in depth" in many areas of the curriculum, there is a valid responsibility for the state to shoulder a much greater share of this function. Resource specialists, on an advisory basis, should be available to assist all school districts as required in a large variety of grade level or subject areas. With this advisory assistance, the local district supervisors and administrators can assume primary responsibility for development of the supervisory program.

How can the services of one of these units strengthen other units? If the state is providing more adequate supervisory services to strong local school districts, then it remains for the intermediate district to provide central, coordinated services to the small or weak school districts. It is the responsibility of the state department of education to formulate state-wide guidelines as to the coordination and utilization of organizational units so that overlap or lack of supervisory services to local school districts does not become a problem.

Will strong supervisors in the central office tend to make the school principal ineffective in the instructional program? If the principal, as the head supervisor for his school, is a strong instructional leader, the answer is, "No." Frequent conferences with the central office supervisor should provide the principal with the assistance that he needs in making instructional decisions with his faculty at the school level that are in keeping with district policies and procedures.

Will special supervision in physical education, art, music, science, etc. survive? With greater emphasis being placed on subject-matter specialization, particularly at the secondary level, there currently is a need for a greater numbers of persons with special skills and techniques to work with teachers in these highly specialized areas. As a change agent, the special supervisor must be competent in all major aspects of his subject field as he gives guidance to teachers in committees, workshops, individual and group conferences, demonstrations, staff meetings, and through the issuance of supervisory bulletins. This is an age of specialization and the special-subject supervisor is a product of that age.

Is vertical or horizontal supervision more functional? Expressed in another way, line (or vertical) supervision is less functional than staff (or horizontal) supervision. In matters of administration or evaluation, central-office supervisors should be eliminated from this task as their effectiveness is lessened when the teacher who needs help is aware of this. The principal, of course, must assume both of these functions and also take the responsibility for line (or vertical) supervision. In the final analysis, horizontal supervision is the best technique for the central office to pursue, while line supervision is a necessity for the fulfillment of the principal's role.

How can supervision help people to think about the purposes of the school and then devise programs to implement these purposes? Supervision can help all persons in the community to develop an awareness as to the school's role in curriculum development and practices. It can foster the idea that no curricular program is ever final, that there is constant socio-economic change going on in any community with a resultant effect on school needs, that the faculty and students of the school are constantly re-evaluating and changing their ideas as to the basic educational objectives that should be attained, and that in an era of rapid technolgocial growth the school has continual need for new materials, resources, and services. Following this dissemination of information, persons in supervisory positions must facilitate the implementation of purposes through the solicitation of cooperation in these aspects: curriculum development, organization design, staff implementation, facility provision, material requirements, in-service programs, and educational program measurement.

Is supervision essentially a telling or helping process? With the advent of highly trained teachers it is apparent that supervision is a "helping" procedure. The supervisor uses his special skills and techniques to assist the professional person in the classroom to do a better job. As an agent of change, he can never expect the teacher to be motivated to innovate in the classroom unless the teacher wants this on his own. Moral support, consultation, recognition, and sharing of ideas are possible only when supervision is used as a helping process.

Administrators and supervisors must be prepared to analyze basic questions of this nature in the light of new developments and evolutionary changes. They will recognize, however, that today's answer may not be appropriate for tomorrow—and this is as it should be in a time of flux and vitality.

SUMMARY

The new strategy for supervision relies on many fundamental concepts and innovations. The pressure today is to discover ways in which the functions of supervision can be fulfilled much more rapidly and effectively than in the past. Basically, the renewed effort must revolve around the motivation of teachers and enable them to reach their potential.

Unifying activities in supervision must be fostered in such areas as guidance, student activities, plant administration, community relations, business management, scheduling, and the like. Supervision, in effect, must strengthen and relate to these functions while stressing the improvement of instruction. Even as the supervisor or administrator plans the strategy of supervision, he recognizes that the true uniqueness of this service area is found in its close, almost intimate attachment to the area of human relations. His strategy, in fact, is built on the assumption that one-to-one contacts with teachers will bring the most effective results.

Seldom have professional educators seen a greater cleavage from tradition than the concept of team administration for the purposes of instructional improvement. Cooperative teaching certainly has shown and will continue to demonstrate new and better ways of supervising instruction. Without question, other services and functions of the school —health, library, testing, parent-teacher associations, and community action councils—will assist the team administration in providing a coordinated plan for upgrading the curricular program.

SELECTED REFERENCES

Beckner, Weldon E., and Wayne Dumas. *American Education: Foundations and Superstructure.* Scranton: Intext, 1970.

Center for the Study of Instruction (William G. Carr, editor). *Values and The Curriculum: Report of The Fourth International Curriculum Conference.* Washington, D.C.: National Education Association, 1970.

Conant, James B. *The Comprehensive High School: A Second Report to Interested Citizens.* New York: McGraw-Hill, 1967

Cummings, Susan N. *Communication for Education.* Scranton: Intext, 1971.

Davis, Russell G. *Planning Human Resource Development: Educational Models and Schemata.* Chicago: Rand McNally, 1966.

Griffiths, Daniel E. *Developing Taxonomies of Organizational Behavior in Educational Administration.* Chicago: Rand McNally, 1969.

Johnson, Lois V., and Mary A. Bany. *Classroom Management: Theory and Skill Training.* New York: Macmillan, 1970.

Sachs, Benjamin M. *Educational Administration: A Behavioral Approach.* Boston: Houghton Mifflin, 1966.

Seagoe, May V. *The Learning Process and School Practice.* Scranton: Chandler, 1970.

CHAPTER 4

Investigation and Project Planning

One of the dramatic changes in the role that today's status leader assumes with the faculty is that of turning from a control practitioner to a problem-solving agent and builder of team spirit. There are clear indications that tight controls held by the supervisor or administrator in the past are not successful in stimulating any meaningful spirit of investigation or promoting a willingness to develop or implement new projects or studies. The theory of total participation by faculty in the organization's search for a systematic approach to curriculum development has confirmed the idea that traditional rigid controls do not work.

Contributions to the educative process come best by devising groups that are engaged in many problem-solving situations and are involved in mutually satisfying plans and activities. Curriculum improvement does require the wisdom of alternative courses of action and their respective results. Status leaders are in an excellent position to assist teachers in arriving at such decisions as to what is to be taught and to discover how it may best be taught.

FREEDOM OF INQUIRY

The transformation of an educational institution in an era of great change calls for the thoughtful deliberation and sustained efforts of large numbers of the education profession. The vitally important work of all groups must be recognized as opposed to the special commendations of only a few. The important expressions of judgment over the years that have resulted from the achievements of various councils, committees, or conferences must be made a matter of record for each educational agency so that succeeding groups of teachers and scholars will be in a position to utilize these judgments as they deliberate on current problems and issues.

In many ways the adoption of the educational structure will determine largely the ability of any group to progress satisfactorily in the area of curriculum change. Excessively centralized external controls, excessively diversified internal controls, or other forms of institutional-agency prototypes will have a real and tangible effect on the ability of curriculum-oriented clusters of professionals to preserve their freedom and independence of inquiry to the extent that their voices will be heard and respected by the profession and the community.

Any good educational institution is composed of educators, students, and related bodies who believe in the worthwhileness of their own struggles to achieve a better life for themselves and others. Such an institution reflects the ability to act on its own behalf, to initiate its own programs as well as to reflect and react to the forces and pressures that lie both within and without its walls. It provides a latitude of freedom that will permit its members to make reasonable and honest mistakes, and it supports a spirit of investigation and inquiry that spurs its constituents to contemplate change whenever it appears necessary. The right of dissent and disagreement must be well established so that those who would urge and demand change will be listened to and given valid opportunity to prove that the current structure requires review, revision, and, perhaps, reform. Both good leadership and strong professional commitment, however, are essential to keep matters of dissent and strong disagreement from becoming a battleground for unyielding controversy.

A good school is one in which there is a shared belief in the wholeness of professional spirit and honesty of all to work cooperatively toward basic common goals. It represents a stage in which there is encouragement and opportunity given to strive for an outstanding program; where there is a willingness to invite the scrutiny of others in evaluating the process and the product of every classroom and every activity.

Curriculum change today, no matter how spectacular, is merely in the foothills of the long journey that lies ahead. No one can say for certain when any change or innovation is complete; if its perfection is envisioned and no further improvement in a particular program or situation can be promoted, it may be that the concept itself is outdated and needs a completely new orientation. This is not to say that the best of any idea should not be preserved; it is to assert that the function or need for any otherwise perfect instrument may no longer be required.

If curriculum change is to proceed on a sound basis, educators and students should regard the learning process and attitudes toward learning as the peak of attention for any system of education. It means, further, that such a prevailing attitude necessitates the common efforts of all in assisting one another to attain cherished and sought-after goals. The work of tomorrow must be sheltered in the habitation of today, but it need not shut out or limit the dreams or aspirations of educators for a better world through a progressive educational plan. Encouragement and support by administrators and supervisors to the end that will serve the faculties well is essential for the accommodation of the school to the requirements of an exciting and changing environment.

PROJECT DEVELOPMENT

The search for educational truth can become a powerful agent to unlock, to redirect, and to revolutionize present patterns and practices in our schools. As one discovery of a new concept is made, another concept is waiting for discovery and, after that, many, many more concepts can be unveiled. Many of the present answers to questions about the satisfactoriness of the educational program are based on inferences that have had their derivation in the intuitive method. This approach lacks substantiating evidence as to its validity. Instead, significant research studies and projects are being undertaken to establish some basic evidence concerning educational needs and procedures in today's educational program.

Projects related to the areas of curriculum development and improvement of the instructional program have several pertinent areas of concern. Part or all of these research projects may: bear upon the patterns of curriculum sequences from the bottom up; move from patterns of single-subject study to many subjects so that the curriculum as a whole does not receive superficial consideration; develop and test materials with children and youth representing divergent cultural groups; consider the advantages and disadvantages of various learning styles; be aided by college- or university-controlled laboratory schools to ensure the rigor of experimental design and operation; and be concerned with new styles for educating future teachers and providing in-service growth for experienced teachers. Some examples of projects are described below.

Project MACSI

Three institutions have joined together to form the Supplementary Center for Curriculum and Instruction—Montgomery County, Maryland; Anniston, Alabama; and the NEA Center for the Study of Instruction. The goals of the Center are to help teachers become more skillful in the rational planning of curriculum and instruction, to study the processes of school improvement, and to provide an avenue for constructive change.[1]

In Project MACSI three possible sources of criteria were considered. The first concerned itself with the view of curricular planning as an organizational process. This process raises some interesting questions. First, what types of curriculum decisions should be mandatory and which should be optional for the teacher? Should the teacher have the option of selecting the objectives for instruction? Second, is the purpose of formal planning to tell the teacher how to do his job or simply to outline his broad responsibilities? Does it provide support and help for teachers? Third, what should the approval process be in terms of decisions, documents, and the like? Fourth, should formal plans be based on specific points of view about learning or instruction, and does this imply that all the planners must agree with or conform to this belief? And fifth, should formal planning be based on the assumption that the planners will make rational decisions and, therefore, need not justify their decisions?

A second source of criteria for judging the formal curriculum plans is a theory or point of view about learning and instruction. In most instances the source of criteria from a theoretical or conceptual view does not exclude other sources, but may represent the predominant beliefs of the institution. The third source of criteria is that of models or rationales which identify the types of curricular decisions, the relationships among these decisions, and the bases on which decisions should be made. Goals and objectives should be stated objectively, objectives should identify desired behavioral outcomes, and plans for activities and evaluation should be consistent with the objectives.

Project MACSI promotes the point of view that effective curriculum planning requires that the quality of its products be high and that teachers perceive this quality. Curriculum planning becomes the one aspect of organizational planning that deals most directly with instruction—the school's most important service.

Project PRISM

Typical of the new federal aid projects wherein administrators and supervisors will be called upon to assist in providing leadership is the project PRISM (Provision for Restructuring in Independent Study Models). This project was designed by a western school district to create an instructional system featuring a variety of independent study practices involving English and social studies teachers and students. The project

[1]Arlene Payne, *The Study of Curriculum Plans: Schools for the 70's* (Washington, D.C.: National Association, 1969), pp. 1–40.

will be under a project manager who is responsible for providing assistance to teachers and students in the use of new educational media to promote opportunities for independent learning.

As an educational leader, the school principal will be highly involved in assisting with the specific tasks or projects assigned. The project director will be responsible to the principal in his recommendations for: (1) planning, organizing, staffing, directing, and controlling the instructional learning centers of the school; and (2) the selection, assignment, and separation of all personnel within the learning centers. The responsibilities of the PRISM project personnel will be many. Most important are these: (1) to purchase, inventory, catalog, store, distribute, and maintain the instructional materials and equipment in the various independent learning centers at the school; (2) to keep school personnel informed about new developments in the technology of classroom instruction; (3) to provide creative leadership in the selection, use, and evaluation of all teaching and learning materials for the learning centers; (4) to make these teaching and learning materials readily accessible to the learner and the teaching staff; (5) to produce teaching and learning materials that are necessary to the improvement of teaching and learning in the school; (6) to provide opportunities for staff members to gain personal knowledge and skills in the use of the new educational media; and (7) to serve as a specialist and consultant to all departments in matters pertaining to the teaching and learning materials available in the learning centers.

New positions such as this will call upon the skill of the supervisory staff to recruit and assist personnel who will have the ability to plan, organize, direct, and coordinate a multi-media instructional program. Supervisors and administrators should be well versed in the whole area of teacher effectiveness and how it can be influenced by introducing new techniques and materials of instruction. New projects of this type will demand a high level of supervisory leadership to induce and maintain a vigorous projection of faculty and student body cooperation to assure the success of such a venture.

Quality Measurement Project

The Quality Measurement Project in New York has proven enlightening to the supervisor or administrator in the evaluation of good educational practice in several ways. First, any supervisory or administrative organization should focus consistently on evaluation. Unless it is willing to give careful attention to evaluating the work of the school or district, there will be little improvement in the instructional program. Second, the measurement of quality differences could readily be done on a small scale in either a school district or individual school situation. The results from testing programs of intelligence and achievement should be of considerable value in fostering a dialog with members of the faculties involved as to needed curriculum revision, identification of remedial cases, providing information needed for the grouping of students, and the like. All of this has a close relationship to counseling and guidance programs as such information can be a most useful tool in the hands of the counseling staff. Third, any negative results from such a project can result in the identity of low-scoring schools, the relaying of this information to the administration and faculty, and the initiating of an intensive program to bring that phase of the program back to an acceptable level. Fourth, schools, like individuals, should not hesitate to be tested in terms of an agreed-upon definition of excellence. The quality of the product or process is a relative description of its effectiveness in meeting specifically defined objectives. Each school recognizes that it may be better or worse in comparison to other schools in terms of certain educational goals, but it should not be satisfied with remaining at a low level of performance in certain areas once they have been identified through such a study.

The "Quest for Quality" studies of 28 school districts by the American Association of School Administration (AASA) and the National School Boards Association also have provided much valuable information in the whole area of evaluation of educational programs, and their importance cannot be overlooked.

Model Schools Project

Thirty-four secondary schools in twenty states, the District of Columbia, Canada, and Germany were selected in 1970 to participate in a five-year project that may help provide the pattern for 21st-century education. Although approaches will vary from school to school, the central idea of the project is to gather, for the first time, all of the major practical new ideas in secondary-school education under a single roof. The basic goal is comprehensive change.

One objective of the Model Schools Project is to explore the effectiveness of different degrees of relationship between the project staff and the participating units. The project staff, for example, will spend most of their time with seven schools in the first group, whereas they will not visit the schools in the third category. All thirty-four schools, however, will have made the same commitment and will seek a similar high level of results from their innovations. In addition, the project staff feels that innovations have become a passport to studies in education in recent years but actually have been disappointing. Many schools have adopted one or two new approaches to education, but not one school has incorporated all, or even most, of the major developments in a systematically related total program. Thus, the potential gains in one area have been cancelled out by time-worn practices in another.

Among the modern methods that the Model Schools may adopt are team teaching, flexible scheduling, varied student groups with small groups predominant, increased use of independent study, extensive curriculum reorganization, greater reliance on community agencies and other outside resources as direct roads to learning, and other new ideas that have been found workable as well as exciting.

Computer Projects

One of the most promising proposals related to the introduction of technology in the individualized instructional process has been that of Computer Assisted Instruction (CAI) which has been explored in a number of research projects. As an assist to individual instruction, the computer is used to select and sequence instructional material for a student, store data on his progress, and provide him with immediate progress evaluation. Such information can include course material, test results, statistical data, and continuing diagnostic information for each student throughout a course.

Supervisors and administrators are working closely with foundations and universities in examining the multiple uses of CAI for individualized instruction. Sixth graders in Yorktown Heights, New York, are using a computer to play games by which they learn the principles of economics. A group of first- and second-graders in a western state are studying arithmetic under the guidance of a computer. Pennsylvania State University is attempting to determine the best ways of using the electronic computer for instruction. A high school is applying CAI experimentally to the laboratory work of a chemistry course in qualitative analysis. These and many other experiments are under way as a means of improving the opportunities for making individualized instruction in the classroom possible.

Some Examples

Illustrations of school curriculum development functions previously mentioned are these. One high school district engages a director of guidance who spends at least 50 percent of his time in curriculum work. Another district develops and coordinates the *what* of the curriculum and gives the local schools freedom and latitude in working out the *how*. A large high school district assigns a high school principal to coordinate the curriculum work of approximately four departments on a district-wide basis as he works with department chairmen from all the high schools. Placing the principal on the school level on a working basis with department chairmen and district-office personnel works very well in another district. Each principal is in charge of a curriculum study group representing all schools. The school-within-a-school concept is used by a district experimenting with school reorganization with each unit principal working with three or more departments in the school. Finally, a small district gives much responsibility in curriculum development to building subject chairmen while a second believes that the principal must be the educational leader of his school and should devote 50 percent of his contractual time to this area.

A large urban district has become engaged in an attempt to find new ways of making local schools more responsive to local needs. It is called "Project 18" and is providing some approaches to pave the way for significant educational changes across the district. The project has three basic goals: to identify desirable changes in policies, procedures, and district support structure; to discover the processes and resources necessary to develop a locally-conceived educational program; and to determine how principals, teachers, and community representatives can participate effectively in planning a school's program of education that meets the needs of pupils and the community. Eighteen schools are participating in this project as a key effort to decentralize decision-making. Organizational models have been devised for each school. Resource teachers have been made available to participating elementary schools on a part-time basis to aid in planning and carrying out new programs. Ten days of substitute teacher time in each school is available to relieve key teachers of classroom duties so that they can assist in planning new programs; additional community resource persons are hired to assist the faculty; and teachers engaged in project planning beyond the school day can be compensated.

SUMMARY

The posture of education as related to the spirit of investigation and the planning of experimental projects is not an easy one to take. James Russell aptly stated in his book *Change and Challenge in American Education,* "Since the development of minds is the main business of schools, the modern age challenges schools to redefine their role." A basic task of American education in the seventies will be to sense a need for curriculum change, define its requirements, and then organize a frontal attack on the areas that require change as a step toward improved educational programs.

The premise of search and research has become a way of life for the public school, pushing it beyond the level of mere perceptory experience and into an area in which theory and research are prime factors in leading to enlightened improvement. In fact, it is likely that our human and natural resources have hardly scratched the surface in terms of the changes that will be on the threshold of reality by the last two decades of the twentieth century.

SELECTED REFERENCES

Brubaker, Dale L. *The Teacher as a Decision-Maker.* Dubuque: Wm. C. Brown, 1970.

Center for the Study of Instruction (William Pharis, *et al.*). *Decision Making and Schools for the 70's.* Washington, D.C.: National Education Association, 1970.

Dettre, John R. *Decision Making in the Secondary School Classroom: Toward Preparing the Diagnostic Teacher.* Scranton: Intext, 1970.

Flanagan, John C., William M. Shanner, and Robert Mager. *Behavioral Objectives: A Guide for Individualized Learning.* New York: Westinghouse Learning Corporation, 1971.

Gronlund, Norman E. *Stating Behavioral Objectives for Classroom Instruction.* New York: Macmillan, 1970.

Harnack, Robert S. *The Teacher: Decision Maker and Curriculum Planner.* Scranton: Intext, 1968.

Howes, Virgil M. editor. *Individualization of Instruction: A Teaching Strategy.* New York: Macmillan, 1970.

Johnson, M. Clemens. *Educational Uses of the Computer: An Introduction.* Chicago: Rand McNally, 1971.

Plowman, Paul. *Behavioral Objectives: Teacher Success through Student Performance.* Palo Alto: Science Research Associates, 1970.

Professional Development and Instructional Services. *The Professional Association Looks at the Role in Instruction.* Washington, D.C.: National Education Association, 1970.

Thorndike, Robert L. *Educational Measurement.* Washington, D.C.: American Council on Education, 1971.

Zeigler, Harmon. *The Political World of the High School Teacher.* Eugene, Oregon: Center for the Advanced Study of Educational Administration, 1966.

PART TWO

Personnel and Programs

Part Two takes into account the broad nature of supervision in the 1970's and the cooperative nature of the supervisory process. The status of persons who exist in the school system for the purpose of supervision must be considered and evaluated in the light of their duties and responsibilities in providing for a dynamic program of instructional growth and development. Teamwork is an important interface situation in which instructional leaders face the central problem of how people can be helped to change. In a larger sense, a strong administrative organization for supervision must be devised, and curricular decision-making is central to the role of the supervisor in good educational practice.

A large problem in school district organization hinges on the relationship of the principal to the central office, to other supervisory personnel, and to the faculty. What is the relationship of the principal vis-à-vis these hierarchical groups within the organizational structure? These are questions that must be resolved at the local level before satisfactory supervisory services can be performed. The principal does, in fact, assume primary leadership for the quality of education at the building level and the central office must support his endeavors.

To become acquainted with new directions in classroom organization and instruction, as well as in research and development, is important to status leaders if they are to serve the faculty and the community with effectiveness. Additional emphasis is placed upon the dynamics of change, the research that is pertinent to the dynamics of change, the role of change agents, and the formulation of change as it will take place during the next decade. A good example of this is the role of the National Council for the Accreditation of Teacher Education (NCATE) in accrediting programs of teacher education and its current effort to rewrite the standards for accrediting teacher-education institutions. New standards of this type will provide greater recognition for the character and nature of programs for the preparation of curriculum coordinators, directors of curriculum, supervisory personnel, and others who provide these services.

The planning of supervisory programs represents a critical task area in which the faculty must be guided into having more than just a tolerance for experimentation; rather, it needs to engage itself in a total cooperative approach to the improvement of instruction as a characteristic of developing an acceptable, workable pattern of operation. The issue of academic freedom, working with teachers through collective bargaining and negotiation, and utilizing the systems approach to educational planning are predictable concerns of those persons who are engaged in curriculum and instructional improvement.

CHAPTER 5

Supervisory Personnel and Teamwork

Many administrative and supervisory personnel coordinate their efforts in striving for optimum development and improvement of the instructional program at the local district level. Each of these positions is predicated on the needs of classroom teachers in providing for the variety of their students' individual differences. As the complexities of interpersonal classroom behavior increase, the teacher becomes confronted with inescapable pressures that would exhaust his intellectual and physical output were it not for the assistance of an organizational plan that provided him with supervisory assistance whenever or wherever needed. Beyond individual help for members of the professional staff, there must be a coordinated effort to assimilate the multi-fractional efforts of many individuals into concerted and unilateral channels that will lead to coherent program development. The magnitude and complexity of this task calls for the assistance of highly skilled status leaders who constitute the instructional service arm of the district.

SUPERVISORY-ADMINISTRATIVE ROLES

Under the leadership of the superintendent of schools, there are several key posts in the educational organization that should be examined in detail if the supervisor and/or administrator is to have a keen understanding of their specific roles and responsibilities. These persons should function in the supervisory enterprise in an intrinsic manner that demands a rather thorough examination of the services that they perform. In effect, when a school district makes a decision to engage in a cooperative curriculum venture it has the basic responsibility for providing leadership for the task. It is important to recognize the responsibility that each office in the district, separately or cooperatively, must assume. Also, it is essential that provisions be made to free professional workers so that they can accomplish that appointed task. As a result each group so involved should be prepared to review closely its organization and working procedures and make any necessary modifications along the way.

A Memorandum

To better implement the sensitive relationships that exist between supervisory personnel and the many professional colleagues with whom they will be working, a few practical guiding principles are enumerated here.

It is important that frequent conferences be held between the supervisor and the principal. Both of these persons must be mutually supportive in their relationships with the faculty and, though they may disagree in some areas, they should present a united front on matters of importance. No instructional innovations within the school should be made without the full knowledge of both, assuming it is within an area of responsibility for the supervisor. The principal may discuss the growth and progress of teachers with the supervisor, but under no circumstances does the supervisor bear any of the rating functions. There should be follow-up conferences or memoranda between the supervisor and the principal while they are working together on any problem.

District office supervisors should expect to attend regularly scheduled meetings with the superintendent and/or the assistant superintendent in charge of instruction. Whenever possible supervisors should attend joint meetings with the district principals at the appropriate organizational or area level. Frequently-scheduled meetings are important for all members of the supervisory staff.

Late in the spring is a good time for the supervisory staff to submit plans for stimulating faculty professional growth for the following school year. In each of their assigned schools, supervisors should work with the faculty and administration on: the planning and conduct of school meetings; the visitation of classrooms at the invitation of the teacher; the conferring with individual teachers, counselors, and department heads; and the conferring with librarians, instructional media personnel, and others assigned to service functions related to the classroom program. Several in-service meetings, discussion seminars, and demonstration lessons should be planned throughout the year. Many types of materials may be assimilated for the in-service programs such as: teaching innovations, sample units, bibliographies, research reviews, illustrative evaluation devices for pupil performance, and new approaches to designing behavioral goals and objectives. Undoubtedly each supervisor will wish to have several experimental programs under way and these should be encouraged and guided whenever the occasion warrants. There should be no hesitation in his participating in grade-level, departmental, or faculty meetings whenever invited to do so. On occasion the supervisor may be asked to speak to community groups and he should encourage this kind of involvement. Student-teacher assignments for the district may fall under his jurisdiction and he will need to work closely with teachers and principals in selecting promising educational environments in which student teachers may best develop professionally.

Adequate professional reading and writing time are essential for the supervisor if he is to remain informed concerning recent trends and developments in education. Also, time should be available so that he may be effective in interpreting these data to teachers through written bulletins and other memoranda. Many professional conferences and meetings will be held where the supervisor acts as a representative of the school district. Here every attempt should be made to acquire new ideas that are being implemented in other places as a basis for further experimentation at the supervisor's local district level.

District Office Leadership

The school district office has a definite obligation to provide supervisory leadership to the staff of the central office, to building adminstrators, to school supervisors, to teaching faculties, and to many outside individuals who are associated with the instructional program. One of the troublesome factors encountered by the district office is establishing clear lines of communication that permit all members of the school community to become aware of the program as well as problems in curriculum that are occurring throughout the district. As study groups become concerned with ways in which the school or the district may solve irksome problems, it is the responsibility of the district office to assist these persons in defining their problems and the direction that they should take in striving toward a solution. There almost certainly will be a demand for resource materials and personnel, and the district office will be in an ideal position to provide these items for the use of any group as they are needed.

More and more professional time is required to attack the highly sophisticated and complex tasks associated with the planning and designing of any curricular program. Central office personnel should be able to provide the necessary released time from teaching and other duties to make it possible for faculty members to work on critical areas related to specialty fields. Groups of this type must, of course, be coordinated to the extent that they are apprised of what has been accomplished before, made aware of the actions that are being taken by other groups that relate to the particular task of this group, and given an opportunity to communicate progress to all concerned at every level. In this way a complete understanding will exist between these groups.

All of these factors are reflected in the actions that must be taken by the district office in facilitating curriculum progress. Strong motivation, good research techniques, and a common bond of understanding between the many splinter groups in any district require strong curriculum assistance on the part of the supervisory staff in the central office.

The Assistant Superintendent in Charge of Instruction

In the typical large- or medium-sized school system, the assistant superintendent in charge of instruction plays a very important role in the over-all development of the instructional and supervisory program. His direct responsibility in this regard to the superintendent and the board of education makes it imperative that he possess certain basic scholastic and ability qualifications. He must have a well-developed philosophy of education; a knowledge of teaching methodology, instructional materials, and curriculum development; an ability to use effective research and guidance techniques; a knowledge of effective personnel practices and the ability to maintain good human relationships; a talent for developing effective procedures for the improvement and evaluation of the instructional program; and the necessary awareness in providing for individual differences in children and meeting the needs of atypical children. In addition to this, he should hold the proper administrative credentials: a master's or doctor's degree from an accredited college or university, at least five years' service as a successful school teacher, and at least three years' service as a school administrator or supervisor.

The assistant superintendent in charge of instruction should spend a large share of his time on and be responsible for the organization and management of the curriculum development program. Further, he will be expected to give leadership in the total district area for the supervision of instruction and assist in the search for proper instructional materials.

In-service training coordination is a major function of his office. Both standing and temporary curriculum committees should work closely with him. He often will wish to serve as a consultant to these groups, thus providing a bridge between the school and the central office in the exchange of ideas and the encouragement of projects and pilot-study programs. Much attention must be given by him to the articulation and coordination of the many curricular programs that will be operating cooperatively at the district and school levels.

As a line administrator, the assistant superintendent will be in charge of many staff meetings that will involve building administrators, supervisors, and teachers. Much time will be required also for the holding of private conferences with these individuals on matters relating to curriculum and instruction that require review and solution. In-service training, orientation programs, college and university work, demonstration lessons, and workshops should represent a major effort on his behalf to upgrade the staff. Teacher inter-visitation on a district-wide basis may be arranged by his office. Also important is the matter of the organization and control of the district curriculum laboratory and assisting in the development and maintenance of various school audio-visual centers and reading libraries.

His concerns with basic district-wide budgetary responsibilities, the approval of instructional supply and equipment requisitions, and the status of the activities of his office with other offices at the district level represent some of his general responsibilities. Certainly his position is both important and rewarding in terms of its many key functions and opportunities.

The Assistant Superintendent in Charge of Business

Although the relationship to instructional improvement may not be too obvious, this individual is in a strategic position to either aid or hinder in this endeavor. As a business expert, the assistant superintendent in charge of business is in a vital spot to assist the principal as they both work together to anticipate future curriculum needs and to reflect this in the making of a sound, defensible budget. Better educational planning, the ability to project the plans of the school into the future, and the development of a sound basis for the reasonable and economical expenditure of funds are the result of good budget administration on the part of this person. His technical advice and assistance to the principal are invaluable in projecting plans that require financial as well as educational forecasting.

The Supervisor

Much that has been said thus far is directly related to the fulfillment of the supervisor's role at the district level. However, a few extra dimensions of the position are discussed here.

The supervisor's basic function is to broaden the role of the teacher so that he is responsible for as many meaningful and essential professional activities as possible. At this critical period in time, the supervisor should be assisting the teacher in seeking and defining new teaching roles that lead to an increase in his influence and productivity. In his relations with the school's administrator, he can encourage those who have the responsibility for designing teacher assignments to provide the differing kinds of experiences for the teacher, at his option and request, whenever possible. For too long the school has been concerned about administrative arrangements rather than teacher wishes. Grade, subject, and room assignments should be designed that free the teacher for the maximum development of his talents and aspirations.

With the teaching staff, the supervisor must coordinate his efforts in determining what needs to be done to assist them in implementing their programs. He will have to help teachers identify the task that they want accomplished as a product or as a service. Further, he must help teachers to identify what is to be done, how much of it is to be accomplished, and how perfect the final product should be. Teachers and the supervisor will wish to take a close look at what condition exists at the present time and what changes are required to reach the goals that have been established by the faculty of the school.

Environment is a meaningful factor in predetermining how well the teacher will relate to the educational system and the curriculum. The supervisor will desire to assist the teacher in discovering the many culturally-based values that are projected by the community, the needs of students, and mandated programs that will influence his work. Performance-requirement specifications for pupils must be designed that will describe the kind of product that the teacher is seeking, how the product will perform, the conditions (in the classroom and elsewhere) under which the performance will take place, and the type of design requirements that must be fashioned to facilitate the developmental process. The supervisor can assist teachers in designing ways in which they can direct a detailed analysis of each task or even a combination of tasks that should be performed in a logically arranged order. Teachers need to understand what elements are required to complete each task and the types of resources that must be at their disposal to assure the success of the learning venture.

The supervisory staff is in an excellent position to assist the faculty in examining all of the learning materials that are relevant, to encourage the personnel available to implement them, and to seek other basic resources that will meet the kind of performance requirements that have been established. The amount of expenditures to be made and the acceptance of this by the community will represent important factors to consider in deciding whether or not to pursue this particular task or to seek other directions. Evaluation of these developmental procedures should be made through data that have been gathered and analyzed as they relate to the initial objectives that were stated earlier.

Coordination and support of teacher action in the area of instructional improvement will be the basis for justifying supervisory services. Teachers can be given help in perceiving how their roles can be enlarged to maximum effectiveness and the supervisor is in an excellent position to help them comprehend how this can be accomplished. Each coordinated act between the supervisor and the teacher should result in a clarification as to the continuing roles of each and provide a pre-judgmental base for deciding how their future cooperative actions might be designed and implemented.

The supervisor, then, is an individual who has had the essential training required for the position, who has the skills and ability to expedite the tasks related to instructional improvement, who communicates well with the professional staff, and who generally is assigned to the central office of the school district. His role is one that is primarily supportive of the classroom teacher as he attempts to improve his teaching performance. The supervisor strives to add new dimensions to the teacher's role by providing creative and helpful assistance whenever requested.

School-Level Functions: Elementary

In an effort to ascertain what functions of the elementary school principal are of the most and least importance in the opinions of both teachers and principals, a study was conducted in a large city school system to determine any significant differences in their interpretation of the principal's leadership role.[1] While 90 percent of the principals rated supervision as their most important function, only 25 percent of the teachers did so. Seventy percent of the principals felt that visiting the classroom to observe the quality of instruction was their most important supervisory function. Only 23 percent of the teachers agreed. Forty-three percent of the teachers ranked conferring on curriculum problems as the most important supervisory function of the principal, although just 20 percent of the principals saw this as their most important supervisory function. Seventy-five percent of the principals stated that they should spend more time in classroom observation. However, 78 percent of the teachers stated that the principal was spending an adequate amount of time in the classroom. Where should a principal give his supervisory help for the improvement of instruction? Seventy percent of the principals named the classroom, while 65 percent of the teachers selected the principal's office. Seventy percent of the princi-

[1]Robert F. Roberts, "The Role and Function of the Elementary School Principal as Interpreted by Teachers and Principals." Unpublished thesis, California State College at Long Beach, Spring, 1963, pp. 1–138. See also Charles F. Faber and Gilbert F. Shearron, *Elementary School Administration: Theory and Practice* (New York: Holt, Rinehart and Winston, 1970), pp. 305–331.

pals stated that they could be most helpful to teachers by making suggestions for their improvement. Only 11 percent of the teachers rated this method as being most helpful.

It must be concluded that teachers do not want to be supervised by the principal on an autocratic basis. They feel that the principal should act as a stimulator and coordinate their activities for the improvement of the curriculum. On the other hand, principals should confer with teachers to clearly outline what is expected of them, both as individuals and as staff members, in terms of educational duties and responsibilities and budget a major portion of their time to conferring on curriculum and observing in the classroom. However, principals should make classroom visitations meaningful to teachers and in the follow-up conference offer specific suggestions for teacher improvement.

School-Level Functions: Secondary

Who generally is directly involved in curriculum development on the school level on the basis of devoting the most time to this operation? A statewide survey of this matter indicated how high school districts have organized for curriculum development and improvement.[2] Twenty-seven small districts stated that the principal had this responsibility; five said an assistant principal; while three revealed that it was a person with another title. Of 33 medium-sized districts, 17 indicated the principal or the principal and department heads; 10 an assistant principal; and the remainder other officials. More than one-half reported that either the principal delegates much of the curriculum development and improvement to other personnel on his school staff or curriculum development and improvement is highly centralized and under the direction of district office personnel. Out of 23 large districts, 14 gave the principal this as his major responsibility, three indicated an assistant principal, and the remaining six designated some other person. In larger districts the principal tends to retain more of this function and delegates some of his other responsibilities.

What percentage of the above persons' contractual time is devoted to curriculum development and improvement? In no small districts did this person devote 75 to 100 percent of his contractual time to this task, while four medium and four large districts reported this person did devote this percentage of time to this activity. From this two patterns emerged. First, the school-level director of curriculum development

[2]Bill J. James, *School-Level Organization for Curriculum Development and Improvement*, reported at the California Association of Secondary-School Administrators' Conference, Los Angeles, California, April 12, 1965. See also David Mahan and Gerald Moellar, *New Faculty Team: School Organization for Results* (Palo Alto: Science Research Associates, 1971), 224 pp.

and improvement in larger districts devotes more time to this area than does his counterpart in smaller districts. Second, when principals assume the direction of school-level curriculum development and improvement, they spend less contractual time than do assistant principals in this regard. Department chairmen were mentioned frequently as being vested with curriculum development leadership and it is most often through them that teachers are involved in this area.

In retrospect, five factors emerged. First, the trend is to have the principal more involved in curriculum development by removing some of his other administrative responsibilities. Second, districts of all sizes are willing now to try different organizational designs to facilitate curriculum development. Third, this task is being accomplished outside of school time. Districts are willing to pay their teachers and other personnel for work during vacations and summer. Fourth, department chairmen have more to do with curriculum development than many school officials realize. Fifth, it doesn't really matter who is in charge of this activity, just so someone is given the responsibility in each local school.

The Co-Administrator's Role

The co-administrator, often referred to as the assistant principal or vice-principal, has a basic responsibility of knowing as much as possible about the school—its practices, regulations, and programs. He often acts as an official representative of the principal in the absence of the principal or in times of emergency. He must be able to fulfill basic functions of a good principal, and this would include giving assistance to the development of the instructional program.

In what ways can he best give assistance in this regard? Most important of all the co-administrator must provide educational leadership by assisting in the conducting of in-service training and orientation programs. Through these programs new teachers can become better acquainted with the total curriculum, individual growth of teachers can be encouraged, help can be provided to improve areas where instructional problems have developed, available instructional aids can become known to the teachers, and instructional policies can be explained and interpreted.

The co-administrator is in a favorable position to act as a liaison person between the principal and the members of various departments in the school. In keeping various civic groups informed about the work of the school, he is in an excellent position to interpret the school's educational program and thereby gain community support for future curriculum change or improvement. Inasmuch as he is concerned about the morale of teachers and students alike, he must give discreet attention to the problems which beset these individuals. On the fringe area of the curriculum, he has to be prepared to work with many persons whose programs, in part, exist outside of the classroom, such as extracurricular activities, student assemblies, and work-experience programs.

As a resource person, the co-administrator brings to the faculty reports of conferences, institutes, school visitations, and community meetings. He faces a large order in keeping abreast of the latest research in the educational field and assisting the principal in making this information available to the staff. He must be available as a resource person for many kinds of meetings and conferences, including curriculum discussion groups, parent-teacher conferences, and the like.

In the development of the curriculum, the co-administrator has many challenging opportunities open to him. Often he will be assigned as a permanent or temporary member of a curriculum study group where he will have an excellent chance to exert leadership and to familiarize himself with the developments that are taking place in a particular field or subject area. He may be given the responsibility of assisting the institution in new pilot or experimental programs in educational television, programmed instruction, team teaching, curriculum-center development, nongraded instruction, the new curricular areas, and in myriad other new-type programs. On numerous occasions he will be called upon to assist in the review and evaluation of new instructional materials like books, audio-visual aids, and other new teaching-learning systems.

The instructional task and opportunities are particularly challenging for the co-administrator in charge of curriculum and instruction who enjoys a full-time or nearly full-time administrative assignment. It would appear that his greatest contribution to the excellence of the school's educational program lies in his active involvement in this critical and sensitive area.

Outside Specialists: A Rewarding Resource

As refinements for education are sought everywhere at the district and local level, the administrator is forced often to look outside the district for expert and high-level assistance. With evaluation, improvement, and redirection needed to promote greater frequency in the cycles of curriculum development, the services of temporary resource personnel from the outside have become extremely important to the growth of educational perspective and insight by the teaching faculty. Research on 200 cases of the use of outside specialists was analyzed and subjected to the Western Data Processing Center's QUAP-4 program to render statistical comparisons to discover: (1) the district situations that called for the employment of outside specialists; (2) proper orientation of the outside specialists; (3) assignment of staff members to work with outside specialists; (4) provision for redirection of specialists' operations; and (5) application of adequate interim activity for district staff between specialists' visits.[3]

Regarding district needs that prompted the employment of an outside specialist, the study identified the need for specialized or technical knowledge or service as the most frequently-mentioned reason (helping teachers learn audiolingual language teaching methods, utilizing programmed learning, etc.). Among other reasons for bringing in outside specialists were the need for inspiration, to brief district personnel in certain practices, to plan or develop a program to help the staff see a problem in proper perspective, and to render objective analyses of existing conditions. Many were brought in because of their unique status and accomplishments.

Concerning the *orientation of the outside specialist* in the school district, he should be briefed as to the background regarding forces and status existing in the district, and information relating to the level of professional awareness of the district staff. The district can make clear the operational framework and the limitations of the specialist-district working relationship, as well as indicate the desired direction or focus of effort and, if appropriate, spell out what the specialist is to accomplish.

In more than one-fourth of the cases, it was felt that the relative appropriateness of the *staff group assigned to work with the outside specialist* was critical to the effectiveness of the service. In 27.5 percent of the cases studied, the outside specialist worked primarily with a large group (over 25 persons), 26 percent worked with a medium group (10–24), 23.5 percent worked with a small group (2–9), and 2.5 percent worked primarily with an individual staff member. The smaller the group assigned to work with the outside specialist, the more likely, to a significant degree, was the service to be rated as highly effective. In terms of any *provision for the redirection of a specialist operation,* there is a trend toward the use of outside specialists in a spaced sequence of sessions. In such sequences no matter how careful the planning, thorough the operation, and complete the communication, some outside specialists tend to become fixed as to their method of operation in the school district. A school district must maintain flexibility to take advantage of strengths appearing in the working relationship or to diminish weaknesses that occur in it. *Interim activities between special-*

---

[3]Tod A. Anton, "Outside Specialists and School Districts," *California School Administrator,* vol. XIX, no. 5, Research Supplement No. 6 (November 1964). See also *Twenty-One Years Later: ETS Today* (Princeton: Educational Testing Service, 1970), 128 pp.

ists' visits are necessary if advice is to be translated into improved district performance, if consultant knowledge is to result in increased district-staff competency, and growth among participating staff members is to be accelerated.

School districts need to identify their own conditions appropriate for the use of outside specialists. They must focus attention on ways in which they can obtain maximum benefits from these services. Guidelines for utilizing outside specialist services are listed in Fig. 5–1

TEAMWORK AND THE PRINCIPAL

One of the questions often asked by building principals is, "How can I obtain the assistance of other personnel in curriculum improvement without appearing to be unequal to the task myself?" Perhaps this is the result of a misunderstanding on the part of the principal and his colleagues as to the basic concept behind the upgrading of instruction. It is not now and should not be in the future a task that includes solely the professional efforts of the principal in such an endeavor. He can become a primary agent of change toward quality education only as he displays a sensitivity to the needs and wishes of those on his staff. This occurs best when there is a "team approach" to the activity. High priorities must be placed on educational outcomes and the school and the principal given every assistance required from each of several categories of individuals to adequately perform this task. Let us then take a look at how each of these persons can be of assistance to the principal in the improvement of instruction.

The Superintendent of Schools

As the executive officer of the school system and responsible for a coordinated, challenging program of education on a district-wide basis, it would be impossible to imagine genuine efforts being made in the instructional improvement without his support at the district level. The superintendent is in a key position to facilitate and encourage curriculum planning. Because of the complexity of many larger school systems he generally provides an organizational and administrative framework within the district that can assist in the over-all development of the curriculum. The Assistant Superintendent in Charge of Instruction, district supervisors, and local school coordinators are often a vital part of this assignment. The superintendent is engaged in many activities that are directly related to instructional improvement at the building level: communicating regularly with members of the board of education, county, and state department of education personnel, lay people in the community, and many others; encouraging local school

[Identify the proposed specialist by name, and state the contemplated period of service; supply the name of the key district coordinator.]

1. State the District's Need or Problem:

   Is there general staff agreement as to the nature, scope and importance of the problem?

2. What Sources of Assistance to Reduce Need or Resolve the Problem Have Been Considered?

3. Which Staff Members are Involved in Selecting the Outside Specialist? Who Has Final Responsibility?

4. Does the Proposed Outside Specialist Meet the District Need as to Level of:

   Technical competence?
   Experimental background?
   Skills in group process?
   Personality characteristics?
   Availability?
   Suitability for the local situation?

5. Check Budgetary and Procedural Factors:

   Administrative approval
   Funds budgeted
   Board of Trustees notified
   Approval of Board of Trustees
   Agreement completed with specialist

6. What Specific Role Will the Outside Specialist Fill in the District?

7. Is There Top-Level Administrative Support for this Project or Program? Will There Be Top-Level Administrative Participation in the Work with the Outside Specialist?

8. What Is the Preliminary Plan for the Outside Specialist's Service in the District?

9. Orientation of the Outside Specialist:

   Background on the problem and progress to date.
   Background regarding forces and status existing in district.
   Information relating to the orientation and level of professional awareness of the district staff.

Fig. 5–1. Guidelines for District Use of Outside Specialist Service.

Mutual assessment of situation by key district staff members and the outside specialist.

Information relating to the operational framework and limitations of the working relationship.

Indication of desired direction or focus of effort.

Spelling out specifically, if appropriate, what the outside specialist is to do.

10. Assignment of District Staff Members to Work with Outside Specialist:

Are staff members vitally concerned with the problem?

Do staff members possess appropriate aptitudes and/or skills?

Is assigned staff group reasonably cohesive in level of professional awareness?

Is their participation concordant with their district responsibilities?

Do staff members have time for effective participation?

Is the size of the staff group appropriate to the task?

11. Provision of Proper Facilities:

Adequate meeting rooms, office space for outside specialist to function.

Necessary audio-visual equipment, special requests.

Necessary clerical assistance.

Necessary transportation, housing, personal needs of outside specialist.

12. Provision for Effective Communication:

Notification of plans in detail to participants and those directly affected.

District publicity and recognition through announcements and displays.

Press releases.

13. Plans for Redirection of Specialist Effort if Early Service Appears to Be Missing District Goals:

14. Plans for Interim Activity by Staff Members Between Visits of Outside Specialist:

15. Plans for District Follow-up to Outside Specialist's Service:

16. Evaluation Procedures to Be Used by Key District Coordinator, Other District Personnel, and Outside Specialist:

Fig. 5-1 (*continued*)

faculties within the district to develop experimental and pilot programs; serving on committees as a resource person to assist in the
development of new ideas; developing curriculum policy at the district
level; keeping the entire district staff aware of significant developments; making wise staff appointments of persons who will be largely
engaged in curriculum work; maintaining district and local curriculum
committees who have tangible influence in this area; and engaging the
services of consultants and experts to assist the central staff in promoting curriculum development.

The Department Chairman

His primary purpose is to provide instructional leadership at the
department level wherein there can exist a grass-roots approach to
solving department problems. In this leadership role, the department
chairman can be of great assistance to the principal in filling a supervisory role. He can aid the principal in these ways: keep the principal
informed as to curriculum problems, plans, and activities in the department; coordinate departmental activities toward the attainment of
previously prescribed goals; visit classrooms on request and confer
regularly with teachers on an individual basis; assist the department in
forwarding requests and recommendations to the principal; hold regular department meetings; and encourage professional growth of staff
members.

Interestingly enough, four research studies completed in the last
few years indicated that department heads can be especially useful to
the principal in assisting him to improve the many areas of the curriculum found in the comprehensive high school, that the organization
pattern of the high school administrative staff must be designed to
permit the greatest potential use of department heads in these areas,
and that department chairmen should have the opportunity to bring in
outside consultants in their areas when the need is apparent. As stated
earlier in the James study, department chairmen have more to do with
curriculum development than most administrators realize.

Team Teaching Leader

Such groups as The Commission on The Experimental Study of the
Utilization of the Staff in the Secondary School and the Claremont
Teaching Team Program have done much to suggest ways in which the
quality of instruction can be improved at the elementary and secondary
level. The team teaching leader has basic responsibilities in coordinating his teaching efforts with that of the other members of the team and
in providing leadership in scheduling, guiding, and coordinating the
team effort. The team teaching leader has these basic functions in

improving instruction: holding daily meetings during planning periods to determine plans for the next few days; devising a master schedule for the activities of the team members and the pupils assigned to the team; obtaining the necessary teaching aids and equipment so that the team can function with large, medium, and small groups; representing the team at a variety of school and district meetings that involve instructional improvement; reporting to members of the team on school and district matters of concern, new research and practice, and the like; coordinating the plans of the individual team teachers; and evaluating the contributions of the members of the team as well as the success of the program. Surely the quality of leadership on the part of the team teaching leader, the effectiveness of the team's members, and contributions that both the leader and the members make toward improving the curriculum of the school make a great deal of difference as to the over-all success of the team teaching approach.

The Teaching Faculty

The teacher represents the heart of the school's teaching-learning situation and the facilitation of a quality program of instruction, in the last analysis, belongs to the teacher. The teacher who is performing in the classroom in outstanding fashion is obviously giving his maximum effort in improving the instructional program. Beyond this there are several ways in which the teacher can be of great assistance: serving on curriculum committees and councils, participating in institute meetings and demonstration lessons, reporting on new research and practice in the field, developing or assisting in the development of new study guides, and becoming involved in any other professional growth activities that are pertinent to the improvement of the school's program.

The Lay Citizen

Perhaps the greatest amount of assistance can be given to instructional improvement by the lay citizen through his active interest in and concern for the quality of the educational program. Wherever the interest of citizens is high and constructive, the schools are encouraged to excel in their efforts to provide an outstanding program. Citizens can assist the principal in improving the instructional program in these ways: acting as resource persons in classrooms, at teachers' meetings, and in assemblies; working with the PTA to develop community interest in educational improvement; serving on citizens' committees to study selected school problems; assisting the school authorities in the passage of bond issues and tax increases to provide better teachers, facilities, and services; selecting and supporting outstanding persons to run for and serve on the local board of education; and promoting such a group as the National Committee for Support of the Public Schools[4] as an agency devoted to instilling a cooperative working-relationship between the school and the community.

BEHAVIOR FACTORS

Leadership Behavior

What is the behavior of school executives which tries to influence the behavior of subordinates who have a claim to professional status? To explore a number of problems in this area of Executive Professional Leadership, a study was launched at Harvard University.[5]

Evidence from the study supported the assumption that the principal's Executive Professional Leadership (EPL) affects teacher morale, teacher performance, and pupil performance. Teachers' professional performance and morale both appear to serve as links in a causal chain between the EPL of principals and their pupils' performance. Sex did not seem to have any relationship to EPL, nor did marital status by itself. The data did seem to lend support to the proposition that older principals offer less leadership. When Jewish, Catholic, and Protestant principals were compared, their EPL scores did not differ significantly. Sex and marital status combined did seem to affect EPL; e.g., married men rated higher than married women. Comparisons of the relationship of sex and EPL, however, should be made with great caution.

The size of the city in which the school is located does not seem to affect the principal's EPL. There was a negative relationship between the size of the student body and the EPL score; the EPL score was smaller when the student body was larger. Also, the relationship between salary and EPL was not significant.

Of notable importance is the fact that the principal is in a position to influence and be influenced. Second, the interaction of individuals in one aspect of their relationship affects other relationships. Third, the concept of role in the mind of the principal, his superiors, and his teachers is important. During his preparation the principal internalizes an EPL conception of his role; on the job, however, he meets obstacles making it difficult to conform to this role. Presumably anything that accentuates blocks to professional leadership will decrease EPL;

[4]*Education U.S.A.*, National School Public Relations Association, January 20, 1969, p. 110.
[5]Neal Gross and Robert E. Herriott, *Staff Leadership in Public Schools* (New York: John Wiley, 1965), 247 pp. See also Dean C. Barnlund, *Interpersonal Communication: Survey and Studies* (New York: Houghton Mifflin, 1968), 727 pp.

anything that reduces such obstacles will increase EPL.

Relative to higher administration, there is a positive relationship between the professional leadership of the principal's immediate administrative superior and the principal's EPL. Managerial support from the immediate superior seems not too important, while social support from above has some effect upon EPL. Superintendents do not seem to influence principals' EPL as much as do the immediate superior, and involving principals in teacher selection and approving the principal's acting as a change agent results in a higher EPL. In relationships with teachers, a positive relationship was found between the staff's involvement in the principal's decisions and his professional leadership, between the principal's egalitarian relations with his staff and his EPL; and between his social and managerial support of teachers and his leadership. Support of teachers in conflicts between teacher and pupils was positively related to EPL.

Principals with high self-assessment scores on providing educational leadership had high EPL scores; the lower their self-assessment scores on managerial skills the higher their EPL. While the principal must give great importance to his role as an education leader, however, he cannot overlook the routine administrative part of his function. A service motive for becoming a principal may influence EPL, but ambitions for financial or professional advancement do not. Intellectual ability is related to EPL as are interpersonal skills.

Persons in supervisory positions should be aware that subordinates, as they perform their relay function in the organization's network, employ a variety of techniques to shape the decisions of their superior.[6] The superordinate may seek to satisfy, rather than disagree, because he has limited access to information and has limited computational capacities for coping with complex problems; in confrontation settings he may make decisions that are frequently guided by the goals and demands of subordinates; or he may yield to the preferences of subordinates because he wishes to avoid the real or imagined costs of noncompliance. Subordinates may exert power by creating an illusion of personal influence, by supplying information which points to one particular definition of the problem, by exerting influence through others in the organization's power structure, or, in some cases, by resorting to disguised flattery. Decision-making requires that status leaders recognize the kinds of influences that can be placed upon them and comprehend their use in establishing a heuristic value to understand how decisions can be guided, shaped, and even controlled by subordinates.

[6]Edwin M. Briges, "Administrative Man: Origin or Pawn in Decision Making," *Educational Administration Quarterly*, Winter 1970, p. 21.

Openness and Satisfaction

As the supervisor or principal strives to improve teacher job satisfaction, he should concern himself with the "openness" of the climate of the school accompanied by a high esprit as compared with a closed climate in which group members obtain little satisfaction in respect to the achievement of tasks or the meeting of social needs. Insofar as climate is able to influence satisfaction, modification of that climate should result in a change in the level of satisfaction. With respect to the number of years in the teaching profession, there is good evidence that as the years increase there also is a progressively higher level of job satisfaction. Younger teachers, suprisingly enough, appear to be the most dogmatic members of the staff. Principals and supervisors, in working with these young people, should use different approaches with them as they attempt to improve the educational program. Research at Stanford, for example, found significant differences in secondary schools between the various departments. A ranking of departments from the highest levels of reported job satisfaction to the lowest levels of job satisfaction were as follows: foreign language, social science, physical education, fine arts, mathematics, science, business, home economics, English, and industrial arts.[7] The tendency of teachers from certain academic departments to perceive the climate of their school to be more closed than teachers from other departments suggests that the supervisor consider what factors might be at work in the school setting that affect these particular groups of teachers more than the others.

PLANS FOR SUPERVISORY SERVICES

Earlier discussions have revolved around the concept that the principal is the educational leader in the school while the teacher is the instructional leader in the classroom. With the curriculum continually expanding and changing to meet the needs of a modern society, it is essential that the principal and the teacher keep pace with changing developments and contribute to a program of instruction of the highest quality. To assist in this effort, most districts provide supervisors and/or consultants as professional resource persons.

What is the new concept of the role of the supervisor as he works with principals and teachers? In brief, he emphasizes the human-relations aspect of professional guidance as well as giving leadership to the interpretation of content and method; he uses the team approach with

[7]Robert M. Hoagland, "Teacher Personality, Organizational Climate, and Teacher Job Satisfaction." Unpublished dissertation, Stanford University, December 1967.

the principal, teacher, and consultants working cooperatively in small group conferences, workshops, and in-service classes for the improvement of classroom instruction; he contributes a resource team from the central office as needed; he serves as an interpreter and coordinator of the district's approved curriculum; he interprets desirable and necessary change in relation to new concepts, materials, and research; and he is an energizer who releases the potentialities of others and develops leadership among the teaching faculty.

Teachers will play a heavy role in their associations with supervisors, consultants, and others who will be working with them on the improvement of instruction. In many instances the teacher will be playing the role of a learning diagnostician as well as that of a learning therapist. So important will be the position of the teacher that he will act as a stimulator and developer of learning activities for all pupils who come under his control. The supervisor will become highly involved with teachers as they seek assistance in discovering ways to identify better the difficulties in learning experienced by their students and in determining the types of learning experiences that will meet the expectancy levels of these young people. As the number of sophisticated computer devices increases, the learning specialist will have to be assisted by the supervisor in being posted and trained in his development of a basic plan for programming learning situations that will enhance pupil progress.

As an illustration of the large variety of plans that may be devised for supervisory services, a medium-sized school district (Garden Grove, California) in 1970 adopted a new organizational pattern. Teachers, administrators, and board members consolidated their views related to the requirements that had to be met in improving the instructional service structure of the district. This is shown in Fig. 5–2.

SUMMARY

There are some specialists who do not feel that there is any difference between curriculum development and supervision. Their argument is that whatever is done to improve the curriculum does, in fact, involve the techniques of good supervision. In agreeing with this concept, we have taken a searching look at the make-up of supervisory personnel and their task which gives undeniable evidence that their role is inextricably tied in with the development and improvement of the curricular program. Stated another way, the relationship is analogous to the wedding of two basic curriculum forces—human and material.

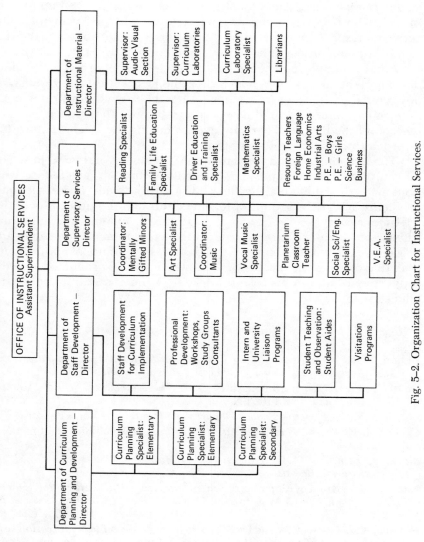

Fig. 5–2. Organization Chart for Instructional Services.

In reviewing the basic supervisory-administrative roles, it has been stressed that the principal assumes primary leadership for the quality of education. Not only must the principal be a primary curriculum leader, but it is one of the most important jobs of the curriculum specialist to establish a strong working relationship with the principal. The curriculum specialist, regardless of title, acts as a contributor to the role of the principal in curriculum development, not as a threat.

Fundamentally, one of the basic reasons for supporting curriculum development on a single-school basis is the fact that this represents the best unit for a teacher-to-teacher and teacher-to-administrator communication base. Meaningful experimentation in the curriculum area is accomplished at the classroom level by having the teacher interested in promoting experimental programs.

The principal should recognize that he has several ways in which he can discharge his supervisory functions: through face-to-face relations with the individual teacher; through the study of instructional problems by various groups of teachers; through the utilization of district supervisory resources; and through the development of numerous supervisory measures that can alert the faculty to new knowledge and procedures. The other supervisory positions are of no less importance than that of the principal; they are, however, to be recognized as being supportive of him in his role as a leader in the contention for quality education.

SELECTED REFERENCES

Bishop, Lloyd K. *Individualizing Educational Systems: The Elementary and Secondary School.* New York: Harper and Row, 1970.

Bradfield, Luther E., and Leonard E. Kraft. *The Elementary School Principal in Action.* Scranton: Intext, 1970.

Callahan, M. G. *Effective School Department Head.* New York: Parker, 1971.

Greene, J. E. *School Personnel Administration.* Philadelphia: Chilton Book, 1971.

McCarty, D. J., and C. E. Ramsey. *School Managers: Power and Conflict in American Public Education.* Westport, Conn.: Greenwood, 1971.

National Association of Elementary School Principals. *Humanizing the Elementary School, Part 5.* Washington, D. C.: National Education Association, 1970.

National Association of Secondary School Principals. *Secondary Education in an Environment of Change.* Washington, D. C.: National Education Association, 1970.

Sullivan, Neil V. *Walk, Run, or Retreat: The Modern School Administrator.* Bloomington: Indiana University Press, 1971.

Webb, Holmes, and Doris Webb. *The Secondary School Teacher: A Casebook.* Scranton: Intext, 1970.

CHAPTER 6

Educational Programs and Projects

As a result of the nationwide rethinking of the educational curriculum, there has been an impressive and vigorous effort in the profession to determine directions that various reforms are taking as a guide to future action. Over the past few years, a wide range of subject areas and specialized educational programs have undergone major revision. Dissatisfaction with the wide gulf which had come to exist between the practical educators and the professional scholars has been a significant factor in the revitalization of interest in curriculum revision. To escape the monotony of routine and the tradition of conformity, the classroom teacher must look to the supervisor for ideas and suggestions that will lead to the development of creativity and talent. The supervisor, within this innovation framework, supplies and interprets new information that can be gleaned from experimental programs and projects that can be readily implemented by the teacher. Attempts to identify an organized multitude of new and challenging curriculum concepts is a difficult task at best. The search for improved ways to assist teachers, better methods of developing skills subjects, and more successful attempts to organize the curriculum are common concerns of every supervisor and administrator.

Supervision in a sense really implies "super" vision. It means, in effect, the ability to analyze larger curricular programs in their entirety, yet at the same time be able to join the small bits and elements into one cohesive whole as they fit into the larger curricular pattern. Such knowledge demands a continuous, current understanding of the research and programs existing in the field, as well as those classic studies that have not yet been superseded by newer data. As illustrative of this approach, several significant educational programs and projects are presented as suggestive of the many areas in the curriculum in which the supervisor must have deep and intelligent understanding.

NEW DIRECTIONS: CLASSROOM ORGANIZATION AND INSTRUCTION

When historians review the pattern of educational transition in the decades of the sixties and the seventies, it appears that this era may well be known as one characterized by rapid change and experimentation. With the developments in education as proposed by such groups as the Fund for the Advancement of Education, the report on the AIBS Biological Sciences Curriculum Study, the Project English and Project Social Studies, the National Science Foundation, the School Mathematics Study Group, and many others, the interest, and even controversy, in the entire curriculum area is evident. Further, it is representative of a retooling and reshaping of the attack on an improved teaching-learning approach by scholars, teachers, supervisors, and administrators. Even such a traditional field as physical science has reduced its total field, in its simplest form, to 34 basic concepts to be utilized as a basis for comprehending the logic related to natural phenomena.

Independent Study and Research

What are some of the most notable trends in classroom innovations? An extensive survey of the recent literature on the subject shows that much progress is being made in the area of independent study—how students can progress at various rates, utilize a variety of learning materials, and continue to be stimulated to learn at a pace that represents maximum output. The feasibility of such independent study programs has been experimentally proven through the development of learning laboratories in all basic-skill areas, the utilization of the teaching machine and educational television, the improvement of computer data processing for workable, flexible scheduling plans, the improvement in the balance between and the range among various courses in the curriculum, greater sensitivity to productive and realistic grouping and related activities, and the decentralization of school facilities and curricular programs as they relate to improved learning.

Many questions baffle youth and in their curiosity they are anxious to learn the answers to many of these puzzling questions. Independent study relies on the ability of youth to be able to study by themselves, to have the advantage of flexible and meaningful assignments, and to have the foresight and vision to pursue tasks of long duration through to their conclusion. Experimental studies have shown, as in the Quest Phase and Independent Study Plan at Melbourne High School (Florida), that only those who have demonstrated the ability and enthusiasm to work on their own on an unsupervised basis should be admitted to follow any independent study plan. Through the use of an instructional materials center, independent study can become a reality. Audio-visual aids, teaching machines, educational television, journals of all kinds, and study spaces (supervised, less supervised, and unsupervised project areas) are all important facilities that need to be found in such a center. In addition, student laboratories should adjoin as many classrooms as possible.

The school library can become a significant place in the school for implementing and enriching all phases of the educational program as well as facilitating independent research. Recordings, films, filmstrips, microfilms, prints, and transparencies are important library resources that can be procured by students in their search for a wealth of information. Some newer libraries are experimenting with programs for computers, making retrievable information possible, and expanding varied media holdings for use with the new automatic equipment that is coming on the market. Increasing numbers of students are being encouraged to share in the meaningful employment of all kinds of valuable library resources. Librarians can be of much help in encouraging experimentation by explaining new methods and techniques that will support and enrich independent study and research.

Educational Television

The long-term effort of The Ford Foundation, the creation of the National Educational Television and Radio Center, and the Mid-West Airborne Program are but a few examples of the forces in this country that have provided a breakthrough in the whole field of ETV. Many schools today are expanding their entire curriculum through this medium. Witness, for example, those western schools that were forced to offer a foreign language as a legal requirement for all 6th, 7th, and 8th grade students for the first time. Faced with the impossible task of finding sufficient qualified teachers of foreign language, where did many of the schools turn? To educational television, of course. Many schools, through this medium, provided advanced subjects and more teacher time for both individual and small group instruction.

Basic problems that are being solved as educators become more accustomed to ETV are the provision of adequate transmission and reception facilities, the training and recruitment of outstanding studio teachers, the proper classroom use of this medium by the faculty, and sound scheduling of a variety of programs for maximum classroom consumption. In particular, studies have shown that ETV is excellent for the introduction of complex material. Beyond this it has become apparent that this medium is not expensive. Plainedge (New York), for example, now has a new low-powered, low-cost transmission system that leads directly into classrooms within a twenty-mile radius furnished only by a ten watt transmitter and at a total cost of $50,000.

The Denver Public Schools and Stanford University's Institute for Communication Research conducted a four-year joint research project to determine how instructional television could best meet a total teaching situation by combining it with other educational phases of the program. The Denver-Stanford project demonstrated that although television alone is a valuable teaching tool, it is much more potent when reinforced with other elements of the total teaching-learning contest. The individualizing of instruction that a classroom teacher can provide after the basic teaching has been accomplished by a television teacher is extremely important. There is growing evidence that programmed instruction, of certain kinds and under suitable conditions, can be used effectively in the schools but that a carefully chosen combination of teaching devices is better than any device used alone.

A five-year study of the Anaheim (California) elementary schools' closed circuit television programs was completed recently. The effectiveness of the instructional program was measured by specially district-constructed objective type tests in science, social studies, and Spanish and by gains from fall to spring on standardized tests of the basic skills in reading, arithmetic, and language. The district-constructed tests provided direct comparisons in subjects taught conventionally (without televised lessons) and with the aid of televised lessons in large and regular-size class groups. The standardized tests assessed achievement in the areas of the basic skills. The results indicated that the pupils receiving televised lessons did better on the district tests than pupils without the televised lessons. In comparisons of pupils in large class groups with televised instruction and pupils in regular-size classes without televised instruction (control), the comparisons favored the pupils in the large class groups by a statistically significant margin in most instances. In comparisons of pupils in regular-size groups with televised instruction and pupils in regular-size groups without televised instruction (control), none of the comparisons favored the pupils in regular-size classes without televised instruction. The results of the five-year study indicated that television is a decidedly useful tool in the hands of a competent instructional staff, and large class groups in the "redeployment plan" (see Fig. 6–1) with the teams of resource (large class) teachers and skills teacher are especially promising.

The Center of Applied Research in Education found in studies, based upon responses from 1203 elementary school children and 2845 high school children who had been exposed to a wide range of different

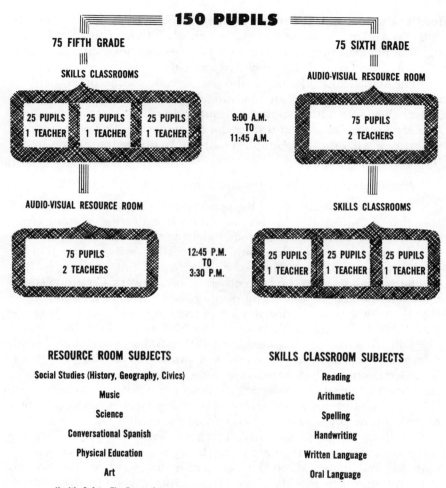

Fig. 6–1. Redeployment Plan.

types of instructional television, that younger children believe they learn more from television classes. Only one third of the high school students, however, believed that they received more benefit from televised classes. In an Indiana study, it was revealed that television is accepted readily by children of elementary school age and adults engaged in home study, but most high school and college students frown on it. It covered subject-matter somewhat more efficiently than conventional methods, but appeared to be less effective in achieving changes in group structure, attitudes, and socialization. The National Program for the Use of Television in the Public Schools project involved nearly 200,000 students in some 200 public school systems. Out of 251 comparisons made during a two-year period between television and control students, 165 favored the television students.

The statistical evidences of the past decade on the potentiality of instructional television as an educational tool has been well established. The challenge to administrators and supervisors is to discover imaginative ways of exploring and testing the uniqueness of this new medium in terms of what it can accomplish best and to utilize those ways to the fullest.

Teaching Machines and Programmed Learning

The one-to-one concept of the teaching machine has revolutionized the idea of "self-study" in the classroom. Because the student is required to give a written response in following the programmed instructional material placed before him, an immediate self-evaluation of his work is made possible without the usual loss of time waiting for the teacher's analysis as to the correctness of his answers. Continuous student activity, too, is provided for over a reasonable period of time. Now that the production and distribution of teaching machines has become a $200,000,000 business, there are many basic types of machines available: simple write-in, computer (such as the IBM digital), punch board, scrambled book, automatic rater, and programmed textbook types. Some excellent machines are as low as $30 to $50 in price and these are readily adaptable to many types of classroom work.

Of all phases of the utilization of teaching machines, the selection of appropriate programmed instructional materials is the most critical. In searching for these materials, teachers should study carefully the methods under which the data were obtained as a basis for writing the materials and investigate the kind of learning that will take place as well as the retention span of the material once it is learned by the student. An astounding development by one company has provided for the programmed learning used by the various machines to be monitored by a computer that adjusts the level of the programmed material automatically for each pupil. The computer easily makes adjustments for several hundred pupils on a split-second basis.

Donald Bushnell, in his work *The Role of the Computer in Future Instructional Systems,* has forecast that the computer-run classroom also will integrate television, films, and slides with regular learning methods, as well as mass day-to-day information to take and record student attendance, make curriculum changes, administer grade records, and even schedule and register students. The future involved in the implementation of computer systems in the classroom will revolutionize the possibilities in integrating and directing individual-student study programs charted on an independent basis.

In an experiment to expose both control and experimental groups to the same material in a concentrated effort over a period of time, two sixth-grade classes in two elementary schools were selected. The programmed method of instruction was at least as effective and successful in teaching the material as the conventional method. Teachers using the programmed materials testified that the use of these materials freed them to do other things in the classroom. Another study of programmed instruction vs ordinary instruction concluded that programmed instruction was more efficient than conventional instruction when time was considered as a measure of efficiency, study habits did not differ, and there was no significant change in student attitudes between the two groups. It is apparent that study habits and student attitudes are important when using programmed learning if a real gain in these two areas is to result.

Testing

The Joint Committee on Testing, established by the American Association of School Administrators, the Council of Chief State School Officers, and the National Association of Secondary School Principals, recently completed a two-year study of external standardized testing. Since that time a Gallup Poll Survey has discovered that 77% of the public favor standardized, national achievement tests for high school youth. The joint commission, however, has serious reservations about the current proper use of these tests and is quite critical of the rather negative effect that might befall curriculum development and improved teaching methods through their indiscriminate administration. Although there is no question that individuals will be evaluated in the classroom, the question is how will they will be evaluated. The Joint Commission has made these recommendations: that every school system periodically evaluate its *total* testing program to determine if it can be justified in terms of individual pupil growth and the over-all instructional program; that all external tests given for the purpose of awarding scholarships be administered without cost to the student; that test scores not be used to compare students, schools, or states; and that all external tests be given outside of class time. In effect, the techniques of measuring knowledge, understanding, creative power, skills, and appreciations are manifold and require the benefit of many types of observations of pupil growth: teacher examinations, anecdotal records, and many other types of data.

In terms of recent developments, new type tests are being correlated as an integral part of the classroom instructional procedure in practically all of the new courses in the curriculum (Project English, Project Social Studies, and the like). Such features as listening, speaking, reading, and writing are becoming intimately involved in many of these testing programs with the aid of electronically-equipped laboratories. Even essay writing can now be analyzed in the latest external standardized testing approach.

An Indiana study investigated the influence of achievement motivation and test anxiety on performance in programmed instruction. 139 undergraduate students took three pre-tests—the Iowa Picture Interpretation Test, the Test Anxiety Questionnaire, and the Achievement Pretest.[1] To adequately score the students' performances on the programmed instruction, three separate measures were obtained: the length of time each student took to complete the material, the number of frames answered incorrectly, and the student's proficiency on an achievement test administered at the conclusion of the programmed instruction. The results of the study indicated that high-achievement-motivated students required less time to complete the programmed learning material, made fewer overt errors on the material, and received higher scores on a short-term retention test than did low-achievement-motivated students. The study reported also that the high-test-anxiety students worked faster and made fewer errors than low-test-anxious students, but failed to exhibit higher retention scores.

These studies give limited evidence that programmed learning does offer some advantages over the conventional type of instruction. With greater familiarity of teachers with programmed learning techniques, it appears likely that real progress can be made in utilizing this type of instruction to advantage with other instructional techniques.

The Fort Lincoln New Town (Washington, D. C.) educational system[2] is moving toward constructing tests based on behavorial taxonomy, a hierarchy of learning objectives, that will enable each student to reach his short- and long-term objectives. Each type of learning begins with the operational level of the student and ends with a different level of performance. The taxonomy enables the system to guide the student to the achievement of his goals and to evaluate his progress. Whenever the student does not seem to be making progress, alternate approaches toward achieving his goals are presented. A student's failure to learn is considered a system failure and a problem for the staff to solve. A computer enables the system to provide accurate and up-to-date records on all students and relieves the staff of time-consuming efforts of record-keeping.

[1] Howard R. Kight and Julius M. Sassenrath, "Relation of Achievement Motivation and Test Anxiety to Performance in Programmed Instruction," *Journal of Educational Psychology*, vol. 57, no. 1 (February 1966), pp. 14–17.
[2] Mario D. Fantini and Milton A. Young, *Designing Education for Tomorrow's Cities* (New York: Holt, Rinehart, and Winston, 1970), pp. 37–38.

Team Teaching

With an increasing amount of evidence being discovered that team teaching provides even greater measures of pupil initiative, enthusiasm, and creativity than the traditional teaching methods, team teaching is now finding acceptance and support in areas that ten years ago would surely have rejected such a practice. Perhaps the strongest argument for the creation of a teaching team is that it makes better use of human talents and classroom materials at a more reasonable unit cost. In its basic element, the organization of team teaching activities calls for 40 percent of the student's time to be spent in large-group instruction, 20 percent in small-group situations, and 40 percent in independent study. Utilizing the services of professional teachers, paraprofessional assistants, clerks, general aides, community consultants, and staff specialists, it has given an advantage to the improved adaptation of many kinds of teaching resources to the classroom program. Currently the Harvard-Lexington Summer Program to train teachers in participating in team teaching programs is an example of overcoming one of the biggest hurdles in the preparation of teachers to assume this responsibility.

Under team teaching students of low ability have been found to do better in English than with a conventional class but this is not true of social studies. However, students have accomplished as much in social studies with team teaching as those who have been assigned to homogeneous groups under one teacher. In biology, superior students in a team teaching situation were able to cover basic course units more rapidly than those taught by conventional methods, thus allowing students an opportunity to investigate several areas of interest extensively. These students also had an opportunity to work in depth with teacher specialists in a variety of fields and to engage in numerous seminar experiences related to several important phases of the science curriculum.

Training Team Teachers

An experimental program of cooperation between the Louisville Public Schools and the University of Louisville has been under way in which student teachers train through team organization. The program consists of a regular team of three English teachers in a city high school plus university specialists in the subject field. A lay aide is assigned the clerical work of the three teachers and each semester three student teachers are assigned to the team.[3]

[3]F. Randall Powers, "Team Trains Teachers," *The Educational Forum*, vol. 30, no. 2 (January 1966), pp. 205–208. See also Leslie J. Chamberlin, *Team Teaching: Organization and Administration* (Columbus: Charles E. Merrill Publishing Co., 1969), 152 pp.

There are three dangers normally associated with student teaching that the team organization tends to lessen. These dangers are: that student teachers' contacts with one set of classes or one class will limit the outlook the student teacher has on student populations; that there is a provincial experience in being confined to one supervising teacher; and that there is the danger of a personality clash where two people are closely associated. The team approach, then, allows the master teacher to shoulder the main burden of training while the student has the opportunity of seeing three regular teachers perform frequently. There is less danger of a block between personalities because pairing is not the training pattern. Finally, students experience the differences of approach needed for various levels of ability and interest.

The benefits lie in the fact that professional educators perform regularly before their colleagues and submit to the sophisticated criticism of procedure that is available from such an audience. This results in improved instructional techniques observed by the students. Also, the team environment offers a more realistic and less secure approach to eventual classroom practice than the solicitude provided by the supervision of a single teacher.

Differentiated Staffing

Increasing staff and competence in the seventies has given rise to a new concept based on the premise of additional remuneration for increased professional responsibilities. As the role of the teacher changes under differentiated staffing, new responsibilities demand additional training and increased task performance. Position definitions provide a model for differentiated staffing as developed at Temple City (California): 1) Teaching Research Associate (twelve months and a doctorate or equivalent); 2) Teaching Curriculum Associate (eleven months and a master's or equivalent); 3) Senior Teacher (ten to eleven months and a master's or equivalent); 4) Staff Teacher (ten months and a B.A. degree plus one year); and 5) Academic Assistant (ten months and an A.A. or B.A. degree). This combination of teacher specialists with the status leader does much to institute the development of a vital and relevant educational program. Teachers are intimately involved in sharing the decision-making process with administrators in determining how the instructional program needs to be strengthened and improved. Teachers have a real voice in disciplining the members of the teaching corps and they have a basic responsibility in exercising leadership as professionals.

Laguna Beach (California) has made maximum utilization of its differentiated staff model by analyzing three functions that take place in the classroom: 1) teacher input information (large group); 2) teacher listens and interacts (small group); and 3) student goes to work (directed or independent study). To provide for these functions, large-group teachers, seminar teachers, and lab teachers have been assigned on a differentiated basis. The Hewitt Engineered Classroom concept has been utilized which provides for a hierarchy of student involvement with the classroom designed for each of the activities appropriate for each level of involvement. Fallbrook (California), in 1971, instigated a new differentiated staffing pattern with varying monetary allowances that incorporated the positions of division chairmen, department chairmen, staff members, intern teachers, and teacher aides in three different classifications.

At present the research staff of Program 20, now being conducted by the Center for the Advanced Study of Educational Administration, is studying how new differentiated staffing patterns are working in schools that are attemping to use them. A longitudinal, in-depth study of the implementation of this concept is under way in four schools in the Northwest. In each of the schools a research assistant has been assigned to watch classes in session, attend staff meetings, and talk informally with teachers, administrators, and other staff members. Observers are concentrating on how instructional personnel divide the labor, how they coordinate their work, what their relations are with other school personnel, and how accommodations are made for conflicts and strains that arise in the course of implementing the program. Space layouts and time scheduling are of special interest to the observers. Such observations will single out central issues of differentiated staffing and will provide the basis for developing systematic interview and questionnaire schedules to be applied later to a large number of schools with exemplary differentiated staffing programs.

Nongraded Classrooms

The most notable change in the revamping of classroom practice is found in the organization of nongraded schools. Although considered best for the elementary school, the nongraded plan has merit in terms of being adaptable to the secondary level. The nongraded plan has several advantages over the graded form of organization: it permits the student to progress at a pace best suited to him; pass or fail pressures do not have to be exerted during the September to June months; parent-teacher conferences become the key to accurate pupil-progress reporting; grouping within the class as well as between classes becomes a reality; and pupils who complete curriculum requirements before the end of the year are not forced to arbitrarily wait until another school year arrives before moving on to new and challenging material.

Current studies indicate that there appears to be a correlation between the graded school and drop-outs. To avert this rather tragic loss of potentially able students, the nongraded plan of organization has received rather notable support in some quarters. Inasmuch as reading ability is the basic criterion for placing students in class and then grouping them, it is considered that a much healthier atmosphere will exist in the classroom due to the homogeneity of students' abilities based on similar reading levels rather than chronological age. The best descriptions of this plan are to be found in John I. Goodlad and Robert H. Anderson, *The Nongraded Elementary School* (Harcourt, Brace, and Co.); B. Frank Brown, *The Nongraded High School* (Prentice-Hall); and the materials produced by Melbourne High School (Florida) in *Space Age Programming*.

Nongraded Schools in Action

The University Elementary School of the University of California, Los Angeles, has been on a nongraded basis since 1960. Children enter school before the age of four and move upward through the twelfth year of age without encountering grade levels. They do not receive grade promotions nor do they fail a grade level and have to repeat.[4]

The premises for nongrading are these: (1) children are much more different from each other than we have realized; (2) because of the many differences, educational diagnosis of and prescription for the individual is necessary; (3) there must be alternatives from which to fill the prescription; (4) the question is not, Is this child ready for school? but, What is this child ready for? (5) criteria replace normative standards as the measure of pupil progress—these standards arrange a sequence of difficulty or a meaningful progression in work assignments which can eventually form a profile; and (6) sound learning is cumulative as nongrading requires different assumptions, expectations, teacher behavior, and language.

Studies have shown no significant advances in learning through homogeneous grouping as grouping is productive only to serve a given purpose. The crucial significance to learning is individual instruction.[5]

The UCLA Elementary School has nine nongraded clusters of children and teachers with 25 to 75 students in each cluster. Each child is assigned to a cluster and several sub-clusters within the larger ones on the basis of diagnosis and prescription. The clusters differ in number

[4]John I. Goodlad, "Meeting Children Where They Are," *Saturday Review of Literature*, vol. XLVIII, no. 12 (March 20, 1965), pp. 57–59, 72–74.

[5]John I. Goodlad, *The Schools vs Education* (Melbourne, Florida: IDEA Reprint Series, 1969), p. 5.

and size each year. The budget is slightly higher than before, yet there are fifty percent more people on the payroll. Not all teachers are on a team teaching basis, although team teaching is essential to the program. There is a great deal of flexibility in the program itself.

The school has two broad levels of function and expectations: (1) ages 4–7 are the early childhood level with an emphasis on the development of the self concept and a satisfying, productive interaction with children, adults, and the environment; (2) ages 8–12 represent attention to the development of the ability to understand and use man's approaches to studying social and natural phenomena. The age limits vary in each cluster; sub-groups work on separate tasks; the child is moved whenever placement seems desirable, yet the attempt is to keep the child in a cluster for one year. Teachers, parents, and children are necessary parties to complete placement, although teachers and the principal determine the students assigned to each cluster. Placement is held up until a cluster is developed.

Nova High School in Florida represents one of the newest and most unique approaches to the nongraded school. Nova is the first unit of an educational complex which eventually will include schools from kindergarten through a private four-year university with graduate studies. Nova is nongraded in regard to grade level while retaining a report card and grades for each unit of work completed. The focal point in the instructional program is the study unit which already outlines the nature of the areas to be studied and includes the factor of continuity and challenge in completing the work.

By 1972 the experimental John Dewey High School in New York City will have incorporated an independent study program based on a nongraded plan. The school will be scheduled year-round and an eight-hour school day will be in effect. The traditional semester system will be replaced with five 7-week phases, with an optional sixth phase offered during the summer. Computerized, flexible scheduling will be capable of arranging seminar-type classes with three to twelve students or providing lecture groups of 250 or more pupils. The nongraded plan will eliminate the distinction between major and minor subjects as a means of presenting a more balanced curriculum.

The findings of the nongraded plans tend to demonstrate that there needs to be constant orientation of parents who are unable to rely on the usual concept of progress in terms of students who advance from one grade level to another on a yearly basis. Considerable orientation of faculty members to the plan is essential and the Board of Education needs to be briefed regularly on the plan's progress from one stage to another.

To substantiate the nongraded concept, a midwestern study of non-graded seventh and eighth graders in two classes showed that all but one of the students made significant gains in achievement of twenty percent more than the national norms. Students were more comfortable and relaxed in their learning experiences and social and emotional growth were as good as that found in the traditional program. More individual help for students was a notable contribution of the nongraded plan.

Flexible Scheduling

New plans for scheduling have been devised to provide a variety of institutional arrangements that include a common characteristic of flexibility. Commonly known as the flexible scheduling plan, modular arrangements of from twelve to thirty-five minute modules have been devised to enable students to take a larger number of subjects. Some subjects are scheduled only once or twice a week, while others meet five times a week or oftener. Teachers and students are allowed much freedom in the use of time and space as well as in determining the content for instruction. Teachers may make daily requests as to the schedule that needs to be followed, and students are given reasonable latitude in decision-making in reference to their own schedule.

Teachers have found that the element of flexibility in scheduling has made it possible to increase the class-time factor whenever there is a need rather than being rationed with an inflexible period each day. Teachers have greater freedom of time to spend on class preparation and to counsel students who need help. A greater opportunity for group effort exists as the teacher is able to work on a more intimate basis with other teachers and students benefit from the smaller, seminar-type of class patterns that may be established under such a plan.

The range of choices under a flexible scheduling plan is greatly extended. New alternatives to both required and elective courses may be offered by shortening their time span; independent study plans may be devised in which the pupil can follow his own research activities; offering course alternatives in which pupils may follow similar but more individualized subject-matter areas under a teacher-advisor—these are only a few ways in which the student can be given greater individual instruction opportunities under the flexible scheduling plan.

Brookhurst Junior High School (Anaheim, California) has combined the efforts of both students and teachers to develop a daily demand variable schedule. Basing their decisions upon daily evaluation of student progress, teachers decide who should be called to their classes, what specific lesson should be taught, how long it will take, what teachers should teach the lesson, what size and type of group the class should be, what educational equipment should be used, and what space is needed to contain the learners. These faculty decisions are submitted daily and the subject and time request are placed on a master schedule. Students report to their teacher-counselor each morning before school begins to make decisions regarding their school schedule for the next day. Because teacher demands and student needs change daily, there is a different schedule each day of the school year. Each student has modules committed for him by the teachers; however, the modules or time not committed by the faculty may be utilized by the students as they wish. Students, therefore, can make decisions daily regarding subjects to be taken and time to be spent in the electives, various resource centers, and laboratories.

Why is there a different daily student schedule? The answer is that it produces a more effective educational program. Brookhurst students have demonstrated superior achievement in some areas with significant critical ratios in comparison to comparable control schools. Daily decision-making has developed initiative and creativity on the part of the faculty and the students. As the bells and the rigid walls have disappeared, so has the lock step of student achievement.

Gaining Support for Flexible Scheduling

The school newspaper, the community newspaper, and talks by school personnel are typical methods of informing parents and others about flexible scheduling plans and programs. One high school faculty spent months attending community coffee klatches and another arranged monthly home seminars once a month in three geographic areas as a means of reaching people in the community. Some high schools have used parents successfully as clerical and teacher aides in a bid for greater parent participation in assisting with the development of the new program.[6]

In-service training programs for faculty are essential to help them adjust to the changes required in moving from a conventional program to a flexible one. In addition, some schools have: 1) invited experts to speak to the faculty to explain the new program; 2) recruited only those teachers who were interested in teaching under a flexible schedule program; 3) operated certain subject areas or departments on a pilot, flexible-scheduling basis for two or three years before complete adoption; 4) scheduled sensitivity training sessions to make faculty personnel more aware of the needs of other people; and 5) offered orientation sessions in the fall and spring for new teachers.

[6]John F. Beacon, *A Survey of Administrative Problems of Flexible Scheduling.* Unpublished Thesis, California State College at Long Beach, 1970, pp. 73–79.

Conclusion

In tomorrow's classroom it becomes obvious that there will be more individual student learning through the use of teaching machines, educational television, tapes, learning laboratories, linguaphones, films, and data-processing machines. More and more the testing and guidance movement will focus earlier attention on students at all ability levels. Team teaching will permit teachers to become better prepared and far more scholarly in their approach to classroom learning. Basic resources, both human and material, will require continual testing and refining as the educational enterprise attempts to devise a more effective organizational pattern in the years to come.

Much that has been happening in education today attests to the ferment that describes the new directions in which the public schools have been moving. The entire educational system has been undergoing a notable restructuring and many new techniques and devices are finding their way into the curriculum. As described earlier, there is a quickening recognition that many of these new procedures call for the attention and evaluation of the education profession. The learning process in the contemporary school needs to be strengthened and there are clear indications that it may be done by utilization of some of these new techniques that are receiving widespread promotion in many educational circles.

STUDIES RELATED TO PROGRAM CHANGE

Undoubtedly one of the most determined efforts made during the last decade has revolved around the questions of what to teach and how to organize for teaching. An important review of this effort in one area was developed by Dorothy Fraser, *Current Curriculum Studies in Academic Subjects,* as a part of the Project on the Instructional Program of the Public Schools. As described by Fraser, the twentieth century school in the United States now presents a broader range of content than any to which young people have been exposed previously. New pressures have formed to teach the disciplines as disciplines in the schools, to start a number of subjects at an earlier grade level, and to stress the structures of the separate subjects. In part, the pressures arise from recognition that all citizens, if they are to understand the complicated questions of public policy in the modern world, must work from a broader and deeper base of knowledge than was necessary in earlier days.

Studies of this type have done much to assist supervisors and administrators in developing guidelines that would lead to the formation of new programs of instruction. In recognition of this, several important studies are reviewed with an analysis of their significance to program change being given later.

Basic Educational Practices

There are a number of ways in which the elementary school must meet the needs of children and young people.[7] The school must have clearly stated purposes that represent its commitment to children, to knowledge, and to society. It should have a responsibility beyond the teaching of the basic skills and reflect a concern for self-concept and the personality development of children. Relating the learning experiences of children to their world and to reality as they know it represents an important task. Far more opportunity can be given children to share in the planning and organizing of their classroom activities, and the school must be more responsive to children's needs that arise from conditions peculiar to the home, the community, and the neighborhood.

Many of today's schools will wish to evaluate carefully the way in which they are utilizing the time of children and the staff so that they are consistent with the purposes of the instructional program. Further, the school needs to be attentive to the problems created by transitions from grade to grade and from school to school, and it must be willing to extend its influence beyond the four walls of the classroom and beyond the physical limits of the school building.

Such criteria provide much insight to the administrator or supervisor in examining the purposes of the elementary school. The current emphasis on excellence and quality of services and instruction makes it imperative that the instructional staff of any elementary school critically review its own program to determine if it is showing real concern for the intellectual and physical growth of children in all aspects of their young lives.

Equality of Opportunity

The Conant studies have found that public education has been making notable strides in moving ahead toward greater equality of opportunity, although much remains to be done.[8] Greater sums of money, however, are required now for the improvement and expansion of public education and this will necessitate new methods of financing.

[7]George Manolakes, *The Elementary School We Need* (Washington, D.C.: Association for Supervision and Curriculum Development, 1965), 40 pp. See also Luther E. Bradfield and Leonard E. Kraft, *The Elementary Principal in Action* (Scranton: Intext, 1970).

[8]James B. Conant, *The Comprehensive High School: A Second Report to Interested Citizens* (New York: McGraw-Hill), 1967, 95 pp.

The technological revolution will demand greater financial support as teachers will have at their disposal televised instruction, photographic devices, tapes, and similar aides that will transform the school into a vast resource center for learning. The spectrum of the comprehensive high school of the future will be shifted toward the highly gifted; the chief variable in school learning will be less the ability of the student than his desire to learn; more and more emphasis will be placed on motivation; and attention will be shifted to the development of social ideals.

Some real improvements in secondary school organization and the curriculum are being made in these areas: instruction in calculus; four years of one modern foreign language; Advanced Placement Program; ratio of English teachers to students (1 to 120 or less); three years of social studies required; vocational education courses; ratio of certificated personnel staff to students (1 to 20.4 or less); ratio of counselors to students (1 to 349 or less); new physics, chemistry, or biology; distributive education; summer school; and courses for slow learners. Later studies should show even greater strides in these areas vital to equal educational opportunity.

Educational Change in the Next Decade

By the middle of the 1980's education and the world around it will be vastly changed. Change will occur not only in the material aspects of human life, but change will take place in the areas of family life, human values, relations with the world, and even in terms of feelings and attitudes. Children and adults will be required to place implicit faith not in the solidity and stability of the environment but in themselves as living, vital organisms that have the capacity for growth, adaptation, and creative interaction in a rapidly changing world. Educational change, then, will occur in several different ways.[9]

1. *Education will be valued as experience, not only as preparation.* In the future, learning will not serve only as preparation; it will be designed to be a richly rewarding human experience. The experience of the moment will be valued because it will have served to enrich the lives of human beings.

2. *Education will be life-long.* Education will become such an integral part of life that it will never end. People will demand the right to study and to learn because it will be a source of great satisfaction. As facts erode quickly, educational needs will be great at all ages.

3. *Education will be fun.* Learning situations will be arranged theoretically and practically that are stimulating, joyfully involving the

[9]Richard E. Farson, "The Education of Jeremy Farson," Western Behavioral Sciences Institute, La Jolla, California, 1968.

learner, and which will evoke the best in him. Learning environments will be constructed in which the experience of learning is, in itself, a sufficient reward to produce great changes in human beings.

4. *Education will include noncognitive dimensions.* Whereas the present educational system is focused almost entirely on cognitive learning (the ability to store and give forth facts), in the future other dimensions will be emphasized as well. Esthetic, sensory, and emotional development, in addition to achieving satisfying interpersonal relationships, will be fostered. People will become better acquainted with their feelings and emotions as the affective side of life is improved.

5. *Education will be, in part, student designed.* To a great extent students know what they need to learn and they know something about how to learn it. As individuals move toward realizing their higher potentials, they are increasingly insistent on self-determination in all their activities.

6. *Education will be directed toward constellations of people.* Learning is best facilitated when people learn together in meaningful groupings, and by living and working together the learning that takes place is mutually reinforced.

7. *The teacher will become the facilitator.* Teachers and students will be partners in the learning enterprise, abandoning the "we-they" concept of education. The gulf between teacher and student will be bridged and students and teachers will discuss and explore their subject matter in a variety of informal settings.

8. *Education will not be restricted to classrooms and courses.* In the future all the resources of the community will be used for experimental learning. Many modules of learning will be used such as games and simulations, systems analysis, and the like. Educational activities of business, religions, and community organizations will continue to grow to supplement the school's programs.

Program Change

It is not enough to indicate that continuous program change has become an important factor in the never-ending attempt of the public school to improve itself. In the final analysis, the educator must be able to demonstrate those factors that should be considered in the promotion of program change and to incorporate these into patterns of action.

Any planning for program change will involve a consideration of the wide range of differences among children so that the offerings of the school will be realistic for each individual. The school faculty must establish learning priorities for the entire school as they take into consideration the many unique problems that face youth and the concomitant responsibility of the school to aid them in the solution of those problems. The staff must evaluate carefully the selection as well as the organization of content so that the learning experience provided in and out of the classroom will be meaningful.

There are many implications of change related to the current pattern of teaching and learning time in the school and these should be reviewed for possible consideration and action. In each classroom, there should be possibilities provided for both success and failure on the part of the children, overweighed by the concept that if failure does occur it should be accepted as a challenge to attack the problem once again.

Program change requires that meaningful information and statistics should be gathered continuously for the purpose of evaluating the success or failure of any program. In viewing any program's adequacy, there must be abundant opportunity for each teacher to understand and diagnose each child's difficulties and to be given information that will prescribe possible differences in accomplishments according to such factors as sex, attitude, chronological age, and the like. Any proposed change should consider the effect that it will have on the interests or abilities of the able as well as the less able students. It should include a means of expanding and improving such intangible factors as the values, ideals, and attitudes that are held by children in and out of school.

The educational leader must consider the forces and pressures that will be involved in the reaction to any program change and be able to compensate for these. He must include any orientation necessary for students and staff as a means of winning their acceptance of the new program. Perhaps the fundamental step to take in establishing this new alignment is to develop first a pilot or experimental program that would serve as an indicator of the possible success or failure of such a venture. If successful, the impetus for program change will be hastened by the demonstrable evidence that improvement can result from the adoption of this new approach.

PROBLEMS AND PROGRESS

Lisbon Falls Solves a Problem

Faced with a legislative enactment that required the teaching of a foreign language in grades seven and eight within the next two years, the supervisory staff at Lisbon Falls investigated three problems in meeting this demand: finding school time for these offerings, finding qualified teachers, and obtaining financial support for the program. Several steps were taken. First, the Junior High School Curriculum Committee was apprised of the situation. A subcommittee was organized to review the junior high school foreign language program, make recommendations for modifications as needed, and coordinate its studies and recommendations with the Foreign Language Subcommittee of the Elementary Division Curriculum Committee. Second, six months later the Foreign Languge Subcommittee gave their recommendations, which were accepted by the Junior High School Curriculum Committee. In effect, the recommendations were that there should be two tracks for the foreign language program and that the state requirements be met by track 2 (two days per week for 30 minutes) while track 1 would continue as a regular subject elective (one period five days a week). Third, representatives from the subcommittee reported the recommendations and plans for implementation to all school faculties. Opinions and reactions of teachers and administrators were reported back to the subcommittee. Fourth, a general meeting of interested district personnel was called for consideration of the plan and to hear arguments for and against. The Director of Curriculum for the district chaired the meeting. Finally, as a result of the aforementioned meeting, a somewhat revised and improved plan was submitted by the subcommittee to the Junior High School Curriculum Committee. This plan was officially adopted, forwarded to the central administration, and then approved by the board of education.

Homeville Institutes a New Program

Faced with an increasing population of children who were classified as "culturally disadvantaged," the Homeville Public School System decided to take advantage of a new state program that provided assistance to those who, although potentially capable of completing the public schools, are hindered from doing so by cultural and socio-economic handicaps. The district supervisory staff was requested to organize the plan on a pilot basis for the ensuing school year. Early in the fall the supervisors enlisted the aid of a teachers' steering committee which met weekly for several months to make plans for the pilot study. As guidelines to the program, the steering committee agreed on these characteristics for the program: more teacher time for youngsters, enriched learning experiences, establishment of practical experiences, enlisting the total support of the community, utilizing flexibility and creativity, and providing staff orientation and training. In addition to this, the committee requested for this group smaller classes, the enlistment of parent support, intensified and extended counseling and guidance, an emphasis on language skills, tutorial instruction, and extra library facilities.

To implement the program, the supervisory staff, based on the recommendations of the steering committee, provided three extra services for these compensatory students. First, *group counseling* was given daily for students who had been identified as eligible for the program. Each member was encouraged to accept himself for what he was, but support was given in making a personally meaningful and responsible appraisal of himself as a human being, particularly with reference to earning a high school diploma. These counseling sessions were conducted over a four-month period until it was felt that the group was ready to enter a special classroom situation. Second, concurrent with the group counseling effort, an *in-service training program* for potential teachers and counselors was in progress. Each participant was given a dynamic understanding of this type of student, based on case study material, along with specific skills in how to meet the student's needs with appropriate and meaningful learning situations. Third, when the students had been oriented through group counseling and the teachers through in-service training, they were brought together in a *classroom situation* for a two-hour period each day. This class was in place of English and Social Science classes. Counseling sessions continued as an adjunct to the classroom situation approximately once each week.

At the end of the first year the results of the pilot program were evaluated. In less than one full year many of the project children's language scores measured by standard achievement tests had improved as much as in two years. Library card usage had greatly increased. Students were not ashamed or apologetic about their cultural background. Many students showed a marked improvement in attitude toward school and this correlated with a large number improving their grades. Instead of one-half likely to drop out of school before graduation the fraction dropped to one-quarter.

The supervisory staff, as a result of the successful first year of the project, was given a request by the board of education to expand the compensatory program in the district. A Community Advisory Committee was established to coordinate its activities with the district steering committee. The findings of the supervisory staff are now being circulated to interested school districts in the region.

SUMMARY

Any improvement of the educational program calls for a familiarity with basic programs and projects that have found acceptance by knowledgeable persons in the field. New ideas and trends relative to improving the learning-teaching process in the classroom must be viewed with balance and sensitivity so that both the strengths and the weaknesses of such ventures are known. In a most significant way, the supervisory staff must be able to relate the experimentation going on in the field to the needs of the local school classroom. The staff must recognize the value of important studies or indicators to signal the need for curriculum change, as conveyors of factual information that can make meaningful change possible, and as vehicles for ascertaining alternative patterns that can lead to the selection (based on the structuring of logical hypotheses) of a directional path which shows promise of improving the instructional program. In effect, the input of the staff in terms of research and evaluation will determine largely the output of the instructional product and its excellence.

SELECTED REFERENCES

American Association of School Administrators. *Year-Round School.* Washington, D.C.: National Education Association, 1970.

Association of Classroom Teachers. *Classroom Teachers Speak on Differentiated Teaching Assignments.* Washington, D.C.: National Education Association, 1969.

Bennett, William, and R. Frank Falk. *New Careers and Urban Schools: A Sociological Study of Teacher and Teacher Aide Roles.* New York: Holt, Rinehart, and Winston, 1970.

Cooper, J. M. *Differentiated Staffing: New Staff Utilization Patterns for Public Schools.* Philadelphia: Saunders, 1971.

Dreeben, Robert. *The Nature of Teaching: Schools and the Work of Teachers.* Glenview, Illinois: Scott, Foresman, 1970.

Frey, Sherman H., editor. *Adolescent Behavior in School: Determinants and Outcomes.* Chicago: Rand McNally, 1970.

National School Public Relations Association. *Differentiated Staffing in Schools.* Washington, D.C.: National Education Association, 1970.

Netzer, Lanore A., et al. *Education, Administration, and Change: The Redeployment of Resources.* New York: Harper and Row, 1970.

Rollins, Sidney P. *Developing Nongraded Schools.* Itasca, Illinois: Peacock, 1968.

Schafer, Walter E., and Carol Olexa. *Tracking and Opportunity: The Locking-Out Process and Beyond.* Scranton: Intext, 1971.

Towksbury, John L. *Nongrading in the Elementary School.* Columbus: Charles Merrill, 1967.

White, William F. *Tactics for Teaching the Disadvantaged.* New York: McGraw-Hill, 1971.

Interaction and the Curriculum

Part Three fully recognizes that the teacher is a specialist in his field and that he may be more knowledgeable about teaching his subject than the principal or some other status leader. It becomes, then, the task of the instructional leader to coordinate his efforts with members of the staff who are highly qualified and competent to work together cooperatively on the improvement of education for the community's youth. Rigorous certification standards require that these people are professionally well trained for their respective positions of responsibility. To be of real assistance to these people requires a high degree of collegial effort on the part of both faculty members and status leaders.

Certain teachers in any staff need assistance from the status leader in implementing classroom instructional techniques that require vision and foresight. In aiding the new teacher, making the weak teacher strong, providing assistance to superior teachers, encouraging change in the resister, and working with the student teacher, the supervisor must give all of them a spirit of enthusiasm and zest to fulfill both personal and organizational goals. The prevention of militancy in teachers, in part, will be found in the expert fashion in which status leaders can be helpful to teachers confronted with many problems within their classroom environments.

The process of in-service education involves a total emphasis on how instructional leaders should be working with teachers in groups of various sizes, kinds, and shapes in the development of a better program of education. Included in this effort, of course, would be a notable number of individual activities that would be essential to the development of a modern educational program. The status leader must expect to be involved in great depth in the whole process of designing an in-service program that will lead teachers to identify with common purposes values essential to the success of the work of the school.

Within the last twenty years the curriculum laboratory has come to be an integral part of the in-service training facilities available for faculty. In addition, new movements have occurred in the origin of regional laboratories (frequently funded by federal monies), publication centers, professional libraries, media centers, and development centers. These latest services facilities represent a considerable advancement in the kinds of services and assistance that can be provided faculty personnel. These agencies have done much to improve educational practice in numerous school systems, and the range of influence of these new laboratories and resource centers is proving to be one of the most effective agencies for the cooperative improvement of modern education.

CHAPTER 7

Supervisory Help
for Certain Teachers

The supervisor, director of learning, or principal must be an expert in understanding teachers of many types. His knowledge of the teaching profession must include an understanding of the behavior of a truly fine educator, a basic comprehension of the curriculum that permits the teacher to perform at his best, and a realistic view of the learning needs of students within the various classrooms that fall under his jurisdiction. The supervisor continually must assess the skills and attitudes of teachers as they work toward acceptable and recognizable goals. Such projects as those conducted by the Center for School Experimentation, Ohio State University, have provided the education profession with fundamental research data that have been of great assistance in recognizing a variety of teachers and their particular needs.

The role of the supervisor, to successfully cope with a magnitude of supervisory tasks, must be meaningful to teachers of all types. The vision of the supervisor must be conspicuously discernible by teachers as their attitude toward supervision moves toward acceptance and approval. Theoretically, ideal supervisory practice is designed to bring teachers, administrators, and supervisors closer together on a cooperative basis. In reality, however, the wide variation in teacher performance, skills, and attitudes, makes this goal of mutuality difficult to attain at times. Each teacher brings to the school a unique philosophy in terms of the role he feels he has to fulfill, a wide variation in understanding the learning process and its relation to the curriculum, and his own background and experience as both a subject-matter expert and a community participant. In many ways the accomplishment of an outstanding job in supervision relates primarily to the immediacy with which the supervisor and administrator can assist the teacher between the origin and the solution of classroom problems. Research data have made evident the need for a well developed program of supervision by teachers of all types.[1]

What, then, constitutes the readily recognizable types of teachers with whom the supervisor and administrator will be working? What problems will these individuals face and how can supervision be adapted to give these people much needed assistance? In answer to these questions the following types of teachers will be discussed: the new teacher, the weak teacher, the superior teacher, the teacher who rejects change, the student teacher, and teachers with unique problems.

HELPING THE NEW TEACHER

Since many new teachers harbor a feeling of insecurity and loneliness, the administration must assist in their development in an effort to establish a confident, well-adjusted professional attitude. The approach used by the administrator may well determine the success or failure of a new teacher.

An orientation program for new teachers should be progressively programmed on three levels: district (and community), building, and departmental (or grade level). This approach affords a systematic method of imparting a wealth of helpful information in addition to establishing a feeling of "belonging." In this fashion the administration should provide the new teacher with helpful information on curriculum content, policies, and procedures of the district (teachers' handbook), and available instructional aids and services. The new teacher should be informed of in-service programs, district- and grade-level meetings, and workshops. Furthermore, it should be clearly evident to the new teacher that the purpose of all this is to aid him in his professional growth and to extend and complement his ability in the classroom.

If possible, released time should be scheduled which would allow the new teacher to visit and observe master teachers. This type of program permits a new teacher to become exposed to many practical situations and methods of coping with everyday occurrences in the classroom.

Every effort should be made to assign the new teacher to classrooms and laboratories where he will have spacious, well-equipped facilities that will have an important but subtle effect on the improvement of

---

[1]See George R. Redfern, "Evaluation by Objective: A Route to Better Teacher Performance," *Croft Educational Services*, December 1969, pp. 1–2.

learning. In as many ways as possible, the physical facilities should offer an opportunity for the enhancement of the student-teacher relationship on a one-to-one basis as an essential element in evolving a strong intellectual and personal relationship. The library, too, should be considered to be an integral part of the classroom program and represent an attractive environment to work in for the teacher as well as the students. Every occasion should be taken to make easily and readily accessible for the new teacher the book, journal, and audio-visual holdings of the library.

Perhaps, most important of all, avenues must be designed that will permit the opinions, questions, and concerns of the new teacher to be heard and heeded by the resident faculty and the administration. The employing institution should listen carefully to what the faculty members have to say about their own needs and the perceptions that they have about their ability to perform their tasks satisfactorily in a new and demanding environment. This involves much discussion and understanding on the part of both new teachers and administrators as they search for better ways to teach and to learn.

Aiding the Beginning Teacher

Because new teachers face many problems, supervision must be carefully planned and implemented. To assist supervisors in discovering the kind of help that these beginning teachers require, a survey of the reactions of first-year teachers was conducted by the Northern Illinois State Teachers College.[2] The items most significant in regard to encouragement received in trying new ideas and instructional improvement were: talking with other teachers, reading professional books and magazines, attendance at professional meetings, recognition of their efforts by school authorities, membership in professional organizations, professional discussions at faculty meetings, suggestions made by the principal or supervisor after observing their work, programs of in-service education, and participation on curricular committees. The new teachers thought that the characteristics of a good supervisor for the beginning teachers were: making the novice teacher feel wanted and secure, providing fair and equal treatment, stimulating the novice to professional growth and success, helping him to develop effective classroom techniques, assisting him in staff and community relationships and in first-year planning, and showing him where improvement is needed and how to achieve it.

[2]Brother James Moroney, C.S.C., "Helping the Beginning Teacher," *The Clearing House*, vol. XXXVIII, no. 6 (Feburary 1964), pp. 360–364. See also B. J. Chandler, *et al.*, *Education and The New Teacher* (New York: Dodd, Mead, 1971), 245 pp.

These new teachers recommended that a good supervisory program include: a thoroughly planned orientation program, workshops and group conferences, individual interviews or counseling sessions, classroom visitations, directed readings, and individual guidance from experienced teachers on the staff. Three especially important areas to the new teacher are discipline, motivating students, and gaining professional competence. A final word of caution was that new teachers should not be weighed down with extracurricular activities as the first year should be spent in learning how to teach well. Sacrificing professional growth for school activities is sacrificing the entire profession.

Problems of Beginning Teachers

Under some conditions young teachers are overwhelmed by the problems of everyday teaching. In order to assess new teachers' problems, a study was made to determine the degree of difficulty of several problem areas.[3] Queens College (New York), in surveying first-year teachers, found that their problems in descending order of difficulty were: discipline, relations with parents, methods of teaching, evaluation, planning, materials and resources, and classroom routines.

It has been hypothesized that "brighter" teachers would see themselves as having less difficulty. However, those who did well academically actually saw themselves in more difficulty in the areas of classroom management, materials and resources, and planning. It is possible that they understand the learning process better—having more insight or awareness of needs. The old adage that city teachers have problems with students while suburban teachers have problems with parents was not borne out by this study. The city teachers reported more difficulty in all problem areas, including relations with parents.

The New Teacher at Oak Park

During the first few weeks of school at Oak Park (Illinois) it has been found that new teachers ask about discipline, study halls, underachievement of pupils, lack of motivation, and other questions.[4] It is believed at Oak Park that school administrators and supervisors should attempt to answer questions, allay the concern of new teachers, and not set up arbitrary rules to take the place of intelligent action, sympathetic understanding, and confident procedures.

[3]Stanley Dropkin and Marvin Taylor, "Perceived Problems of Beginning Teachers and Related Factors, " *The Journal of Teacher Education*, vol. XIV, no. 4 (December 1963), pp. 384–390. See also Glenys Unrich and William Alexander, *Innovations in Secondary Education* (New York: Holt, Rinehart and Winston), 1970, pp. 137–139.

[4]Russell J. Fuog, "The New Teacher Needs Help," *Bulletin* of the NASSP, vol. 46, no. 273 (April 1962), pp. 124–128.

In terms of *discipline,* it has been learned that most discipline concerns deviation from the accepted normal pattern of behavior to a much lesser degree than incorrigibility. Teachers at Oak Park learned to develop the philosophy of helping students with personal problems and to recognize that their responsibility to the school extends beyond the four walls of the classroom. From the point of view of both the school and the pupil, *study hall* is considered very important. Study halls are maintained for study purposes and students are expected to acquire a discipline of work and a respect for the rights of others. It has been discovered that the *underachiever* most hurts the learning program because of the teachers' tolerance of classroom work that is significantly below the pupils' tested ability to achieve. Four important causes of underachievement that need to be explored by new teachers are emotional disturbances, unambitious companionship, lack of motivation, and poor work habits. *Lack of motivation* permeates the entire learning spectrum if pupils fail to see the purpose or value in what teachers ask them to do. New teachers must realize that their task in its best sense is a "selling" job and that pupils will get to work when purposes and values are made clear.[5] Further, new teachers must be excited about their subject and their teaching. A vital, active, expressive teacher is a major force in the motivation of students.

A Synthesis

The previous studies concerned with the beginning teacher give much assistance in developing a plan that will be effective in aiding this person to be successful at the outset of his career. Briefly stated, any plan for the new teacher should encompass these elements: offer encouragement to any new ideas; show support and understanding as he attempts to develop his professional ability; make available relevant and meaningful in-service training opportunities; encourage the revelation of any teaching difficulties so that they can be solved before becoming serious problems; give assistance by demonstrating how unusual problems (such as discipline, underachieving, and lack of motivation) can be solved; and provide self-rating opportunities in which he can review his teaching techniques in terms of success or failure and know what to do about them.

New teachers must understand and accept the fact that teaching is a profession and not just a job. The professional person should be concerned primarily with his task and how his skills and services can be

---

[5]See Mario Fantini and Milton Young, *Designing Education for Tomorrow's Cities* (New York: Holt, Rinehart and Winston, 1970), pp. 33–34.

utilized best by the school. Undoubtedly many beginning teachers with a difficult first-year assignment would not survive beyond the end of the spring term if it were not for the professional help of the administrator or supervisor. These persons must provide assistance if the beginning teacher is to reap any of the rewards that later accrue with several years of successful teaching experience. Research indicates that the greatest aid for beginning teachers from supervisory personnel is needed in the areas of discipline, relations with parents, and methods of teaching. Even though the average beginning teacher can cope with problems in these areas, there is a great variation in the skills with which the first-year person meets these challenges.

The administrator or supervisor should provide adequate guidelines for new teachers as they embark on their first classroom experience. The new person should make every effort to impress upon his classes that he considers the lesson at hand a matter of serious concern, requiring not only his best efforts but that of the class as well. He should set the pace of the lesson at a reasonable rate so that everyone in class is able to comprehend the material that is being covered. As he proceeds with the various elements of the lesson, he should carefully note the response that he is receiving from the class. If, for instance, the planned lesson is meeting with little enthusiasm from the group, the teacher should be willing and able to shift to another avenue of attack. His rapport with the class should be so designed that they can accept him readily in many roles if necessary: as friend, disciplinarian, leader, counselor, or partner. He should be so imbued with the establishment of good relations with the class that he willingly moves from serious reflection to humor as the occasion demands. Great emphasis must be placed on making the lesson challenging and interesting, on stimulating students to think for themselves, and on adopting a true spirit of inquiry. Each child in the classroom needs to feel that he can achieve according to his own needs and abilities and the new teacher should encourage him, whenever possible, to exceed his own limited ambitions. He should inculcate democratic values and procedures in the classroom so that class activities become an integral part in the learning process which is directed toward preparation for living in a democratic society. Overshadowing all of the classroom enterprises should be the matter of good classroom control. The beginning teacher should make certain that students understand that exemplary behavior is a basic requirement for membership in the class and no instances of disrespect or discourtesy can be tolerated.

In essence it is obvious that new teachers should be striving early to become interesting, creative people. They must assume that they have a real obligation to the school and to the profession to instill democratic values in their teaching experiences. Only by fostering the skills of good communication and making readily apparent to students the fact that they are warm, understanding persons, can they hope to establish happy, productive relationships in the classroom.

MAKING A WEAK TEACHER STRONG

The educational community should devise criteria that would enable the administrator to identify (objectively) a "weak teacher." Such criteria should be formulated through the cooperative effort of the administration and certificated personnel. The measurement instrument, based on a collegial approach, should permit the administrator to arrive at an early identification of a weak teacher.

When a teacher has been deemed "weak," the administration should strive to establish a feeling of rapport which would foster "free and open" discussion with colleagues and supervisors. This should be followed by counseling and observation of the weak teacher to help him assess his strengths and weaknesses.

Scheduled conferences at predetermined times should accompany any observational technique. At this time the principal should offer his assistance to solve any problems that have been perceived. After a thorough self-examination (on the part of the teacher) and discussion, specific recommendations that might be helpful should be suggested relative to learning procedures and techniques, classroom organization, student control, room environment, and adequate planning and preparation. Further conferences should then ensue to heighten the progress of the teacher in question.

The teacher should be encouraged to read and react to current professional journals and research material. In addition, he should be urged to attend relevant and promising institutes, workshops, and conferences. The administrator, at the teacher's request, could review lesson plans as a basis for discussion and action. This technique would be advantageous in assisting the teacher to evaluate his skill in classroom management as well as offering some insight into his planning and knowledge of subject matter.

Scheduled visitations of other teachers and conferences with master teachers and department heads proffer supplemental aid to the weak teacher. If additional conferences and observations indicate little or no change in attitude and ability, the administrator should inform the teacher that his teaching performance must be reviewed by others as a basis for striving for *significant* improvement.

Incentive Structure

A basic objective of the supervisor in assisting the weak teacher is to facilitate a positive change in the behavioral characteristics which he exhibits through the identity of elements that the teacher can control as he strives to work effectively with children. This will involve the creation of a variety of educational forms and patterns that can assist him in his quest for greater and more creative knowledge about the teaching art. In his relationship with colleagues and supervisory personnel, he must be persuaded to develop a commitment to educational change—not only on a personal basis, but on an institutional one as well. He must recognize that the pattern of school life is not one that is timeless and non-moving, and that many new forms and patterns emerge over relatively short periods of time. Too often the weak teacher is confronted with the substantive shifts that occur in the educational milieu to such an extent that he: 1) is unable to recognize the suddenness with which his own teaching has been rendered obsolete; and 2) lacks the ability to select the necessary alternatives that are available to him as a means of solving his own instructional techniques. It then becomes incumbent upon the instructional leader to awaken his interest in experimenting with a number of teaching and learning activities that might provide a solution to the problems he has encountered. In some instances it may mean a period of retraining for the teacher in which he may feel free to borrow from the strengths and the experiences of others in his special field of endeavor.

Often the weak teacher faces a dilemma in which he is not sure of the goals that should be attained in his classroom or the methods by which those goals can be reached. Even as he exhibits a willingness to change, he must recognize that many alterative patterns of educational pursuit in the profession are being explored and promoted from time to time. He must, in fact, be given every opportunity to indulge in self-orientation in the search for new objectives and improved procedures that will enrich his role as an educator. If his role is to be strengthened perceptibly, he must be challenged to do more than merely conform to the existing educational model; he should be encouraged to move in novel and positive instructional directions that have promise of releasing his latent and unfound pedagogical sensibilities. Independent reflection and thought must be fostered so that he can make decisions that will lead to promising educational practices at the level that will prove most assertive to him—that level found in the world of the classroom and in the drama of real-life interaction between teacher and student. Only through the creation of new educational configurations can the weak teacher anticipate improved receptivity and productivity on the part of pupils.

How can this new educational form be provided as a basis for action for the weak teacher? First, it relies on the installation of motivation to the extent that he desires improvement and has greater expectation for his productivity. Second, his personal motivational experience will arouse the encouragement and support of his colleagues to the extent that he no longer feels isolated, but instead has been accepted as one of them. Third, the level of uncertainty that he has experienced as a potential failure will be eradicated and he will begin to make decisions relative to learning experiences that will meet with the approval of pupils and parents alike. And last, he will recognize new hypotheses concerning his role as a teacher that will enable him to make situational as well as psychological adjustments that will lead to the improvement of teaching and learning in the classroom.

Psychological Help

With teachers in the school system being confronted with more problems and situations than they could cope with, Woodbridge (Connecticut) decided to do something about it.[6] These involved both personal and student problems, so the system turned to psychiatrists and psychologists for help. An experimental program was organized in which psychologists offered help to the teachers. According to the report, after a two-year trial the program turned out to be successful with 85% of the staff who were involved in the program.

School officials felt that these factors were significant: rapid sociological changes that all rapidly growing communities must undergo; reactions to modernizing educational programs such as the new primary-intermediate organization, nongrading, departmentalization, homogeneous grouping, and greatly stepped-up curriculum programs. The Beers Child Guidance Clinic of New Haven (Connecticut) and the Connecticut State Department of Mental Health joined forces with the school system to find classroom solutions to mental health problems and to adjustment problems. The State Department helped finance the program, the school system worked directly with the children, and the clinic worked with the teacher. Minor adjustments were made during the first year according to need and much progress in the program was reported. By the second year the school staffs were joined together in large-group meetings, smaller group discussions on a grade level basis were requested by the teachers, and the psychologist observed classes at least one day a month.

A private poll was taken which indicated that two-thirds of the

[6]"Do Your Teachers Need Psychological Help?" *School Management*, vol. 7, no. 12 (December 1963), p. 74. See also Jacob W. Getzels, *et al., Educational Administration as a Social Process* (New York: Harper and Row, 1968), pp. 250–285.

teachers used the services offered and 85 percent of the people involved wanted the program to continue. An official report at the end of two years made these recommendations: the program should be expanded, the work with the clinic should stop, and a psychologist should be hired.

An Analysis

The weak teacher, if efforts to assist him fail, should be encouraged to leave teaching. If this move is unsuccessful, this person should expect to face dismissal proceedings. Many of these individuals are incompetent on a number of grounds, namely: they are physically or mentally ill themselves; they are unable to properly relate to or communicate with students, members of the profession, and persons in the community; they are ineffective in the classroom in terms of providing proper learning experiences; or their presence in class may be upsetting or disturbing to children with whom they associate. In each instance, however, in the event of a dismissal proceeding before a judge or hearing officer, two of the main questions will hinge on : (1) whether or not the teacher has been notified of these shortcomings; and (2) whether or not the school or district has tried to assist the teacher in improving his performance in the classroom. Most states have legislation that pertain to dismissal procedures and these should be adhered to closely. In any event, all matters relating to the eventual dismissal of any teacher should be documented so they become items of record in the event the dismissal is challenged and the case goes to court or becomes a hearing procedure.

As indicated earlier, any school psychologist who is hired to work with faculty members and students should have highly specialized training and experience. Also, he should have had classroom experience and the advantages of performing clinical field work. His training should include extensive work with adults as well so that he could, where permitted or required, offer psychological services to the faculty at the request of individual members. There is a serious need to safeguard the mental health of teachers as well as that of children and these services should be available when requested.

HELPFUL SUPERVISION FOR SUPERIOR TEACHERS

Although classroom observation of the superior teacher should be minimal, individual conferences should be encouraged. The occasional individual conference can establish a close communication linkage between this teacher and the administrator. This technique enables many ideas and suggestions to be discussed cooperatively in an effort to improve the educational curriculum of the school and its relationship to the upgrading of student experiences in the classroom.

If the superior teacher is overburdened with menial, time-consuming tasks, his attitude towards his educational role could become lethargic and thereby stifle his willingness to accept leadership functions. Superior teachers can become "stagnant" in their modus operandi. Therefore, many provisions for professional growth and expansion should be offered. The cliché, "killing two birds with one stone," could be accomplished if handled tactfully. For example, if the superior teacher was requested by his colleagues to direct educational meetings, committees, demonstrations, workshops, and the like, he would be in a position to contribute much to faculty growth and attainment. This, in effect, would bestow recognition on his efforts and increase his leadership and participatory role in many areas related to the activities of the academic community.

The role of the superior teacher could move in several directions within the framework of the total school setting. He could spark the efforts of school-community planning committees that are involved in the organizational design for more realistic and functional school programs. His talents could be directed toward both theoretical and action research projects which would lead to the acceptance of pilot projects that enrich the total program of the school. His example of productivity in this area could lend itself to the creation of teams of teachers who would be concerned with the implementation and experimentation of new educational purposes and accomplishments. In an era when investigation is often the only way in which program stagnation can be avoided, his work might be allied closely with the activities of the curriculum laboratory. Closer coordination with institutions of higher learning could be fostered by freeing his time so that the school would benefit by working on curricular projects on a cooperative basis. In many ways, with a flexible and limited class schedule, the superior teacher could be freed so that he might perform creative services for both the faculty and the student body. Through modification, inductive and deductive reasoning, stimulation of a broad base of school activities, and developing basic strategy for experimentation and change, the superior teacher offers much promise in the realm of increasing the effectiveness of collegial inspiration and precept.

The Superior Teacher: A Challenge

An Illinois report presents good evidence that superior teachers' talents are often wasted. In identifying the superior teacher, he is assumed to be one who is academically well trained, has a love for children and young people, is emotionally well balanced, enjoys the respect of pupils and fellow teachers, has the confidence of the administration and the community, and is not afraid to experiment.[7] Often the superior teacher motivates and inspires the learner to continue his education after graduation, regardless of the academic level he attains. In fact the success of the superior teacher is reflected in the improvement and accomplishments of his pupils.

No one does the thinking for the superior teacher. At best, the instructional supervisor helps him do a better job of teaching. Unfortunately, the poorest teachers get most of the attention while the superior ones achieve unnoticed and with little time or attention given them.

The Illinois report stated that superior teachers are divided into three categories: those already recognized as superior teachers; those not yet discovered, but who are superior teachers; and those not doing superior work, but who could if properly supervised and motivated. The factors that seemed to help teachers enjoy being superior ones are characterized by: a good background, teaching in their major field of interest, no home worries, having ample teaching supplies, utilizing adequate classroom equipment, teaching small classes of bright pupils, and benefiting from the leadership of a forward-looking administration.

Helping Superior Teachers

There may be occasions when the superior teacher will consider his teaching to be outstanding and, therefore, will not require the assistance of a supervisor or his colleagues to help him improve. Cases of this nature are in the minority. The superior teacher generally has risen to his peak of performance on the basis of his eagerness to seek suggestions elsewhere, and he more than likely will welcome any constructive, concrete ideas that can assist him in maintaining his teaching excellence. Experience has shown rather conclusively that the teaching ability of the superior teacher will eventually degenerate if he is not given planned, formal assistance through an in-service training program and other supervisory services. Adequate recognition, too, must be provided the superior teacher. Further research must be devoted to this critical area so that these persons can be encouraged to stay in the profession. One possible method is the provision of merit pay. The Utah School Merit Study, for example, concludes that merit pay is feasible and, under certain conditions, is desirable. Basic conditions require that there should be no fixed limits or percentages imposed upon the member who can qualify and that merit pay should represent a substantial

---

[7]Roye R. Bryant, "Supervision of Superior Teachers," *Illinois Education*, vol. 51, no. 8 (April 1963), p. 327. See also Louis J. Rubin, *A Study on the Continuing Education of Teachers* (Center for Coordinated Education, UCSB, 1970), pp. 13–21.

reward for merit. It would be fallacious, nevertheless, to consider that merit pay is the sole answer. Only when strong support for merit pay programs exists at the local level should they be considered.

Every opportunity should be provided by supervisors and administrators to encourage the superior teacher's interest in wide-spread reading, both in and out of his field of specialization. Many professional activities exist that should offer exciting possibilities to expand his knowledge and insights that would relate to his classroom teaching. Opportunities should be provided for the superior teacher to mingle frequently with other faculty members so that his creativity and ideas can be shared with others. As stated earlier, these individuals should hold positions of leadership on the faculty and out in the community whenever possible, and they should be guided into new, innovative programs that require the special abilities that these people possess. Relief from burdensome, non-creative duties will do a great deal to free these individuals for concentration on new and exciting experimental activities.

Opportunities such as these should encourage the superior teacher to continually raise his sights. Once his superior teaching ability is recognized, every effort should be made to make his teaching career a highly rewarding one. No school district can afford to lose the services of one of these persons who has such a salutary effect on children in and out of the classroom.

ENCOURAGING CHANGE IN THE RESISTER

Attacking Resistance

Historically, little attention has been devoted to the development of highly specific agencies that are devoted to the producing of change in education. As a result there has been a similar reluctance on the part of many teachers to depart from what they consider to be a conventional, satisfactory method of presenting learning experiences in the classroom. Such conservatism has had an inhibiting effect on the aspirations of teachers to deal effectively with change as it affects their classroom practices. Lacking a sufficient flow of ideas from a higher source that are accompanied by a "know how" posture, the teacher in such a situation is likely to reject change largely on the basis of the fact that stability is a more defensible position than a changing one.

There appear to be a few characteristics that identify the teacher who resists change. He is apt to be less productive and unwilling to attempt more than the minimum in regard to expected improvements. He often will lack sensitivity in his relationship with others and will make little effort to strengthen his personal bonds with his associates and students. His interests in the area of instruction often will be narrow and largely centered on his own accomplishments in the classroom. He seldom will place a high priority on the directions in which the educational program should be moving and he will give every indication that he considers change a rather awesome, perplexing thing.

All this means that the ability to identify the form of rejection that a teacher will engage in becomes a most difficult task indeed. The educational leader must actively seek to find the value system that the teacher is relying on to reject change. He then must work with him to assist him in recognizing how change can be an awakening to and rediscovery of the basic values in education that can lead to greater teaching satisfactions and rewards.

Helping Teachers Who Reject Change

Who is the rejector of change and what is his proper role? In general, researchers in education have ignored rejection and the rejector. In a study of rejection, forty-five elementary school teachers in five elementary schools were investigated; these were previously identified as rejectors, particularly concerning their attitudes toward the utilization of audio-visual materials.[8] Depth interviews with these teachers showed one or more of five forms of rejection. These were: ignorance —the subject simply did not know about the proposed innovation; suspended judgment—the subject was doubtful and concluded that it was better to be safe with traditional methods than to try unknown ones; situational rejection—the subject was assured that the innovation was good, but he still had reservations about its use; personal rejection—the subject felt anxious about his own ability to carry through the innovation; and experimental rejection—the subject was convinced that the innovation didn't work, based upon his actual experimentation with the innovation. Of the factors influencing rejection, it was found that the number of years taught or grade level taught made no appreciable difference. Also, the important factor in rejection was the subject's personal attitude (his inner state), expressed as, "They constantly change the curriculum and the textbooks, but I keep right on teaching the way I know best."

What, then, are the steps to overcome rejection in each of these five forms? To combat *ignorance*, place professional magazines or information in readily available and accessible spots, such as lounges, the li-

---

[8]Gerhard C. Eichholz, "Why Do Teachers Reject Change?" *Theory Into Practice*, vol. 2, no. 5 (December 1963), pp. 264–268. See also Paul Woodring, *Investment in Innovation* (Boston: Little, Brown, 1970), pp. 79–90.

brary, and elsewhere. Discuss at faculty meetings innovations and changes occurring in other schools. Create informal and formal channels of communication (informal—use personal relationships among teachers; and formal—use routing channels to circulate information). Regarding *suspended judgment,* encourage the few teachers who will accept a new idea to experiment rather than involve the entire faculty. It is a good idea to communicate accomplishments constantly to the entire faculty and encourage their support of the new idea or innovation. Considering *situational rejection,* the supervisor should implement the group endeavor where an individual teacher's fear of personal failure can be alleviated. Having up-to-date materials available and keeping equipment in good condition and accessible are important. In relation to *personal rejection,* the whole matter must be approached slowly and with a sympathetic attitude. The administrator can indicate that some small change might prove helpful and offer assistance in this matter. If possible, the teacher should be led to the trial stage and encouraged to become involved in some experimentation. In the event *experimental rejection* is a problem, then encouragement should be offered for any small attempt in this area. The supervisor should keep in mind that only through the dual process of rejection and acceptance can change be controlled and channeled into its most effective form.

Improving Professional Interaction

As the instructional leader surveys various strategies that can improve the relationship of those who serve on the professional team, he might utilize several aspects of group behavior. These strategies should do much to fuse the staff together and stimulate the resisters to exert their energies to work cooperatively toward the common cause.[9] Within these group-maintenance tasks behavior can be found that will lead to the maximum utilization of the resources of its members.

First, *harmonizing* is an attempt to reconcile the disagreements or reduce the tension within the group. The intent of this strategy is to encourage teachers and others to explore their own differences. Often this behavior results from a motivation to avoid conflict within the group or the inability of its members to stand continued disagreement. Second, *gate keeping* is an attempt to keep the communication channels open by facilitating the participation of others in the group discussion. Gate keeping is exemplified when a group member suggests procedures that permit the sharing of remarks or the interaction of people in a non-threatening atmosphere. Third, *encouraging* can result

---

[9]Jerrold Novotney, *Viewing the System: Human Interaction.* Unpublished paper, Orange County Schools Office, 1968.

from providing friendly, warm responses to the statements of others. Non-verbal cues, such as facial expressions or hand motions, can also help others to make a contribution. Fourth, *compromising* is a matter of offering to modify a strongly-stated position, yielding status, or admitting to error in a situation as a means of modifying behavior. Compromise is often motivated by the desire of the participants to help the situation improve or the group to move forward. Fifth, *standard setting and testing* recognizes that all groups have norms that are either written or unwritten. At times it may be necessary for the individuals concerned or the group to determine whether they are satisfied with their own procedures or operating norms. Testing implies the questioning of the continued suitability of these norms or standards.

Supervisors must recognize that human organizations will tend to disagree with goals and means as representative of a singular point of view. To the teacher who resists change, the mere suggestion of a change might very likely bring him into conflict with the organization. It may be, however, that the conflict situation will not be merely disruptive, but may accelerate the movement of the group to modify a static situation. If there was no resistance and conflict was lacking, it is conceivable that there would be little stimulation and few incentives to accomplish the goals of the human organization.

It is possible that the effort to attain change in a teacher's performance will demand confrontation and ultimately some type of consensus. The supervisor must know whether the issues involved in the resistant teacher are important enough to demand the time and investment of a confrontation. If this is the case, every effort must be made by both parties to state their positions fully so that their respective positions are understood.

Assisting Unstimulated Teachers

Teachers need to feel that they are an essential part of the school organization. Research studies indicate that a fundamental factor in this respect lies in the on-site administrative staff organizational structure. Schools having a prevalence of diversified leadership positions appear to be more successful in motivating teachers than those which concentrate leadership on a few individuals. Unwilling teachers, however, should not be forced into positions of leadership.[10]

Key staff members should be given released time to assist teachers in areas of instruction, guidance, and student activities. The existence

[10]William J. Stone and Bette Pegas, "Stimulating the Tenure Teacher," *Journal of Secondary Education*, vol. 44, no. 4 (April 1969), pp. 167–170.

of these leadership positions within a school often will serve as an impetus for the tenure teacher who may feel that there is nothing for which it is worth striving. Team teaching, cluster grouping, back-to-back scheduling, cooperative teaching, and flexible scheduling can result in the development of a more enthusiastic staff who are anxious to improve the quality of instruction.

A Faculty Member Is Dismissed

Poor recruiting procedures at Gorham Place caused a public relations problem within a year after a poorly qualified teacher was hired for a special class of slow-learning students. With little effort being made by Gorham Place school officials to locate the best possible individual for the position, a teacher was issued a contract after only two or three candidates were considered. Within two months reports began to reach the district supervisor that students in the class were having problems with the teacher and their parents were becoming concerned. At first it appeared that the new situation was causing the problem, but by November the situation suddenly took a turn for the worse. Students, the teacher said, were purposely antagonizing him and he was taking the liberty of suspending some of them from class for as much as an entire day at a time. Parent contacts with the principal became more and more frequent as did the conferences. During these sessions it was observed that the teacher had an extremely hostile attitude toward the parents as well as the students involved. When parent conferences were requested with the teacher, he often concluded them by berating the parents and belittling their understanding of the situation. By this time the district supervisor had made several visits to the teacher's classroom and reported these observations to the principal: in one incident the teacher demanded a public apology to the class by the student who was accused of making a disturbance earlier when it was obvious that the boy was in no way directly responsible for the disorder; at another time the teacher forcibly removed a girl from the room when she was obviously frightened and shaken by an accusation that was not true; and during the last observation made the teacher literally was screaming at the entire class in an effort to force their attention on a portion of the lesson that was notably dull, uninteresting, and the result of poor planning.

In each instance the principal or the supervisor at Gorham Place held a conference with the teacher following the classroom visitation. During these conferences the teacher rejected the concept of changing his approach to and understanding of the children. He considered that he was doing an outstanding job of teaching and it was the fault of the students and parents that things did not go well in the classroom. After three months of serious, concerted efforts on the part of the supervisor and principal to develop a better understanding of the needs and abilities of these children, the joint recommendation of these two was that the teacher should not be rehired. During the spring an effective recruiting campaign was developed to attract a fully qualified teacher to assume this post and by May of that year such a person was found and issued a contract.

This situation, of course, should never have been allowed to occur. Proper selection procedures at Gorhan Place would have prevented the assignment of a teacher in a classroom position where he would almost certainly be doomed to failure. In each instance, however, the instructional leader must do his utmost to bring about self-improvement, to involve the individual with the identification and examination of the teaching-learning potential that exists within the group, to discover how behavioral objectives can be structured to measure accurately the quality of the product, and to make available the entire resources of the school system in an attempt to improve the teaching capabilities of the teacher. If these and other procedures fail, the administrator must be prepared to convince the teacher that he should not continue as a member of the teaching profession inasmuch as his efforts will fall far short of the teaching excellence demanded by the educational institution.

THE STUDENT TEACHER

The education profession has been making rapid strides in the assistance being given student teachers as they begin their field or internship experiences in the school situation. Such projects as those supported by the Rosenberg Foundation to develop and implement effective programs of supervision for intern teachers hold much promise. The Rosenberg study gives high priority to the improvement of methods that will lead to the identity of typical problems of student and beginning teachers and to the development of suitable techniques and skills that are applicable to these individuals. The success of on-the-job training programs for students engaged in teacher education, coupled with the development of understanding, skills, and abilities of school principals who work with these young people, has been authenticated at such institutions as the University of California (Berkeley) and the College of the Pacific. Strengthened pre-service teacher training programs, improvement in the supervisory skills of administrative personnel, and improved student teacher performance in the classroom have resulted from major advances in this critical area of supervision.

Conceptual Patterns

James Conant, in his book *The Education of American Teachers*, has declared that each state should develop a loan policy for future teachers aimed at recruiting into the profession the most able students.[11] In any institution engaged in educating teachers, the board of trustees should determine that there is a continuing and effective all-university or interdepartmental approach to the education of teachers. This should assure the institution that there is a coordinated program of teacher education both in general education and in programs of concentration. Ample opportunity should be given for exposure in the fields of mathematics, physical science, biological science, social science, English literature, English composition, history, and philosophy.

Bruce Joyce (Teachers College) has designed a model related to the preparation of teachers that conceptualizes a variety of curricular modes and teaching strategies. Professional tools must be readily available at all levels of inquiry and the organization responsible for the supervision of teachers in training must have the capacity for inventing and producing more supports than are now available. In this fashion the support system idea includes ideas, people, material, and services.[12]

This institution-building model would include three integral parts: (1) a small think tank operation with a movable and moving faculty; (2) a teacher-support center stocked with the material, technology, and services needed by teachers to study themselves, the teaching-learning act, and the environment and school organization required to create schools as centers of inquiry; and (3) learning centers for children, also well stocked with organized instructional materials.

Most important would be the establishment and maintenance of an open two-way communication system between the differentiated parts. The whole internal system should be tied to the parent organizations so that the entire operation would function in a synergistic fashion. For teacher preparation programs, an inter-agency coalition could be staffed jointly by members of the collaborating university or college and the school system on the basis of mutual contracts. Easy access to a series of scholar consultants, close relations with forward-looking and dynamic institutions and associations, a small "think tank" group of individuals recruited for varying periods of time, and a corp of teacher leaders who are shapers and movers are essential to the development of such a model. The quality of leadership required for this task calls for

[11]James B. Conant, *The Education of American Teachers* (New York: McGraw-Hill, 1963), pp. 73–111.
[12]Bruce R. Joyce, *The Teacher-Innovator: A Program to Prepare Teachers* (Washington, D.C.: U.S. Office of Education, October 1968), pp. 124–126.

the assistance of the teacher scholar who can assume the colleague authority and who has the intelligence and the power to focus the school upon its primary functions related to the nature of the learning process and the institution which supports it. Teacher preparation under this schema would be endowed with a huge step forward toward a meaningful and significant approach in solving a critical problem syndrome.

Some Concerns

Much more emphasis today has been placed on the use of anecdotal records, interviews, and conferences than on rating scales to evaluate student-teaching effectiveness. Student teachers should be informed as to the behavioral characteristics that will be evaluated whenever classroom observations are made by the supervisor or administrator. Many informal meetings should be held with the student teacher to assist him with the development of his teaching skills.

Many institutions of higher learning have had much success in providing observation opportunities correlated with intensive work in related education and subject-matter areas the semester prior to student teaching. During the semester that student teaching occurs, many conferences on an individual basis are held with the college supervisor and master teacher. Any classroom problems that arise are quickly detected by the observer who discusses them later with the student.

Considerations such as these are important aspects of student-teaching supervision: Are the students properly motivated? Are interesting and challenging assignments given? Is there sufficient identification and selection of problems as a basis for classroom work? Is there a plan for testing and evaluating the results of student efforts? What kind of records are kept that will furnish evidence of student success or failure? Is there an opportunity for the class to have access to good resource materials? Does the class have an adequate chance to involve itself in numerous democratic situations in which each person can practice citizenship techniques? Is a variety of learning situations used in which the pupils can discover their own best learning techniques? These and many other questions related to teaching effectiveness should be pursued carefully by the supervisor in his discussions with the student teacher.

Pupil creativity and the ability to learn on one's own must be emphasized by the student teacher as he works with his class. To kindle this spirit, many new avenues of in-serivce opportunities should be made available to the student teacher by the supervisor. Also, he must be given assistance in gaining insight into the behavior of the students with whom he works as well as his own classroom behavior. Only in this way can he be assured of becoming a good teacher.

TEACHERS WITH PROBLEMS

In a study to ascertain what major problems of teachers beset administrators, forty-two administrators were interviewed, all of whom had at least four years of administrative experience. The problem teachers were found to be classified into five general types: (1) problems involving incompetency; (2) problems involving teachers who refused to abide by reasonable rules and regulations prescribed by the State and local governing boards; (3) problems involving unwillingness to cooperate with the district program; (4) problems involving morals; and (5) problems involving psychological maladjustment.[13]

Teachers with Problems Involving Incompetency. These problem teachers usually come to the attention of the administrator either by complaints of parents, personal observations in the classroom, noisy and disorderly students, or by a kind of insight an experienced principal has gained from talking to and observing a given teacher in the school situation. To determine if a given teacher is really incompetent, and if so, to what degree, the administrator observes the teacher with his students both in and out of the classroom.

The problems of incompetent teachers might be classified into four categories: (1) lack of knowledge of subject matter; (2) poor and ineffective teaching methods; (3) lack of discipline in ability to control students; and (4) a combination of two or more of the first three categories.

Incompetent teachers are seldom found to be tenure teachers; usually they are in their first year at a given school. Age or sex do not seem to be significant factors.

If the incompetent teacher can be brought to realize his inadequacies, and if he has a sincere desire to become a successful teacher, usually help from the principal and from other faculty members will save this teacher and after a short period of time he will cease to be a problem.

Teachers Who Refuse to Abide by Reasonable Rules and Regulations Prescribed by the State and Local School Governing Boards. Teachers in this category generally fall into one of three types: (1) teachers who are persistently late, either to school in the morning, or at noon, or to yard-duty assignments; (2) teachers with poor attendance; and (3) teachers who are lax in their duties and responsibilities to pupils, such as leaving school early or leaving the class alone in the room for prolonged periods of time. Many of these people have a poor attitude

---

[13]Robert A. McAfee, *Problem Teachers and the Administrator.* Unpublished study, California State College at Long Beach.

toward the profession and tend to be self-centered. Most of these people are non-tenure teachers, they do not respond to help and encouragement, and about fifty percent are not hired for a second year.

Teachers with Problems Involving Morals. Moral charges against teachers seem to fall into five general types: (1) obscene or suggestive remarks in the presence of students; (2) seducing or attempting to seduce a student; (3) attempting or succeeding in committing immoral acts with students; (4) teachers found to be deviates; and (5) teachers involved in charges of adultery.

In discussing the courses of action administrators take, it is necessary to distinguish in each of the five categories between teachers who are only suspected and teachers who have actually been proven guilty either by court action or a predominance of evidence available to the administrator. When a charge has been proven or there is substantial evidence against the teacher, the matter is usually turned over to the district attorney and the teacher immediately removed from the classroom. In suspected cases, administrators seem divided on the course of action, some removing the teacher and others transferring him to another area, the latter being prevalent in the larger school districts. In many cases involving items four and five the teacher concerned is prevailed upon to resign.

Teachers Unwilling to Cooperate with the District Program. These are the most numerous kinds of problem teachers administrators must face. The more outspoken and overly uncooperative teachers are often quite capable individuals who, because of jealousy or lack of recognition, spend their efforts making trouble for the administrator. Some administrators have found that by giving these people challenging responsibilities, some semi-administrative duties, or more recognition, they can be converted into outstanding supporters of the educational program.

Sometimes one overtly uncooperative teacher can be a ring leader, agitating a great deal of dissension in the school against the administrator. If this problem cannot be solved by any other means, the administrator "must stand on his own two feet" and present the issue to the superintendent, the board of education, and/or the professional ethics commission. Either the teacher will have to be removed or the principal will resign.

The uncooperative teacher presents the most perplexing problem to the administrator, because he, more than any other kind of problem teacher, tends to make the administrator's leadership role less effective.

Teachers with Psychological Problems. These individuals have the following kinds of problems: (1) unsatisfactory dress and appearance; (2) being sadistically cruel to students; (3) suffering from neurotic tendencies; (4) alcoholism; (5) being ultra-authoritarian; and (6) domineering toward students.

The courses of action here varied a great deal according to the severity of the problem and the effect of the problem on the students and the school. In serious psychological cases the help of a family physician was sought to aid the teacher in solving his problems.

PERSONNEL STANDARDS COMMITTEES

Several state associations have initiated formal groups to conduct investigations at the request of educators as a means of arriving at a solution to personnel problem cases. The Connecticut Education Association, for example, has organized a Professional Practice Panel to conduct inquiries as a means of settling disputes involving the professional conduct and competence of educators. The panel's primary function is to provide expert witnesses in cases in which it is asked to arbitrate. The Connecticut Education Association considers it essential that a professional third party be brought in to assist in the settlement of many of the cases that cause serious friction in the schools. The panel, in particular, attempts to assist boards of education in this fashion. No single individual or group likes to face a serious personnel situation alone and the inviting of such a panel to participate in the deliberations can prevent this from happening.

On occasion strong disagreements can cause disruption of the educational program of the school or district. Students as much as the general public are often the victims in these clashes. Whenever the various parties are unable to reach an agreement or discover some way in which they can compromise their situation, an objective outside party needs to be invited to assist. Basically, when firm stands have been taken by the parties in the case, someone needs to review the problem and suggest ways in which it can be resolved.

One state organization (the Association of California Secondary School Administrators) has developed some procedures that should assist in the recognition and elimination of strained personnel relations. Through this procedure problems have been observed and solutions sought in the developmental stage as a means of avoiding a breakdown of local educational effort.

A set of procedures has been devised that can assist in the recognition and elimination of these problems. An informal request for assistance in a personnel problem received from an association member goes to the chairman of the Personnel Standards Committee. The committee chairman assigns a committee member to conduct a personal interview with the party initiating the request. The requestor is informed that a full report will be made only to him and that certain findings of the investigation pertaining to district policy and procedures may be given to the board and the superintendent upon their request. After hearing the requestor, the interviewer may be of considerable assistance in considering all aspects of the problem and some possible solutions. In the event the requestor still wants the investigation, a request form is sent to the association to be evaluated. If the request is accepted, two Personnel Standards Panel members are appointed to conduct a preliminary investigation. If the preliminary investigation vindicates the requestor, appropriate steps as determined by the situation are taken on his behalf. The Personnel Standards Committee will later determine whether or not its recommendations have received proper attention. In the event the recommendations have not been followed, the Personnel Standards Committee will ask both parties to participate in a complete investigation of the problem.

If a complete investigation is ordered, both parties will be contacted by the association office and invited to participate in the investigation. Assuming that both parties accept the invitation, a Panel of Adjudicators will be appointed. All members of the panel must be approved by both parties. A calendar will be developed and a place will be arranged for the investigation. Copies of the report of the preliminary investigation will be sent along with the agenda to all interested parties. The investigation will be conducted as a hearing where both parties will present evidence and witnesses.

Following the conclusion of the hearing, the Panel of Adjudicators will meet to develop conclusions and formulate recommendations. These conclusions and recommendations will be forwarded to the Personnel Standards Committee which, in turn, will transmit them to the interested parties. The association underwrites all expenses incurred in the conduct of a complete investigation, including the provision of a stenographer.

Investigation Preparation

Any investigation brings into focus several important aspects of supervision that need to be clearly delineated before such a situation becomes a matter of public controversy. In effect, in any case where dismissal is sought, the principal should be prepared to show concrete evidence that: (1) the teacher has persistently refused to change a pattern of unsatisfactory behavior relative to the teaching-learning situation in the classroom; (2) there have been sufficient classroom visits on which to base evidence of unsatisfactory performance; (3) following classroom visitations the teacher has been given the benefit of whatever suggestions the principal has to offer; (4) a low rating should be looked upon by the teacher as a warning that there is need for special supervision and assistance; and (5) the teacher, if probationary, will not be re-employed unless he shows satisfactory improvement and a potential for competent service. In the event the teacher refuses to abide by the decision of the administration and the board of education, help should be sought from a state organization that has formal procedures for the adjudication of such matters. In an era of highly sensitive personnel matters, instructional leaders should be prepared to bring similar difficulties before such a hearing body.

Preventive Strategy

Board of education policies should include the procedures to be followed in any grievance case. Regardless of the precision of the description of the proper procedures to follow, there will be failure if both parties do not consult with good faith and intelligence. The administration of any personnel-problem investigation is particularly crucial in determining the level of staff morale and the consequent effectiveness of the entire contractual relationship between all parties.[14]

All personnel (teachers, supervisors, and administrators) should be permitted to express dissatisfaction and obtain necessary adjustments in a fair and impartial setting. Dissatisfaction may be very real even though a valid problem does not exist, and an open climate should prevail that will lend itself to reasonable and calm discussion of the problem and its resolution. Any grievance procedure should strive to maintain a balance between the wielding of authority by the administrator on the one hand and the prevention of abuse of that authority on the other.

Supervisors and administrators must thoroughly familiarize themselves with the terms of any district personnel operational agreement. Local educational associations should study the agreements and distribute their interpretations and recommendations so that all would be better informed as to their implications for personnel relationships. In-service instruction, workshops, institutes, and other types of training programs should be made available to all personnel as a means of creating greater tolerance and better understanding of personnel problems related to instruction. Supervisory leaders must become highly trained and sophisticated in this field if they are to cope successfully with individual faculty members and local teachers' associations as grievances are brought to the fore and demand a solution.

[14]Louis I. Kramer, *Principals and Grievance Procedures* (Washington, D.C.: National Association of Secondary School Principals, 1969), pp. 5–7.

HELPING ALL TEACHERS ACCOMPLISH COOPERATIVE OBJECTIVES

One of the basic tasks confronting the status leader is the development of a unifying concept of supervision that will help all teachers accomplish the objectives which they set for themselves. Even though the instructional leader has taken into account the needs and requirements of certain types of teachers in improving their performance, a well-defined thrust must be made to work with all teachers in developing educational plans and projects and carrying them forward to a successful conclusion. The concern of the status leader is to center attention on the development of the best possible conditions for encouraging learning and to ascribe certain basic criteria that will aid the entire faculty in unifying its efforts in meeting the demands of self-generated goals and objectives. Seven fundamental aspects to this process are described on the following pages.

1. *The teaching faculty will expect to be given every opportunity to define varying teaching tasks as it views them cooperatively in relation to basic goals and programs.* As the faculty considers the many facets of the teaching-learning act, assurances must be given that all teachers will be recipients of new concept developments. Highly rated techniques will be found in the organizational development of small group meetings and the scheduling of individual conferences in which the status leader and the teacher can relate to one another on a one-to-one basis. Seminars, workshops, and other group devices will do much to assist teachers in similar areas of specialization in working together on the fashioning of commonly agreed upon objectives. Small groups of these specialists can share their talents in cooperatively discussing uniform commitments to a particular educational program, in planning together how they will attain these commitments, in determining through group action how they will proceed, and in presenting a plan to the school community to which they subscribe. Following this group planning and action calls for constant recycling of the entire process and its success depends upon the whole-hearted support of status leaders. Joint action between the teachers and the status leader should come after the teachers have formulated their group and individual goals and are now ready to translate these into total-school goals and objectives. At this juncture the status leader may wish to explore with the staff the time and energy investments that must be made, as well as establish the kind of schedule that will be required. His main function at this point will be to determine the type and amount of support that he will need to invest to achieve the goals the teachers have enumerated for themselves. As the work unfolds, the ultimate task of the instructional leader

is to provide an ever-broadening service to the teaching force in assisting them to attain these goals. In addition, he will wish to be considered an integral member of the group so that it will look upon him as being so strongly related to other members of the group that his presence is essential for maintaining its structure.

2. *After the goal-setting function has been established, all teachers will wish to improve their skills in the ability to solve the problems in instruction that confront them and to make the kinds of decisions that are essential to a proper goal-work orientation flow.* In a sense, every faculty member needs to become involved in both individual and group problem solving and to determine the kinds of actions that are needed. The organizational structure of the staff can now be designed so that representative groups hold regularly scheduled meetings, discuss the difficulties and problems that face them, and make decisions as to the appropriate action to take for their solution. As currently exhibited by many faculties in higher education, public school staffs would, in effect, represent the basic power structure that wields a strong hand in shaping the curricular and instructional program of the school. The status leader's role would be reversed from the conventional pattern as his control of the faculty's involvement in decision-making would lessen greatly. Communication would now flow primarily from the faculty to the status leader and his response pattern will be one of advice and support. Complete sharing of powers by the status leader with the faculty, then, is basic to the success of teachers in attaining self-determined goals.

3. *Teachers require, in addition to the basic physical needs related to their profession, expressions of respect and esteem by others as they labor toward the fulfillment of their objectives.* They need to feel that they are accomplishing the tasks they set out to do in a personal, self-directed fashion that truly represents their own real life style. Through individual or group effort, the status leader has the responsibility to defend the teacher's right to seek the truth as he sees it and to reflect this knowledge in a teaching style that is uniquely his own. He will wish to build an organizational climate that is healthy and vital as a means of encouraging teachers to study, meet, and confer with one another at every opportunity. Teachers should not be denied the right to share in all phases of the educational task. This is vital to the building of a sound self-image of themselves and their work as cooperating members who are structuring the institution's growth. The status leader then becomes the person who allocates and integrates the tasks, personnel, and plant to bring into realization the true function of the educational program. The demands of the institution and the fulfillment requirements of its personnel are elements that require integration

if the organization is going to be productive and self-renewing.

4. *Helping all teachers achieve their objectives imposes a responsibility on the status leader to avoid making any administrative-centered changes for the staff.* This need not, however, negate the opportunities that will be presented to make the faculty cognizant of the many new directions and innovations that are taking place in the area of curriculum development. Sharing this information with grade-level chairmen and department leaders can make these persons readily aware of innovations and new developments and make it possible for them, in turn, to assess their potential in meeting the instructional needs that exist within their area. The sharing of such information lends encouragement to department and grade-level leaders to review and reflect upon new and interesting ideas and to refer them to the appropriate committees for consideration, recommendation, and action.

5. *New organizational patterns, such as differentiated staffing, also will assist teachers in attaining their objectives.* Curriculum associates, clinical professors, part-time personnel, auxiliary specialists, and paraprofessionals will aid veteran and new teachers in restructuring and redeploying their efforts to meet their optimal professional obligations. New teaching strategies, closer student-teacher contacts, and data-resource banks will offer many heretofore unknown possibilities for reaching realistic behavioral objectives. Teaching-research specialists will assume new status leadership positions and will give assistance in the development of interdisciplinary curricular programs and specialized teaching procedures. Greater utilization of human resources will be possible, more interaction can take place between the teaching faculty and the community, and the educational experience of pupils can become more meaningful. The school staff can become structured to the extent that all personnel will be encouraged, within their professional training limits, to undertake increased responsibility as reflected in greater status potential within the organization.

6. *The role of the status leader will change perceptibly as he works with teachers.* His position will become more specialized as the decision-making process within the school takes on a strong decentralized structure. His basic relationships with teachers and with the instructional program will undergo constant evaluation and his own leadership functions will tend to be directed toward his areas of greatest ability and accomplishment. Greater numbers of teaching and research specialists from the faculty will assist him in coordinating his overall responsibilities as they relate to in-service growth and staff development. In some cases he may become known as a project specialist or manager. As new projects or missions are formed within the organizational framework, his task will be to provide continuity, flexibility, and encouragement to

highly trained teaching professionals whose talents are both scarce and valuable. The work performance standards of the status leader and the faculty group can be nothing short of being of the highest order and both parties can expect to be held reasonably accountable for the productivity that will result from their efforts.

7. *PPBS (Planning-Programming-Budgeting-System) offers a new approach to organizations pursuing objectives that require resources to initiate and sustain purposeful programs of instruction.* Utilization of this technique does give the status leader and the faculty the advantage of long-range planning and the development of a variety of alternatives in program direction. As it classifies budget items, it also exhibits differing arrangements that can be considered in the generation of alternative courses of action. The staff can view the structure of its plans, analyze the flow of activity toward established goals, and make appropriate decisions as to the processes involved. Clarification of time and energy factors, in moving ahead toward the desired goal, will be important benefits derived from the PPBS approach. Increased expectations as to what the faculty considers that it can and should accomplish will make this conceptual framework a bright, new tool for the status leader. Problem-solving, decision-making, and long-range planning are concerns that will require a broad understanding of instructional tasks, skills, and personnel development. PPBS offers a unique approach to solving educational problems.

In conclusion, teachers can and should expect much assistance from the instructional leader in accomplishing their own predetermined objectives. The leader must give a good deal of thought to the planning of the organizational structure as he tailors the supportive services to meet the needs of both individuals and groups. Personalities and attitudes are as important as the software and hardware that will be required to sustain the various projects and activities. People, budgets, time schedules, and a host of other concerns will require his undivided attention if he is to serve the profession in a competent, accountable manner. The teaching faculty may produce the ideas and the concepts that it wishes to see fulfilled, but the status leader will be expected to integrate and devise a logical plan of operation that will transform dreams into realities.

SUMMARY

The spectrum of the abilities, make-up, and dispositions of the teaching force are many. Even though the previous discussion has identified rather neat, discrete prototypes of teachers, it would be absurd to make the assumption that there are not teachers who fall into more than one of these categories or who may be identified as representative of "grey" areas in between these types. The administrator or supervisor, nevertheless, must be in a position to have some objective means of developing working methods of dealing with the reasonable number of teachers who are not readily placed in an "average" teacher category. These persons represent a special class of individuals who need some highly professional assistance that will be unique in its approach to instructional upgrading.

Reduced to barest terms, the new teacher needs encouragement and support as he begins his career as a member of the educational enterprise; the weak teacher must be motivated to improve and become a contributing member of the educational team; the superior teacher must be placed in a position where his many personal talents can become diffused for the benefit of those less precocious as educators; the teacher who rejects change must be surrounded with new ideas that will make continued rejection a most uncomfortable and insecure position; and the student teacher should be exposed to a modern, realistic training program that will assure him success when he enters the classroom for the first time as a regular teacher.

The large range of all teachers who are seeking to accomplish their own objects requires the development by status leaders of alternative routes to satisfy numerous and complex demands. Greater specialization on the part of both teachers and status leaders will require more supportive personnel; increased involvement in the decision-making process by teachers will make mandatory the establishment of new supervisory patterns; and enlarged segments of unstructured teacher time will give all concerned more opportunities to think, plan, and relate to one another on a new cooperative basis.

SELECTED REFERENCES

Association for Supervision and Curriculum Development. *The Supervisor's Role in Negotiations,* Washington, D.C.: National Education Association, 1969.

Association of Teacher Educators. *A Guide To Professional Excellence in Clinical Experiences in Teacher Education.* Washington, D.C.: National Education Association, 1970.

Brown, Thomas J. *Student Teaching in a Secondary School.* New York: Harper and Row, 1968.

Carver, Fred D., and Thomas J. Sergiovanni. *Organizations and Human Behavior: Focus on Schools.* New York: McGraw-Hill, 1969.

Chandler, B. J., *et al. Education and the New Teacher.* New York: Dodd, Mead, 1971.

Eddy, Elizabeth M. *Becoming a Teacher: The Passage to Professional Status.* New York: Teachers College Press, 1969.

Gerhard, M. *Effective Teaching Strategies With the Behavioral Outcomes Approach.* New York: Parker, 1971.

Grant, B. M., and D. G. Hennings. *Teacher Moves: An Analysis of Non-Verbal Activity.* New York: Teachers College Press, 1971.

Green, Thomas F. *The Activities of Teaching.* New York: McGraw-Hill, 1971.

Student National Education Association. *New Teachers: New Education.* Washington, D.C.: National Education Association, 1970.

CHAPTER 8

Design for In-Service Education

Supervision implies that the role of the instructional leader is one in which the inner resources and creativity of the faculty are released by his efforts. To perform this task adequately, the supervisor must make his professional skills known to and desired by the teaching staff. As teachers express a willingness to discuss their programs and problems with him, the supervisor must display an attitude of encouragement, a willingness to offer constructive suggestions, and an ability to advance reasonable and valid criticism in a helpful, forthright fashion. In many ways he provides teachers with challenging opportunities to perfect their unique teaching talents. Through effective in-service interaction, teachers are given faith in themselves coupled with enthusiasm and zeal.

Although some teachers can and do work constructively alone, there is such a growing body of human knowledge that individuals must from time to time coordinate their efforts in seeking solutions to problems on a group basis. The task of extending learning opportunities, coupled with the development of new techniques in teaching, requires the involvement of many persons on the teaching-administrative team to provide a coordinated approach to curriculum development. Stated in a different fashion, the tangible combinations of group forces working together have a striking influence upon the attitude of the individual teacher as he relates his activities to improved instruction.

GROUP PROCESS

One of the chief concerns of the educational leader is to change the behavior of the professional groups with which he works. He recognizes, however, that mere changes in the organization, its officers, its lines of communication, and the like, are no assurance that the behavior of the individuals in the group will change or, in fact, be improved. What the group ultimately needs is the assistance of a working force that can personally play an important role in helping them become motivated to the point that they are willing to do something that will improve their own capabilities. There is no substitute for the development and expression of a warm, personal relationship between the educational leader and the members of the professional groups to assist them in the performance of their task.

There is good evidence that the effectiveness of any group as it performs its task is largely due to the abilities, professional background, and self-assurance that the individuals have in themselves and their leaders. There is little doubt that group members must be given an opportunity to play an independent-action role if they are to emerge successfully from their deliberations and to parlay this action-prone attitude into a changed behavior pattern. Educational leaders, who may be hesitant to permit this libertarian climate, will have to reassess their own attitudes toward teachers and the expectations they have for them. A leader's strong authoritarian attitude toward the group has no place in the permissive atmosphere that must be fostered if individual and group potentials are to be realized.

The educational leader must provide many facilitating conditions for the group, such as support, availability of information, reinforcement of decisions, and helpful instructions. A differentiation of approaches must be used among various groups: for example, teachers only recently employed by the district as compared to those who have been with the district for a long career period. From time to time the educational leader will wish to assess carefully when various groups are ready for cooperative ventures and, if the need is apparent, to provide psychological inducements to move in this direction.

Objective task performance is generally the result of a perception of the task by the group in which they feel that the enterprise at various levels of accomplishment has been successful. As long as the group members view the objectives of the group as being similar to their own, they perceive the necessity of the group's actions being aimed at reaching a successful conclusion. Group leaders must capitalize on these two aspects of group work: (1) that the group is meeting with reasonable success in its various stages of task achievement; and (2) that the objectives of the group are identifiable with those of its members.

One of the most difficult tasks that the leader of any group faces is that of preventing members of the group from assuming group identity to the extent that they no longer reveal their own individual capabilities and behavior characteristics. Leaders must permit reasonable avenues of individual action and dissent to exist within the structure of the group's activities if there is to be a realistic balance between individual and group identity. The group must provide the opportunity for individuals to work together on common problems and concerns, but it must not subvert or disallow individual talents or creativity.

Some important findings from small-group research and a close look at group problem-solving techniques will be discussed next.

A Synthesis of Small-Group Studies

A research program designed to integrate knowledge in the small-group field has yielded some interesting results.[1] 250 small-group studies were classified on the basis of a set of data collection and data-analysis properties and several major conclusions were drawn from these analyses. One major generalization from the data compiled in this study is that groups whose members have high abilities, training, and/or experience are more effective than groups whose members are lower in abilities or experiences. Another proposition is that group members who have high social or task status in the group are likely to have high power and to react favorably to the group. It was found that favorable attitudes toward the group's task and toward the situation seem to be partly a consequence of high social or task status in the group, job autonomy, cooperative group conditions, and induced perceptions of task success. High authoritarian attitudes seem to be associated with low popularity and low choice as a leader. Conversely, members who have low authoritarian attitudes and high group rank or status are likely to be personally attractive to group-mates. In terms of perceptions of task effectiveness, these are more likely to occur for individuals with high status in the group.

Relatively small group size is likely to be accompanied by less perceived need for guidance and a definite leader, by fewer expressed ideas and changes in attitudes by members, and by better performance in operational settings. Members who have high status in the group and who are central in the group's communication net tend to be high communicators. Communication tends to be directed toward other members who are personally liked or disliked, rather than toward those to whom the communicator is personally indifferent. Effective leadership behavior seemed related to: individual personality characteristics such as extroversion, assertiveness, and social maturity; education, but

[1]Joseph E. McGrath, *A Summary of Small Group Studies*. Prepared for Air Force Office of Scientific Research, Office of Aerospace Research, Human Sciences Research, Inc., Arlington, Virginia, June 1962, 29 pp. See also Ben Harris and Wailand Bessent, *In-service Education: A Guide to Better Practice* (Englewood Cliffs: Prentice-Hall, 1969), pp. 253–267.

not age; intelligence, general abilities and task abilities; high group status; and training in leadership techniques. Obviously the person who will emerge as a leader is the one having the highest status, skills, and training. Effective group-task performance is characterized by: general and task abilities of members, and training or experience on the task; systematic distribution of task information, and rapid, direct access to it; cooperative conditions; group rather than individual reward for success, and continuation of expectations about the nature of the task; individual praise and criticism; and little hostility and disagreement within the group.

Several propositions about small groups can be formulated: (1) the degree of conformity is a function of amount and continuousness of conformity pressures—this is particularly effective for members who see themselves as rejected; (2) job-decision autonomy is associated with favorable attitudes toward supervisors and greater satisfaction with the job; (3) exposure to task-relevant materials, in the form of films or discussion, is effective in producing attitude changes and in increasing problem-solving effectiveness; (4) reduction of ambiguity increases problem-solving effectiveness and reduces the transmission of rumors; (5) feedback of performance data increases member task effectiveness in experimental settings; (6) appointed leaders, those with low authoritarian attitudes, and those who perceive themselves to have high power, are most likely to attempt to influence other group members; (7) the level of education is associated with leadership in leaderless group situations; and (8) self-ratings of physical prowess and self-reliance, and absence of extreme personality characteristics, are associated with effective group performance in operational settings.

Group Problem Solving

Group problem solving can be described best as the unified effort of an organized group of people to reach an effective solution to a problem situation confronting the group. Administrators and supervisors have found that group problem solving contributes to the achievement of educational goals in these ways: (1) improves the human relations of staff members by uniting them toward a common purpose; promotes an understanding of individual ideas and motives through group discussion, providing an outlet for repressed grievances, and, in general, resulting in better faculty communication; (2) stimulates a more enthusiastic acceptance and implementation of any changes necessary for the solution of the problem; (3) reduces feelings of alienation and improves staff morale because teachers feel that they have a voice in some of the decisions that affect them; (4) contributes to the in-service growth of teachers who become increasingly aware of problems that need to be solved; and (5) assists teachers in developing methods for working together successfully.[2]

A summary of these interrelated principles and techniques that will help supervisory leaders to increase group productivity is presented below:

1. *Obtain a complete agreement as to the nature of the problem prior to any effort toward a solution.* Occasionally, an analysis of a group controversy regarding a solution reveals a lack of complete agreement concerning the definition of the problem. Each member should receive a copy of the definition agreed upon by the group.

2. *Direct initial effort toward locating and evaluating surmountable obstacles.* A solution which is lacking in feasibility or cannot be effectuated serves no purpose except in the "process of elimination." Likewise, problems which require the acceptance of blame often terminate in failure. If no one will accept (or identify himself with) the problem, the motivation to solve it must come as a result of another approach.

3. *Analyze all aspects of the problem on the basis of available data.* Restrict this analysis to the facts while being aware of their limitations. Avoid the use of over-generalizations, imagination, or opinion. The application of a previously effective solution to a new problem often leads to poor results. A thorough analysis of the group's prime objective will usually lead to a starting point and the tentative selection of a course of action.

4. *Continually re-emphasize the problem in order to stimulate new ideas and delay acceptance of first solutions.* Research indicates that in most cases the first solution is inferior to subsequent solutions. When an avenue of approach proves to be a "blind alley," retreat to a position which offers several courses of action, re-examine the facts, and select the most promising direction.

5. *Explore many solution possibilities—"make haste slowly."* People must learn through experience to proceed analytically and to delve beneath the surface for less obvious solutions. Creativity requires the ability to fragment past experiences and permit the formation of new and spontaneous combinations. In contrast, learning depends upon the ability to combine or connect elements that are contiguous to each other in our experience. Both abilities are necessary for effective problem solving.

6. *Inhibit the evaluation of ideas until all relevant thoughts have*

[2]Viola Abercrombie, "Group Problem Solving and the Elementary School Principal," *Monthly Bulletin* (Los Angeles County Schools Office), vol. 22, no. 8 (May 1964), pp 9–11.

been expressed. In order to encourage participation and creativity in solution possibilities, *all* ideas should be accepted and listed. No proof should be required at first. In the use of spontaneous, free expression, as in brainstorming, one idea often "sparks" another. If the evaluative process begins before all ideas have been stated, further expression may be inhibited.

7. *Eliminate personality involvement in disagreement.* Utilize constructive disagreement to stimulate a more thorough analysis of the problem and to inspire creative thinking. Neither conformity nor the avoidance of disagreement necessarily constitutes good human relations. The non-conformist may be the more creative member of the group. Conflict over the support of various solutions may require an entirely new approach.

8. *Look for problems when faced with a choice situation.* In a choice situation, the solution involves choosing between two or more alternatives. When attempting to make a choice, think of the obstacles involved in each.

9. *Look for choices when faced with a problem situation.* In a problem situation, the solution requires the surmounting of one or more obstacles. When attempting to analyze the obstacles, think in terms of possible choices. Both problem-solving behavior and choice behavior are involved in making decisions. In the former, possibilities for solutions are expanded—in the latter, these possibilites are narrowed down to a final selection.

10. *Recognize leadership behavior (skill) as a determining factor in the ultimate success of the group problem-solving situation.* Administrators must realize that skilled leadership is essential if the best results are to be obtained. Considerable skill is required for a leader to deal with personal feelings as conference obstacles, to clarify semantic problems, to increase involvement, to keep the discussion "on course," and to stimulate and guide rather than to direct group effort toward a higher level of productivity.

FACULTY MEETINGS

Small-group theory provides several guidelines that are of concern to status leaders as they consider the dynamics and implementation of faculty meetings as an important interaction tool. The human relations skills that are so aptly exhibited in the small-group situation will be extremely useful in devising the faculty meeting structure so that it aids the staff in attaining organizational effectiveness and efficiency. Facility in the development of goal-oriented changes and feedback techniques through faculty meeting procedures illustrate the fact that large-group success depends upon the existence of many small-group experiences. Relationships that are formulated in faculty meetings will be similar to the relationships that exist among small faculty groups in the school at large. As a result, administrators have a responsibility to make certain that faculty meetings are faculty oriented as opposed to administration oriented. Continuous assignment of faculty planning committees will help give assurance that both individual and small-group expectations of the faculty will be met. Difficult school problems can be solved by a unified faculty approach and school morale can benefit by this device. Interpersonal relationships are subject to strengthening by good faculty-meeting arrangements and the preferences of teachers can be reflected in faculty-oriented planning. What the group expects and what it prefers are central to considerations that will need to be reflected in devising faculty-meeting patterns.

Faculty meetings, if properly organized and oriented, should represent an important augmentation to the in-service training activities of the school. Although a reasonable amount of time and effort in faculty meetings must be given to administrative affairs, the main focus of these meetings should be to provide greater growth and understanding of personnel as to the learning needs and progress of the entire school. Any systems approach to the development of strategies for improving the school should result in the achievement of a better open system of communication, the recognition of the school as an organization that benefits from such interaction, and a polarization toward an attitude for encouraging change. Faculty meetings should promote these qualities in the institution's striving to achieve organizational health and stability. If new ideas are to be given an audience within the framework of the system, faculty meetings must provide this opportunity for each member of the staff to be heard, if he wishes, by all other members in an appropriate, controlled climate.

In some institutions students have been invited to attend faculty meetings. Imaginative leadership has made it possible for them to make constructive contributions to the decision-making process in discussions dealing with curriculum, discipline, activity programs, and related topics.[3] With greater student demands for more involvement in the organizational development of the school's program, this would permit the encouragement of greater cooperation with students in many phases of school life.

Faculty meetings should be planned with a definite time schedule established for the meeting—a day and hour set aside for meetings

---

[3]William W. Savage, *Interpersonal and Group Relations in Educational Administration* (Glenview, Ill.: Scott, Foresman, 1968), pp. 258–259.

when teachers will be available. A definite purpose for the meeting should be stated with the agenda items selected on the basis of broad teacher interest and with an overriding concern for the welfare of the school's program. The meeting should be held in an appropriate place and at an appropriate time with a definite starting and ending time established.

A copy of the agenda placed in the hands of teachers ahead of the meeting (preferably the day before) would be helpful. During these meetings teachers could report on their activities inside and outside of the school from an educational and general-interest standpoint.

A democratic approach is essential to the success of the meeting. Many important input as well as output items of concern to the faculty could be discussed. A faculty forum for the discussion of interests and objectives might be organized during several of the meetings. District personnel, on invitation, could play an important part in discussing some aspects of their work and services to the faculty. In addition, development of faculty leadership could be encouraged by having faculty members chair some or all aspects of the faculty meeting. Lastly, providing refreshments and an opportunity for brief social communication among members of the faculty can be most worthwhile.

Teacher and Principal Attitudes toward Faculty Meetings

A follow-up study on school faculty meetings was conducted by the Group Dynamics Center (Philadelphia, Pennsylvania). The Center considered that since the faculty meeting represents the only time a total faculty is together for cooperative purposes, it offered valuable insights regarding the social-psychological nature of the school organization. Further, it was felt that the perceptions of principals regarding faculty meetings should be investigated to determine the agreement or disagreement between their perceptions and those of teachers.[4] See Fig. 8–1. The results of the study indicated that there was a very consistent trend for principals to perceive what transpires in their faculty meetings differently than do teachers. Principals and teachers tend to operate at different perceptual levels concerning the school and what goes on in it, largely due to the effect of one's status in the organization which colors one's attitude towards it. Principals, therefore, should guard against being insensitive to faculty behavior and not being aware of feelings expressed in faculty meetings. In any meeting there should be a forthright acknowledgment of the differences present so that the

[4]Arthur Blumberg and Edward Amidon, "A Comparison of Teacher and Principal Attitudes Toward Faculty Meetings," *Bulletin* of the NASSP, vol. 48, no. 290 (March 1964), pp. 45–55. See also James E. Jones, *et al.*, *Secondary School Administration* (New York: McGraw-Hill, 1969), pp. 314–316.

TEACHERS   PRINCIPALS

Item I. How does the principal respond to a teacher's comment?

Teachers tend to view the principal as being noncommittal or giving mixed reactions to teachers' comments in the meetings.

Principals see themselves reacting to teacher comments in a very accepting and encouraging way.

Item II. How do teachers respond to the comments of other teachers?

Teachers see their colleagues reacting slightly on the critical side to each other's comments.

Principals perceive that the teachers respond to each other in an encouraging manner.

Item III. How free do teachers feel to express themselves?

Teachers apparently think that teachers as a group are "rather careful in what they say" in a faculty meeting. A strong element of caution is present.

Principals seem to think that teachers feel a great deal of freedom to "say whatever they wish."

Item IV. How free do you feel to express yourself?

Individual teachers seem to reflect their feelings about the teacher group as a whole, as they feel that they, as individuals, are rather cautious about what they say.

Principals apparently feel free to say whatever they wish in faculty meetings.

Fig. 8–1. Comparison of Teacher and Principal Perceptions of Faculty Meetings and Relationships.

Item V. What is your general reaction to faculty meetings in your school?

Teachers tend to react to faculty meetings as being close to a "waste of time."

The satisfaction of principals with faculty meetings is rather high. They see them as an "effective use of time and energy."

Item VI. What do you think is the general condition of the faculty?

In regard to attitudes about the faculty as a whole, the results suggested that teachers view their colleagues as fairly interested in doing a good job.

In regard to attitudes about the faculty as a whole, principals perceive their faculties as being "alert, aware, and interested."

Item VII. How close do you feel to members of the faculty?

Teachers seem to see the general level of faculty relationships as being rather casual but generally cooperative.

The typical response of principals in regard to faculty relationships is that they are "very close, everyone pulling together."

Item VIII. How easy do you find it talking to the (principal) (teachers) about new ideas and suggestions for the school?

In regard to how easy they find it to talk to the principal, teachers suggest that it is rather "easy" if my idea is a good one."

Principals apparently feel little inhibition about talking to teachers. Their reactions are that it is "easy for me at any time."

Fig. 8–1 *(continued)*

problems can be resolved and all facts relevant to a problem can be known. Unfortunately, as this study found, central issues of school concern which should receive open and frank consideration from both principals and teachers seldom seemed to be dealt with on the appropriate levels of understanding.

Committee to Study Special Problems

The principal may sometimes find it necessary to request the faculty to appoint a committee to fulfill a particular function in some special problem area. The function and purposes of the committee should be made known to the participants and the committee made aware that their suggestions and recommendations will receive careful consideration and probable implementation. Otherwise, there is little reason for requesting the services of busy faculty members in such a venture.

Experienced teachers as well as new teachers should serve on this committee. The committee would consist largely of teachers from a specific problem area, but the rest of the faculty should be represented also.

The meetings should be arranged at a time convenient for the teachers, making arrangements for substitutes as necessary. Adequate secretarial help must be provided for producing the minutes following these meetings.

The committee should discuss the problem and make recommendations as to its solution, with the chairman reporting the committee's progress to the faculty. The principal should then review the recommendations of the committee on special problems and be willing to implement its recommendations if possible.

SELF-IMPROVEMENT AND GROWTH

New teaching roles require that teachers become willing to change their task from structuring teacher-dominated learning situations to those dominated by students in which the teacher provides the setting for student inquiry and response. In this fashion teachers must be willing to investigate carefully ways in which they can improve their own competency within personal areas of academic and professional disciplines. They should learn to be able to remove themselves from an artificial role that dominates the learning situation and relinquish this role to the learner. To accomplish this the teacher may be given many opportunities to determine ways in which he needs to grow professionally. Further, he should be encouraged to assess those areas of learning and learning techniques that deserve his utmost attention and immediate, as well as future action.

Self-improvement, growth attitudes, teacher inter-visitation, and self-analysis are all considered below as a means for aiding the teacher in professional improvement. If the teacher is to make a constructive contribution to the improvement of classroom learning, avenues of this type must be opened for him. Greater emphasis must be given to the teacher's role in developing the kinds of growth experiences that will have a positive effect on the teaching-learning situation.

Self-Improvement

The behavior of the individual teacher will not necessarily change just because he has gone through a formal program devoted to teacher growth. Status leaders initially will wish to determine the attitudes of the teacher as he is encouraged to develop his own program that will assist him in growing professionally. The teacher then can be encouraged to consider his own talents and weaknesses and to embark on a goal-oriented program that will improve his behavior as a professional. In a larger sense, this involves building a self-improvement climate for the entire school through changing the interaction patterns among staff members, increasing the opportunities for cooperative curriculum development, and devising means to improve human behavior in the whole organization. Freedom to innovate and experiment is an important factor in encouraging self-improvement and each individual must be held accountable for the change that will or can take place in himself. Better involvement and increased interaction among staff will lead teachers to new perceptions about their role and their potential as professionals.

Attitude for Growth: An Individualized Program

In developing any program of teacher improvement, individual teachers must have a major role if the program is to be successful. Supervisors and administrators need to reaffirm their commitment to individual teacher growth and to practices which develop the following traits: individuality, self-understanding, self-fulfillment, and growth in ability to live and work harmoniously with oneself and others.[5] Programs for teacher growth, therefore, must set inspiring examples of educational objectives. There should be no restrictive and controlling behavior on the part of the administration and the program should always emphasize the development of teachers as individuals. There is a close relationship between self-motivation and teacher attitude. The attitudes the teacher holds as a person and as a member of a profession

---

[5]Karl Openshaw, "Attitudes for Growth," *Educational Leadership*, vol. 20, no. 2 (November 1962), pp. 90–92. See also Ryland W. Crary, *Humanizing the School: Curriculum Development and Theory* (New York: Alfred A. Knopf, 1969), pp. 155–157.

show a significant relationship; the various groups with which he has membership have an increasing effect on the attitudes that he holds.

Any program of teacher improvement should be individually oriented in order to appeal to the interests of individual teachers. The teacher must have an opportunity to help set his goals and plan his individual growth program; he must be able to identify with his program in a personal way. Many opportunities may be provided for the teacher to increase his understanding of his professional role so that he may recognize possible significant areas where growth is needed.

Teacher Inter-Visitation

How are new insights developed in classroom teaching? To provide an opportunity to teachers to view the on-going activities in classrooms other than their own, a Connecticut experiment was conducted in which teachers took part on a voluntary basis.[6] The teachers did not limit themselves to visiting someone in their own department, but visited teachers in other departments. During the project, the respect and dignity of all teachers were emphasized and any teachers not wishing to take part did not have to do so. Visiting teachers did not sit in judgment on their colleagues, they did not write reports regarding their competency, and no names were written on the observation forms. During the first week, five teachers were scheduled to observe. Each observer witnessed four lessons selected from a variety of departments and levels. Each observer was asked to file the following report: Do you feel that this is a worthwhile experience? If so, how? If not, why not? What was the outstanding feature of your observation? Any suggestions or comments? During the second week eight teachers observed.

The teachers felt they learned much about many teaching techniques. They observed differences between age groups, many characteristics about class control, the effect of negative attitudes, the results from lack of motivation, the importance of meaningful materials for the proper grade level and academic grouping, unusual audio-visual techniques, and the like. After five weeks an evaluation meeting was held and all the teachers agreed that it was a worthwhile experience.

The Connecticut plan has some real advantages over the typical demonstration-lesson arrangement. In some districts teachers are given the opportunity of observing other teachers who are demonstration teachers. Since the demonstration lesson is planned it can be observed from its conception to its completion. However, through planned inter-visitation the visiting teacher has an unusual opportunity to witness a

[6]Joseph DeVita, "Teachers Observe Other Teachers," *The Clearing House*, vol. 37, no. 9 (May 1963), pp. 549–550.

lesson develop in a realistic situation with the vital student-teacher relationship ever evident. With average as well as superior teachers being visited the observer has an excellent chance to reflect on the negative aspects of the classroom learning situation as well as the positive ones. Accessibility of inter-visitations within the building provides a wealth of opportunity for teachers to do this easily during a counseling and planning period, if they are so scheduled. It is encouraging to note that the members of this faculty were enabled to learn a great deal from each other through the inter-visitation process.

Self-Analysis Questionnaires

Few supervisory techniques provide greater assistance to teacher growth in the classroom than self-analysis. One procedure requires that a self-analysis questionnaire be developed that will review many facets of the lesson that has just been covered. It might raise a number of questions as to the manner in which these areas were covered in the classroom: effective methods of thought, important social attitudes, work habits, skills in study and research, interest range, student control, involvement of pupils, effort and determination to progress toward task completion, lesson-objective attainment, and time utilization.

Areas like these could form the basis for a dialog between the supervisor and teacher following a visitation. Teachers who are confronted with an unusual number of classroom problems could constructively use such a questionnaire daily for a reasonable period of time as a means of closer analysis of the problems that beset them. Follow-up conferences with the supervisor could be of considerable assistance in helping such teachers come to grips with the very problems that desperately need solution.

In its most meaningful sense, the self-analysis questionnaire offers the teacher an opportunity to study his own performance and how it relates to the problem of his professional growth. He must be able to recognize his areas of greatest success as well as those where weaknesses are found. Exciting learning opportunities cannot be expected in a classroom situation in which the teacher is unwilling periodically to assess his own teaching accomplishments.

INDIVIDUAL HELP

The faculty represents a formidable source for the development of new ideas and attitudes that can lead to instructional improvement and professional development. A notable span exists, however, between the developmental stage for new ideas and the later practices that become an integral part of classroom instruction. Few innovations can afford to wait thirty to fifty years before they are accepted as a regular part of the classroom program.

Little help has been found for teachers merely through the use of printed materials. A large variety of techniques needs to be employed as a means of communicating with the teacher. One of the greatest obstacles to overcome is an attitude, both inside and outside the school, that tends to inhibit the desire for acceptance of new ways of doing things. Somehow the teacher must feel that the community is solidly in support of change and that members of the community are willing, on an attitudinal, as well as a financial basis, to support teacher growth. To promote such an attitude, a major effort must be made on the part of those in the teaching profession to relate the goals and objectives of the school closely to those of the community and to give ample evidence that teacher growth will tangibly promote community progress.

Today's teachers are extremely sensitive as to their relationship with administrative and supervisory personnel. Too often an atmosphere of officialism prevails and the teacher, rightly or wrongly, receives the misconceived idea that the district office is the sole purveyor of worthwhile ideas or suggestions that should be pursued. In some instances a serious lag or omission may occur in the fostering of ideas to teachers by the central agency because no real provision has been made for this function to take place on a planned, continuing basis. Too often the administration is primarily concerned with retaining those ideas and practices that seemingly are successful within the present setting with little thought being devoted to revising or upgrading such practices that already may be outmoded. At times suggestions for change emanating from the school level or the teacher may find themselves vetoed as they are subjected to a number of approvals at differing strata of administrative dictum. Here again a lack of regard may be shown for the inner compulsion that some creative teachers have to rise above their colleagues in terms of innovativeness and challenge.

Oftentimes a closer relationship should be established between the individual and the system that employs him. Without active involvement in a close-knit group situation, the teacher may never really consider that he is an important cog in the formalized system that directs his activities. The overall goals of the organization can be an elaboration of his own, and the intertwining of his activities in part with the informal group structure will give added vitality and meaning to his own image and role-playing within the system. Under these conditions this close relationship with the group will assist the teacher in coalescing his own professional concerns and attitudes with those of the district and its various educational subdivisions.

Administrators and supervisors can actively support the professional development of teachers as they are busily engaged in working with pupils. Every effort must be expended to make certain that teachers not only have the opportunity to assist pupils in small-group situations, but that they are given the opportunity to meet individually with these children, to determine how best their individual abilities may be accommodated, and how the whole classroom program can be structured to assist them toward meeting their own highest level of achievement. In effect, the teacher should be given heady encouragement to become a real decision-maker at the classroom level and to be ever mindful that his ability to garner resource materials can lead to far greater achievements in the classroom.

Research and the Teacher

More evidence is coming to light that action research must become an integral responsibility of the school as well as the teacher. As laboratory experimentation increases and greater support is given to the development of new ideas and concepts in education, there must be established practical avenues for the introduction of these innovations into the classroom situation. The improvement of good learning experiences demands that teachers be encouraged to test hypotheses and try out new theories of learning wherever these findings appear appropriate and necessary to the development of improved learning practices.

On a local basis the classroom teacher must be motivated to review the problems that confront him in the pursuit of his learning objectives. A school action-research committee should be formed that will be available to him for assistance in helping design better methods of achieving the desired learning results in the classroom. Such a committee should have at its disposal a number of consultants as well as supervisory help at any stage of its deliberation. The most important element in the functioning of such a group is the cooperation and willingness of the individual teacher to engage in an action-research program in his classroom.

Procedures to follow in an action-research plan will require several steps. There should be valid evidence that a serious problem does exist that warrants the use of research techniques in a particular situation. Careful gathering of data from the field will be essential to assure the teacher and the committee that an action-research approach to the problem is possible at this stage. Following the development of one or more hypotheses, the research plan can begin in the classroom. Records should be kept of the various stages of experimentation, the progress of the experiment should be reported to the committee, and an analysis should be made from time to time to determine if the research is moving in the right direction. Final conclusions should result from a complete review of the progress of the study and the findings should be disseminated to other segments of the school as a basis for incorporating them into other classroom programs where applicable.

There is a real need for organized experimentation as a method of assisting teachers to attack their classroom problems scientifically. Many problems can be isolated in this manner and the application of scientific methods can be applied as a means of solving them. The teacher who engages in this kind of research activity is taking real strides in making his teaching an exciting and profitable adventure.

Professional and Technical Reading

Greater emphasis is being given to the professional reading habits of teachers. With accelerated changes occurring in all disciplinary fields, teachers must have access to the great reservoir of new knowledge that can be found only through reading. There are many sources available for professional reading; district professional libraries, college and university libraries, local public libraries, and individual collections of resource materials found in departments and various learning centers of the school. All of these should be utilized to full capacity.

Much interest in professional reading can be stimulated through the discussion of interesting materials at faculty and department meetings, the publication of brief book reviews in the district bulletin, the display of new books and journals in the professional library center, and the establishment of a library committee that assists the librarian and the general faculty in selecting new and exciting materials for faculty reading purposes. Wherever reading materials are readily available faculty interest in professional growth is greatly increased. The wealth of professional literature found in the field must be placed in a depository that is close to the teacher and his work if individual professional growth is to be a reality.

Supervisory Bulletins

The good supervisory bulletin will focus on the communication of ideas and activities that are of interest to the faculty. The faculty should play an integral part in the planning of the bulletin and should be given an opportunity to present materials that will go into the final edition. Much material can be solicited from bulletins by neighboring school districts where interesting curriculum development is under way. Book reviews and significant journal articles can be included, as well as information on various meetings at school that are concerned with upgrading the curriculum.

The supervisory bulletin must have as its objective the improvement of learning and the instructional program of the school and/or district. It should cover adequately a number of important areas mentioned above, yet it should be relatively short so as not to discourage busy teachers from reading its contents. Above all, the bulletin can stimulate teachers to be creative and to be desirous of experimenting with new ideas and concepts.

The number of supervisory bulletins should be reduced to a minimum, preferably one or two a week. Written contributions by teachers represent an important contribution to curriculum development as they describe projects and progress on the school level.

Routine staff communications to the faculty may contain daily announcements, the weekly schedule, reports to teachers from off-campus meetings, bell schedules (regular, assembly, long assembly, and faculty meeting), defense drill, fire drill, and the like. Supervisory bulletins, on the other hand, inform the faculty of the availability of new materials, new in-service courses to help the teacher improve instruction, future in-service meetings, new curriculum projects that are being considered by the district, and other items of interest.

Studying Pupil Behavior

Faculty responsibility and influence makes it essential that pupil records are easily accessible to teachers. These must be maintained on a current basis with the student advisor and members of the teaching and clerical staff entering pertinent information on pupil behavior promptly. In-service training for new teachers in the interpretation of pupil-record information is necessary if they are to become acquainted with a wide variety of approaches through which the educational program may benefit these individuals.

Conferences should be available for teachers and staff members who come in contact with and see the need patterns of students who have problems. Teachers must be helped to recognize the cues from learners, identify with their frame of reference, and make the proper learning adjustment. If a teacher-counselor conference is required to solve a student case, the following reports could be ready: test reports, psychological reports, family history, academic record, health record, and disciplinary record.

Studying pupils relies on the components of teacher flexibility and insight and any in-service program in this area should be designed to increase the perceptions of teachers. The process involves helping the teacher to react as follows:[7] (1) The teacher regards each of the behaviors of his students as potentially significant; he believes the learner's

---

[7] Bruce R. Joyce, *The Teacher-Innovator: A Program to Prepare Teachers* (Washington, D. C.: U.S. Office of Education, 1968), p. 247.

behavior occurs in patterns that can be interpreted in terms of an information-processing system; (2) The teacher can shift his style or strategy in such a way as to increase the flow of information from the learner about his frame of reference; (3) The teacher can make educated guesses about the frames of reference of particular learners; and (4) The teacher can modify his style or strategy to build a bridge between the learner and himself and to reconcile his goals and strategy with the mind of the learner. As he continues to study pupils, the teacher can also modify his behavior to: adjust procedures and objectives to the competence level of the learner; build a conceptual bridge between the learner and the teaching objectives; adjust procedures to match learner preferences and feelings of competence; or to accommodate an emotional response by the learner.

Greater confidence can be gained, particularly by new teachers, in studying pupil behavior. Studies of this type do much to break rigid patterns of teacher response that often frustrate and repel pupils. A strengthening of the communicative tasks of the teacher will do much to foster better teacher-pupil understanding and strategy.

Casual Meetings

A principal may use many spontaneous methods of helping teachers during casual meetings. Perhaps of greatest importance is the necessity to develop and maintain good avenues of communication. This may be accomplished by expressing a sincere interest in the teacher as a person. The principal, for example, may distribute materials that will be helpful to teachers. He may also keep teachers informed about meetings, seminars, institutes, and the like. By asking specific questions regarding curriculum, students' supplies, and other possible problem areas, he may identify problems and give meaning to the efforts made to help individuals. Personal examples offered by the principal may also assist teachers in seeking practical solutions to some of their problems. It is extremely important that the principal set an example for the staff in all professional areas, be positive in his relations with teachers, avoid developing an authoritarian attitude, and gain an understanding of each teacher's philosophy of education and background.

COURSES OF STUDY AND CURRICULUM GUIDES

Neagley and Evans have defined a course of study as a formal outline of prescribed content to be covered in a particular subject, group of subjects, or area of study by grades, and it may or may not include some of the elements of a curriculum guide. A curriculum guide is defined as a less formal document for teachers that contains the objectives, aims, and goals of instruction; the suggested, desirable content, learning experiences, and teaching aids that may be used to achieve them; and the evaluation techniques suitable for determining the extent to which they have been achieved.[8] Both courses of study and curriculum guides represent basic types of curriculum publications that serve as an integral part of the curriculum structure in the school and the district.

Developing Courses of Study

A form of in-service education that has proven profitable for faculty growth has been the development of courses of study. Some school systems, through central curriculum committees, have produced flexible guides by which teachers can move toward common goals and yet exercise various types of decisions that allow for both individual and team effort in many specialized areas of the curriculum. Some course guides concern themselves with philosophy, units of work to be covered, resource materials, and bibliographical items. Descriptions of methods for producing individual courses of study are helpful and some guides contain illustrative materials that represent samples of the areas of basic coverage that are important to the development of any course of study. Curriculum workers are in a position to be much more effective in the attainment of their own objectives if they have access to important format and content items that are suggestive of the kinds of instructional development items that are required for individual courses of study.

Department members or grade-level teachers need to have continuing concern for updated courses of study. A committee effort should exist at this level to assume responsibility for annual review and updating of course-of-study materials as the need arises. Individual staff members should be responsible for the coordinated development of courses of study in their area.

The department or grade-level chairman is a key person to work out the details of the course-of-study developmental process. The principal can review progress made by the committee through reports given to him periodically by the chairman and act as a resource person as needed.

It is the responsibility of the principal to determine that the course of study as prepared by the committee meets district and school needs, as well as the legal requirements of the county and state education offices. The implementation and the eventual evaluation of the new

[8]Ross L. Neagley and N. Dean Evans, *Handbook for Effective Curriculum Development* (Englewood Cliffs, N.J.: Prentice-Hall, 1967), p. 5.

course of study is the responsibility of the subject and/or grade-level teachers. The course-of-study descriptions should be acceptable to the majority of the teachers working in that area. Final approval must be given by the central office administration and the board of education.

Within the course-of-study structure, teachers are expected to develop their own daily lesson plans. The principle of academic freedom constitutes a right for the teacher to implement the course of study as he sees fit, as long as he remains within the scope and intent of the guide.

Formulating Curriculum Guides

Faculty members who possess the essential talents and skills in organizing and defining their particular subject matter or grade-level areas are ideal professionals for developing the curriculum guides in their area of specialization. Although curriculum development and methodology may be seen as separate concerns, it appears unlikely that curriculums can be rationally evolved without consideration being given to the teaching media.[9] There seems to be general consensus that what is taught and the act of teaching itself are matters that should be resolved by the professionals. The development of curriculum guides also should be primarily the concern of the faculty, and, when changes in the curriculum are undertaken, the district must provide the orientation to the new shifts in district philosophy and direction so that they can be reflected in new curriculum-material publications.

Teacher-oriented district curriculum committees are often the prime developers of curriculum publications in a wide variety of subject fields. Many districts have an elected representative from each school participating in the committee, with representation from the school system office and one or two administrative representatives from the local school level. These subject or grade-level committees hold regularly scheduled meetings and publish their minutes for distribution to those areas affected at the school level. Besides being involved in curriculum-guide development, these committees are engaged in making recommendations related to the revision of programs, reviewing efforts at coordinating and integrating particular subject programs with others in the district, and making organizational, fiscal, and material recommendations for district and school consideration.

The curriculum guides describe the total curriculum organization within a single subject field. They may designate the coordinated approach that is offered in meeting the main continuity thrust throughout

[9]James E. Heald and Samuel A. Moor II, *The Teacher and Administrative Relationships in School Systems* (New York: Macmillan, 1968), p. 70.

the entire curriculum. Discussion of the basic areas of course content to be covered, the textbooks that are to be used, the objectives to be sought, and the evaluation techniques to be applied, are vital topics in the manuals.

An apparent need in the area of curriculum guides is the development of a handbook that would reflect critical evaluations of theories in curriculum that have been tried and proven on a practical basis. Supervisors should commit themselves to the highly important business of relating theory to practical situations as a continuous process that devotes its attention to increasing our knowledge of "what works" and "what does not work" in this field. All curriculum developments might be subjected to this type of appraisal. Each theoretical proposal could be reviewed on the basis of its applicability to learning theories and how it can be welded into a pattern of teaching and learning. As new curriculums are structured, supervisors, in working with curriculum specialists in colleges and universities, must take the initiative in redefining their roles as pure practitioners to become also theorists and implementers. The enlargement of their role will make possible a lessening of the gap between theory and practice that has existed for too long a time.

WORKSHOPS

Teachers, with their principal, will wish to determine what needs exist for workshops, then request help from district and regional groups in planning them. Teachers should give leadership in setting up the objectives of the workshop as well as participating in this dimension of in-service experience. Utilizing teacher strengths in the various phases of workshop development is essential. The workshop functions best, research has found, when groups of teachers have an opportunity to work together on common problems. One or more workshop directors could be assigned and time made available for individual conferences, talks, discussions, work on projects, visitations, and other activities essential to the success of the group.

In coordinating all group activities, the director will want to show enthusiasm and interest, as well as act as a resource person when needed. If expedient, he should contact special speakers and consultants for the committee. The stimulation of "open end" research is a basic workshop objective.

The schedule of meetings could be made well in advance so that there will be no conflict with other activities. This action necessitates channeling communications to all people who are likely to be involved. It is the responsibility of the administration to provide proper physical facilities and materials as needed. Recognition should be given to members who are participating and arrangements made for extra pay, if travel is involved, when feasible. In some cases college credit may be arranged with neighboring institutions of higher learning.

The principal should observe the workshops in progress whenever possible. Looking toward the improvement of future workshops, he should evaluate the workshops in cooperation with the appropriate committees and together make recommendations to the faculty as to future workshop experiences that may appear necessary.

As an example of regional support for workshop programs, in 1970 the Educational Research Council of America promoted on-site workshops for teachers in various school districts affiliated with the council program. Of special interest were the in-service programs devoted to mathematics, social science, reading, humanities, and science.

Summer Curriculum Work

A north central community has successfully planned summer curriculum work in which parents, students, and teachers have coordinated research and action efforts for a two-week period following the close of school. A laboratory-workroom facility has been made available for the group which considers various intermediate school subjects according to the plan chosen for that summer. Leadership for the curriculum work is provided by a college consultant who brings resource persons to the workshop as needed. Approximately twenty participated in the three-hour daily sessions and good progress has been reported by the group.

In Fountain Valley (California) the district recently developed basic guidelines for the implementation of instructional leadership and evaluation of programs during the summer session months. The activities were as follows:

1. *Supervisors* conducted the Summer School program, led the new teacher seminar, selected teachers to participate in various college or university extension courses, and developed plans for teacher in-service education.

2. *Teachers* pursued and developed approaches to the implementation of new subject-matter guides, wrote information bulletins in many curriculum areas, selected and purchased social studies units, observed social studies units in other county schools, and prepared seventh and eighth grade curriculum organizational publications.

3. *Community Participants,* who were selected for citizen committees, coordinated efforts with the Parent-Teachers Association to de-

velop school-community policy, worked with the Home Owners Association to provide them with information concerning the school district's program, and helped host visitors to the district.

4. *Administrators* prepared new schools for the September opening, managed the physical operation of the Summer School program, ordered supplies, planned the work schedule of both certificated and classified personnel, and assisted the staff in evaluating the Summer School program.

Summer Workshop in Communication

A two-week training workshop for communication consultants was conducted by the Center for the Advanced Study of Educational Administration (CASEA). The workshop dealt with communication in groups and organizational functioning. Through 1970 the workshop trainees spent several months trying out their new skills learned with the help of CASEA staff members. In their role as organizational facilitators, the communication consultants helped others within the school system to increase their skills in objective decision-making within working groups, in diagnosing communication breakdowns, and in using resources within and without the system. Special responsibilities of the communication consultants would include such assignments as designing and conducting in-service training events and consulting with existing intact work groups within the school system.

CONVENTIONS AND LEARNING INSTITUTES

Notifying teachers of existing or planned institutes or conventions is important. When feasible, time off should be allowed to attend these activities and reports on institutes or conventions by teachers who attend should be given in relevant group meetings. Where monies are budgeted for these activities, teachers should be encouraged to file a brief report on the conference they attended, indicating the benefits that accrued to them and the school.

Principals and supervisors are in an excellent position to organize institutes or help coordinate district institutes for areas unique to a particular district that represent facets of felt need by the faculty. They should attempt to organize procedures for financial assistance to teachers attending these institutes and conventions and, whenever possible, arrange district credit for attendance at these institutes and workshops. Printed materials concerning the institutes or conventions can do much to describe the advantages that can be gained by teachers attending institutes and conventions. Good attendance and representation by teachers at these meetings will represent a favorable response to them as a valuable in-service training device.

Summer institutes, particularly under the National Defense Education Act (NDEA) and the National Science Foundation (NSF), have become one of the most potent in-service forces in American education today. Many teachers, particularly in the fields of biology, chemistry, mathematics, and physics, are taking advantage of the NSF summer institutes and are returning to their schools with new ideas, materials, and resources to upgrade the subject content of their particular disciplinary field.

Institutions of higher learning should work closely with administrators, supervisors, and department chairmen in planning any summer institute or conference at the secondary level. Institute or conference planning at the elementary level could combine the efforts of both administrators and supervisors with that of teachers representative of the appropriate grade or subject combination.

The 1969 Learning Institute at Palo Alto, California, as an example, was designed to help interested educators make independence, trust, and personal meaning the strength of their school's ethos. It recognized that learning is an inventive, risky, and highly personalized behavior that demands independence for teachers and students as being more important than their control. Three meetings were held: two weeks in the summer, one week in the fall, and one week in the spring. Small-group discussions were scheduled to establish the level of personal communication necessary for dealing with problems of change in the most meaningful and productive way now known. Expert theorists and practitioners shared their ideas and successes in large-group presentations and personal conversations. Educational wares now in operation or development were observed and pertinent publications were read.

Interestingly, each participant was able to turn to specific problems faced in his own district or school and new information and materials were made available to sharpen his model of communication as well as his own personal goals. In essence the institute was able to devote itself to a continuance of a disposition toward and capability for improvement through an understanding of the extent to which personal behavior was changed and the consequences such change produced. Frequent and cumulative communication with participants throughout the year provided an integration and balance of in-house and out-of-house experience and basis for evaluation and recommendation of each participant's self-initiated program for improvement. This conference is typical of a number of exceptionally fine in-service training experiences for educators within their regional area.

Learning institutes have provided new avenues for the initiation of ideas without fear of embarrassment or reprisal. Under such circumstances, valuable reference materials can be supplied by institute leaders and resource personnel, and unusual opportunities can be offered to work on practical problems that are of immediate concern to faculty. The learning institute may make some teachers aware of the need for taking college or university courses that will update their understanding of new concepts in the field; it may point out new ways in which students can be motivated to take on self-induced responsibilities related to their program; and it may give incentive to teachers to spend more time reading about their particular areas of interest as well as prepare more of their own materials for class use. Newer teachers, in particular, will find the typical institute a most constructive experience, while older teachers may wish to pursue more independent activities as a basis for permitting sufficient attention to the unique problems that confront them. Following any learning-institute program, adequate time is essential for the examination and analysis of the findings of the institute group and for this information to be disseminated to all interested personnel.

Professional Meetings

Attendance at educational conventions, conferences, and professional meetings have proven to be a valuable experience for educational personnel. How do most boards of education feel about these professional meetings? The National Education Association found that school boards believe that these meetings benefit both the individual who participates and his school district.[10] At these conferences, school leaders are given an opportunity for face-to-face contacts with persons in positions similar to their own. Such contacts result in the exchange of ideas and participants return with new ideas and enthusiasm for improvement in the school program.

Relative to *value*, the study found that many school districts have written statements attesting to the value of participation in professional groups. Sometimes professional meetings can substitute for in-service training and some districts find it more economical to send personnel to a special meeting than to organize a program within the district. Many school districts have pride in their programs and send people to professional meetings so that others will learn about the district and recognize their leadership. A recent nationwide survey showed that over 90 percent of the school districts surveyed encouraged participa-

[10] *NEA Research Bulletin*, "Attendance at Professional Meetings," vol. 40, no. 2 (May 1962), pp. 46–47. See also Stephen Knezevich, *Administration of Public Education* (New York: Harper and Row, 1969), pp. 201–205.

tion in professional organizations and attendance at meetings. In terms of *policy*, many school districts have developed written statements that usually specify circumstances under which school personnel may attend meetings and regulations on reimbursement of expenses. Selected in a variety of ways are the meetings to attend and the *delegates* to go. Often the board of education annually approves a list of meetings together with the staff members who will be permitted to go.

What about the *conditions* of attendance? The following questions should be asked: Will the meetings benefit the school system? Is the meeting's subject field appropriate to the assignment of the individual? Is the location convenient? Has the opportunity to attend meetings been fairly distributed among the staff? Is the person who is to attend the meeting a member of the organization? Some school districts have committees to screen applications, select meetings, and make recommendations concerning the representative. *Reports* are often made, either orally or in writing, after meetings. In this way the district assures itself that those who attend conferences and conventions have an opportunity to share their experiences with their colleagues. Finally, a recent Educational Research Service survey of *expenses* showed that more than three-quarters of the districts surveyed provided funds for this expenditure. The funds represented a fraction of one percent of the total budget. Almost all of the districts indicated a substitute teacher is supplied at district expense with no loss of salary to the teacher attending. Some districts allocate budgets for each department in proportion to the number of teachers working in each area. Other districts provide a budget and divide the available money among the different schools in the district according to the number of teachers in each school.

Professional Study and Experiences

The 1970's have ushered in a strong trend for school districts to require evidence that the teacher has been an active participant in professional-growth activities as a condition for new salary increments. Generally this growth is expected to be verified periodically, and it frequently is reflected in the number of institutional credits that must be earned as a matter of board policy. Many school districts require that the teacher earn at least six semester or eight quarter hours of college credit within a five- or six-year period. Extension courses have been a popular vehicle for obtaining the required units, although more teachers are taking advantage of sabbatical leave opportunities to gain additional units as well as advanced degrees and credentials. Large numbers of institutions have been offering clinical experiences for credit, both on and off the campus, as a means of providing greater "reality" to the content of varied courses. Few restrictions have been placed on the type of courses that may be taken for credit. This decision is almost invariably left to the individual; he determines which particular program will be of the greatest benefit to him professionally.

A large percentage of school districts give credit for travel as a means of meeting the district salary hurdle classification. Many state and national associations schedule fascinating and reasonable travel packages to areas all over the world and make this avenue of professional growth ever more inviting and rewarding.

In addition to course work and travel, many districts give credit for a variety of professional assignments that are not only rewarding to the district, but to the individual as well. With "involvement" representing a key element in any stage of self-development, districts are exceptionally anxious to give support to worthy professional activities of this type.

Participation in publication, writing, and research are prime areas of interest for growth credit. Forward-looking school districts recognize these enterprises as some of the most satisfying accomplishments of the professional educator—to become involved in the hard, analytical, and logical processes that must be followed if one is to place himself in a position of creating written materials that are significant, accurate, and interesting. Many larger districts feel a serious obligation to encourage their teaching staffs to engage in this productive research activity and are now more willing to budget funds for this.

Miscellaneous growth credits are acceptable for many activities that are too numerous to mention. Suffice it to say that professional-growth evaluation committees often are established on the district level and have the responsibility of determining growth credits from a variety of experiences. Bulletins and information developed by this committee are extremely helpful to teachers in assisting them to become better acquainted with a large number of unique and challenging professional-growth experiences that are available.

ANALYZING METHODS

There has been much concern with what constitutes the most effective methods for achieving instructional improvement on a widespread basis at the school or district level. In essence, the kind of help that teachers consider most desirable is an important factor in determining the supervisory techniques that will be of greatest assistance in improving the teaching-learning that occurs. Several of these methods shall be anlayzed here.

Most teachers consider school or district workshops as an extremely valuable supervisory technique. They find these sessions to be very productive in assisting them in their work. Department or grade-level meetings have been found to be very helpful, particularly when there are outside resource people present to lend support to the deliberations of the group. In some instances, administrators or supervisors have been requested to chair such meetings and these have been very successful. Special assignment or short-term-committee groups have found great favor with teachers. They consider that these meetings permit an in-depth study of many of the vexing problems that confront the teacher. They have found that the only way to attack them is to band together in a committee organization of this type as a means of seeking some solutions. Some of these groups have met successfully for a year or more and have been evaluated as one of the best in-service training opportunities provided by the district. Classroom observation by administrative or supervisory personnel has been found to be significantly beneficial to the development of improved classroom teaching techniques. When the emphasis is placed upon a mutual review of the kinds of learning experiences that should be taking place, teachers favor this kind of tactic. In most instances, however, teachers prefer to be able to call upon the administrator or supervisor to come in for a scheduled visit that has been requested by the teacher whenever he feels that he needs assistance. After the observation has been made, teachers consider that a conference must be held with the observer so that his thoughts and suggestions resulting from the visit can be made known to them. Also, teachers are anxious to engage in a two-way dialog with the observer to clear up any misunderstandings or unwarranted interpretations that may have occurred as a result of the visit. Teachers feel, too, that there is a need through the personal conference to place the segment of the lesson observed in its proper perspective with the long-range goals of the class. In addition to the conference that is held following the visitation, teachers are anxious to schedule an informal conference with the administrator or supervisor at any time that they consider this to be necessary.

A high percentage of teachers like the opportunity of visiting other teachers' classes as a means of obtaining new ideas that may be used in their own classroom teaching. These teachers feel that they are able to absorb more quickly "on the scene" concepts related to practical methods that they can use in their own classroom procedures. Demonstration lessons are looked upon with favor by most teachers as a method by which highly-skilled teachers or outside experts can simulate typical learning experiences that are related to their own classroom situations.

Of somewhat lesser effectiveness are faculty meetings in which the traditional emphasis has been on routine announcements and the like. Teachers feel that these meetings could be of much more value if they were scheduled on the basis of need and there was a chance to present constructive ideas and suggestions as a main portion of the agenda. Supervisory bulletins were considered most helpful when they were published on a regularly scheduled basis and written by an editor skilled in this area. Too often, however, this was not the case and the supervisory bulletins issued on a sporadic, casual basis tended to lose their effectiveness. Utilizing the services of an outside consultant is not often considered as being extremely helpful to teachers. Too often teachers are uninformed as to the purposes that the outside consultants are expected to fulfill and, furthermore, they are somewhat fearful of the results of a critical analysis of the educational program by these individuals. Only when the teachers themselves wished the help of outside consultants were their services considered of high value by the faculty.

Of least value to teachers in terms of the improvement of instruction are those activities in which there is little or no close working relationship with other members of the faculty. Attendance at required county institute sessions, taking course work at an institution of higher learning, attending district meetings that are called by the supervisory staff, and working on individual projects that are suggested by the administration are illustrative of these. It is apparent that faculty members do not place a high value on experiences that are both individual and involuntary in nature. In each instance, it is the responsibility of the supervisor or administrator to seek for a voluntary willingness on the part of each of these teachers to do that which appears necessary and important to them. No sizable gains in teacher professional growth will be visible until there is a spontaneous desire on the part of the teacher to participate in these activities.

Behavior patterns of administrators and supervisors performing their supervisory tasks must become more discernible and discreet as they relate to the growth of students and teachers within the educational design of the school. New administrators and supervisors may wish to log their activities so that later they can analyze their behavior and compare it with those behaviors that others have found to be highly successful. Each activity should be reviewed as a means of determining whether or not it is representative of a good supervisory approach.

Making Decisions About In-Service Education

The Far West Laboratory for Educational Research and Development has stated that as yet educators are not in a position to be prescriptive about in-service education. The present state of research is not definitive enough to serve as a basis on which to mandate in-service education practices. However, given the present state of knowledge about research and innovations, educators do have some bases for making decisions about in-service education practices. Educators can question whether proposed in-service education practices:

1. Relate to what is going on in individual schools and communities.
2. Involve teachers and administrators in planning.
3. Choose as initial participants personnel who express interest in change.
4. Differentiate various kinds of programs appropriate for various groups and individuals.
5. Diagnose individual teacher readiness for various kinds of programs.
6. Specify cognitive, affective, and skill objectives in performance terms.
7. Emphasize process as well as content (teacher as catalyst in learning process rather than information dispenser).
8. Utilize appropriate patterns (intensive group experience, task team, interaction analysis, microteaching, etc.).
9. Choose appropriate media (open or closed circuit television, videotape, programmed instruction, etc.).
10. Use staff appropriately (staff teams, principal, supervisor, clinical professor, consultant, etc.).
11. Provide prime time and adequate support money.
12. Provide for evaluation and develop evaluation instruments that emphasize feedback based on classroom situations (self-evaluation, peer evaluation, pupil feedback, etc.).
13. Cooperate where appropriate with other schools, districts, colleges and universities, research and development centers, and regional laboratories.
14. Enlist a high level of community understanding and support.[11]

TWO ILLUSTRATIONS

A midwestern school district has utilized its faculty in completely planning and coordinating its early fall in-service meeting. The faculty planning committee concerned itself with educational trends, techniques, and changes that should be considered by teachers as they developed their curricular plans. The all-day in-service meeting devoted itself to stimulating teachers to recognize the needs of pupils, to provide information that would lend itself to the adoption of new ideas that would enrich classroom and out-of-classroom experiences, and to

[11]Dorothy Westby-Gibson, *Inservice Education: Perspectives for Educators* (Berkeley: Far West Laboratory for Educational Research and Development, 1967), p. 42.

give an overview of the many transitions that were taking place in the district curriculum. Two main speakers were provided who set the tone of the day's discussions. Following lunch, informal panel and clinic groups were scheduled to be chosen according to the teacher's interest. Displays were shown for various subject-area groups. Status leaders in the district had been available to the faculty planning committee for any help and advice in furthering the development of the in-service program. Every effort was made to assure the participants that their interest and concerns were being reflected in the development of the program.

A southwestern school district staff has developed an in-service training program for its elementary and secondary teachers that assists them in meeting district requirements for professional growth. Within a three-year period four credits are expected to be earned by the teacher through a variety of ways that the teacher may choose: satisfactory completion of courses at an accredited college or university, attendance at in-service training classes or workshops authorized by the board of education, participation in authorized curriculum-study committees, and by approved travel. The district, through its faculty planning groups, has made every effort to provide exciting and informative sessions that involve faculty participation, include the use of outside resource people where possible, and offer individual follow-up by teachers with status leaders and outside experts after the meetings. An example of the schedule of in-service meetings for elementary teachers is shown below as Fig. 8–2.

SUMMARY

The previous discussion has dealt in part with the process of group activity at a highly sophisticated, professional level. It has given direction to the evolvement of several specialized forms of group work, the strategy that must take place if the group is to be effective, and the kinds of demands that are placed upon the person or persons who assume positions of leadership in such situations. The whole cognitive process demands the highest order of skill in promoting group work so that each of these sessions for the group members can become a self-teaching device. The intricacies involved in the meshing of a multitude of differing personalities, ambitions, and expectations calls for an organizational structure that will suffice to meet the basic purposes for which the group was established.

The status leader must be alert to helping the teacher become aware of the needs of the group. He should be perceptive of the changing climate found in the shifting inter-relationships of the members of

Date, Time, Grade Level	Title	Description	Place
Tuesday January 5 3:50 p.m. All Teachers	MOTIVATION IN READING THROUGH CREATIVE THINKING AND DOING	Motivation as a stimulating catalyst cannot be overlooked in the reading process. Motivation not only acts as a stimulus that makes students read more but gives them a basis that leads to deeper understanding of what they have read. This type of motivation leads to self-motivation, which is the goal we hope to attain.	Instructional Aids Service Center Room 2
Thursday January 7 3:30 p.m. Primary Teachers	SCIENCE OUTSIDE YOUR DOOR	What elements or phenomena are just outside the classroom door, which provide motivation for exploration and discovery of basic science concepts? How do we use these most effectively with primary children? The District's new Teacher's Guide on Science Instruction will be used as a reference.	Mesa School
Thursday January 7 3:55 p.m. 6th Grade Teachers	SOCIAL STUDIES: MEXICO	"Classroom tested" ideas for projects, activities and techniques for a depth study of Mexico. This meeting will be of particular interest to teachers doing a study of Mexico the second semester.	Instructional Aids Service Center Room 2
Monday January 11 3:30 p.m. Corvallis Faculty	IMPLEMENTING MODERN MATH IN GRADE 7 #5	The fifth in a series devoted to familiarization with the new State textbooks in mathematics and development of instructional methods and materials.	Corvallis Intermediate School
Tuesday January 12 3:50 p.m. All Teachers	TESTING IN READING	Reading tests will be evaluated and their values determined. Basic group reading tests will be used as individual reading tests. The selection of tests for various purposes will be discussed.	Administration Building Room 32
Tuesday January 12 3:15 p.m. Wright Faculty	IMPLEMENTING MODERN MATH IN GRADE 7 #3	The third in a series devoted to familiarization with the new State textbooks in mathematics and development of instructional methods and materials.	Wright Intermediate School Room 23
Tuesday January 12 3:15 p.m. Grade 3 Selected Committee	MATH PLANNING COMMITTEE #1	Familiarization and utilization of the new State textbook in mathematics adopted for grade three and development of plans for presentation of workshops in your own building.	Instructional Aids Service Center Room 2
Wednesday January 3 3:55 p.m. All teachers	LEARNING FROM EDUCATIONAL FILMS	Various techniques will be presented for introducing an educational film with examples of follow-up activities.	Instructional Aids Service Center Room 2

Fig. 8–2. A Schedule of In-Service Meetings.

Date, Time, Grade Level	Title	Description	Place
Wednesday January 13 K-3 3:00 p.m. 4-6 4:00 p.m. Hoxie, Nuffer, Glazier, Elmcroft, Morrison, New River Teachers	PROVIDING FOR THE GIFTED IN THE ELEMENTARY SCHOOL (Limited to teachers with pupils identified and screened for MGM program)	Enrichment practices and materials, as they relate to specific endowments of those pupils identified. Beginning of a series of meetings to be set up in seminar-type groups for continuation of the study and implementation of the district program.	New River School
Thursday January 14 K-3 3:00 p.m. 4-6 4:00 p.m. Dolland, Grayland, Nottingham, Moffitt, Hargitt, Waite Teachers	SEE ABOVE	See above	Waite School Teacher's Dining Room
Thursday January 14 3:55 p.m. Grades 5-8	SMOKING AND HEALTH	How to develop a classroom program based upon scientific evidence regarding the harmful effects of cigarette smoking. A "Teachers Resource Kit on Smoking and Health" provided by the State Department of Education will be available for teacher use.	Instructional Aids Service Center Room 2
Wednesday January 20 2:45 p.m. 1st Grade Teachers	SCIENCE WORKSHOP FOR ALL FIRST GRADE TEACHERS	Stimulating first grade children's senses through science activities.	Instructional Aids Service Center Room 2
Wednesday January 20 3:15 p.m. Benton, McNally, Los Coyotes Teachers	PROVIDING FOR THE GIFTED IN THE ELEMENTARY SCHOOL (Limited to teachers with pupils identified and screened for the MGM program)	Enrichment practices and materials, as they relate to specific endowments of those pupils identified. Beginning of a series of meetings to be set up in seminar-type groups for continuation of the study and implementation of the district program.	Los Coyotes Teacher's Lounge
Thursday January 21 K-3 3:00 p.m. 4-6 4:00 p.m. Foster Road, Rancho, Gardenhill, Escalona, Hutchinson Teachers	SEE ABOVE	See Above	Rancho School
Thursday January 21 3:55 p.m. 6th Grade Teachers	SOCIAL STUDIES: BRAZIL	Projects and activities developed by teachers will be presented. This meeting will be of particular interest to teachers who will be doing a study of Brazil the second semester.	Instructional Aids Service Center Room 2

Fig. 8–2 (*continued*)

Date, Time, Grade Level	Title	Description	Place
Monday January 25 3:30 p.m. 'Wright Faculty	INDUSTRIAL ARTS EDUCATION	Specific activities, skills and processes in General Wood and Metal programs will be discussed at this regular meeting.	Wright Intermediate School
Monday January 25 3:15 p.m. Corvallis Faculty	IMPLEMENTING MODERN MATH IN GRADE 7 #6	The sixth in a series devoted to familiarization with the new State textbooks in mathematics and development of instructional methods and materials.	Corvallis Intermediate School
Tuesday January 26 3:15 p.m. Corvallis Faculty	IMPLEMENTING MODERN MATH IN GRADE 7 #4	The fourth in a series devoted to familiarization with the new State textbooks in mathematics and development of instructional methods and materials.	Wright Intermediate School
Tuesday January 26 3:15 p.m. Grade 3 Selected Committee	MATH PLANNING COMMITTEE #2	Familiarization and utilization of the new State textbook in mathematics adopted for grade three and development of plans for presentation of workshops in your own building.	Instructional Aids Service Center Room 2
Wednesday January 27 3:20 p.m. Homemaking Teachers	REGULAR MONTHLY MEETING	This will be a regular monthly meeting of the homemaking teachers. Audio-visual materials will be previewed.	Instructional Aids Service Center Room 10
Wednesday January 27 K-3 3:00 p.m. 4-6 4:00 p.m. Mesa, Dulles, Eastwood, Anthony, La Pluma, Kling Teachers	PROVIDING FOR THE GIFTED IN THE ELEMENTARY SCHOOL (Limited to teachers with pupils identified and screened for the MGM program)	Enrichment practices and materials, as they relate to specific endowments of those pupils identified. Beginning of a series of meetings to be set up in seminar-type groups for continuation of the study and implementation of the district program.	La Pluma School Teacher's Dining Room
Thursday January 28 3:20 p.m. Wright, Centennial, Los Alisos, Corvallis Teachers	SEE ABOVE	See above	Los Alisos Intermediate School Teacher's Lounge
Thursday January 28 3:55 p.m. Middle and Upper Grade Teachers	SCIENCE OUTSIDE YOUR DOOR	What elements or phenomena are just outside the classroom door which provide motivation for exploration and discovery of basic science concepts? How do we use these most effectively with middle and upper grade children? The District's new Teacher's Guide on Science Instruction will be used as a reference.	Mesa School

Fig. 8-2 (*continued*)

any group and be prepared to take any necessary action for the continued well-being of the group. He should assist the group in clarifying its task and help it to move toward the realization of its goals. In a very real sense, he must provide the means for the group to incorporate its concerns and its findings in terms that are meaningful to the individual members of the group. If the latter is possible, then the perceptiveness of the group can be transmitted to the person taking part and become a source of stimulation for his own teaching artistry.

In some respects there are several by-products of the group process: it helps the faculty to understand better the function of supervision; it offers a laboratory-type experience for the mutual solution of group and individual problems; and it provides a means for the supervisory staff to discover and learn about the problems that typically confront teachers. In the final analysis, the group process gives the teacher an opportunity to become excited about his own learning and improvement as a result of being involved in contagious, meaningful group experiences.

Helping the individual teacher demands that field-laboratory opportunities for the study of social and educational change must be afforded each person. Teachers should be encouraged to gather data about the whole entourage of the teaching profession, the dynamics of student learning, the critical role that they play in promoting instructional excellence, and the vast implications of the quality of the school upon the well-being of the community. Viewed in another fashion, the supervisory staff, as it works with the individual teacher, should operate a "clinic" that would provide a permanent, continuing diagnostic treatment center for the solution of problems inherent in its ever-expanding instructional role.

The many techniques described earlier are representative of some of the ways in which the administrator or supervisor attempts to slow down the process of obsolescence that will take place if the teacher ever stops learning. Undoubtedly the ideal situation would be one in which the supervisory environment was such that certificated personnel would become, in fact, self-teachers. Within this context the supervisory staff will become terribly serious about the individual differences of teachers. If, for instance, the individual teacher displays an instructional handicap, it will be the task of the staff to teach this person to harness his handicap and use it as a skill.

As the climate of the good one-to-one relationship develops between the administrator or supervisor and the teacher, the teacher must be encouraged to view instructional matters in a very critical manner, to ask any questions he may wish (even funny, unusual ones), and to feel that the supervisory staff really *wants* him to innovate and to seek change. For too long a period of time in educational history, the schools have tended to ignore innovative teachers—a situation that can no longer be permitted to exist. Through professional meetings, reading, self-analysis, research, and the like, the teacher must be given every chance to become a better teacher. The status leader must create for him a safe place where he can be open about his problems and have the assurance that he will receive the attention and help that he needs.

SELECTED REFERENCES

Association for Supervision and Curriculum Development. *Curriculum Materials.* Washington, D.C.: National Education Association, 1970.

Association of Teacher Educators. *Teaching is Communicating: Nonverbal Language in the Classroom.* Washington, D.C.: National Education Association, 1970.

Educational Research Service. *Attendance at Professional Conferences and Conventions.* Washington, D.C.: National Education Association, 1969.

Kraft, L.E. *Secondary School Principal in Action.* Dubuque: William C. Brown, 1971.

Martin, Jane. *Explaining, Understanding, and Teaching.* New York: McGraw-Hill, 1970.

National Association of Secondary School Principals. *Learning in The Summer.* Washington, D.C.: National Education Association, 1970.

Rubin, Louis J. *Improving In-service Education: Proposals and Procedures for Change.* Boston: Allyn and Bacon, 1971.

Wilson, John A. R. *Diagnosis of Learning Difficulties.* New York: McGraw-Hill, 1971.

Wilson, L.C. *Open Access Curriculum.* Rockleigh, N. J.: Allyn and Bacon, 1971.

CHAPTER 9

Laboratories
and the New Technology

As the new media become more commonplace in educational institutions, the option for those school systems that have chosen to disregard them has decreased. With so much more to be learned by so many in a relatively short space of time, the decision not to turn towards the new instructional technology in the decade of the 1970's becomes a shortsighted and disastrous one indeed. New information and knowledge have not only become more voluminous; they are subjected constantly to the forces of movement and diffusion as the lines of communication are ever more closely interwoven within the educational structure. Even the design of facilities in school houses all over the nation is showing an awareness of the revolution that is taking place, not only in the rapid motion in ideas, but the stress that is being placed on a new technology of teaching and learning. Learning laboratories, curriculum centers, professional libraries, staff-development projects, and system analysis are all fabrics that are being woven into the in-service training programs of teachers to galvanize the schools into action.

New and highly organized techniques have brought about the installation of a variety of controls upon the educational process. To assist the teacher in becoming the controlling agent in executing the most modern and effective learning methods in the classroom, various laboratory and media situations have been organized. These in-service provisions are essential techniques in increasing the self-improvement opportunities for teachers.

185

THE CURRICULUM LABORATORY

Basically the curriculum laboratory is an ideal place for teachers and staff members to rework raw materials into finished items for classroom teaching. In a real sense it is a staging area where data about teaching aids are collected, studied, and put into practical use for teaching children. In a variety of ways it provides for the pursuit of curriculum study, development, and improvement. Individuals and groups have a constructive meeting place in the curriculum laboratory under the professional leadership of those who help plan the curriculum. Perhaps most important, it is a place where teachers participate in experimentation, where they create or invent instructional aids and techniques used with children in the learning process.

The curriculum laboratory is in a unique position to assist teaching personnel in their constant efforts to upgrade and improve the curriculum. Fortunately there are several possible levels on which a curriculum laboratory can function: federal, state, intermediate district, local, and college. Each of these types has its own unique function in furthering curriculum activity by using its laboratories on an experimental basis as a means of encouraging other groups to provide their own laboratory facilities. At the state level department of education personnel can go into the field to work with those who are interested in organizing a local laboratory. A large reservoir of curricular items should be stored in a state depository and be available for distribution to those districts that request them. The intermediate district curriculum laboratory will represent an important link with those local districts that wish to promote laboratory opportunities, but do not have the facilities or the budget. Many reports and materials, as well as counsel, may be offered by the intermediate district to those districts that do have laboratories and are seeking help in developing projects. At the local district level there will be an excellent opportunity for teachers to become involved in many laboratory experiences. It will be possible for teachers to create original teaching aids with laboratory materials; to receive assistance in designing, developing, and using instructional aids; to attend scheduled workshops and demonstrations; to witness the demonstration of new methods and materials; to discover free materials; to see displays of other teachers' projects that could be adapted to their own classroom needs; and to attend study-group sessions and grade-level meetings. Finally, at the college level a great deal of exploratory curriculum work can be accomplished during the student teacher training program. Some colleges and universities assign curriculum laboratory units in which the student develops materials that will aid him in his forthcoming teaching assignments.

The curriculum laboratory has many significant functions at a variety of levels. Through the proper coordination of effort from these various laboratories, much can be done to vitalize curriculum development for the individual teacher.

Developing a Curriculum Laboratory

The planning of the physical facilities of the curriculum laboratory requires that a careful inventory be made of the needs and requirements of faculty members who will be served. The facility should be housed in a centralized area and be easily accessible to members of the staff as a place where faculty personnel fashion new materials into finished products for classroom use. The curriculum laboratory is an ideal facility in which to exhibit teaching aids and to encourage their employment in the teaching of children. Both individuals and groups will wish to be able to schedule their time in the laboratory and to enlist the aid of their professional colleagues who have the responsibility for planning the curriculum. Space requirements demand that several areas be available for small-group meetings, conferences, storage and construction of materials, and workrooms for the creation of new and exciting instructional methods and aids.

The typical district curriculum laboratory will house a variety of filed materials and equipment: manuals, textbooks, courses of study, transparencies, ERIC documents, audio tapes, and many other articles of interest. The director of the laboratory will have the responsibility of providing pertinent information to faculty members as to their use and potential.

The director of the curriculum laboratory will be in a position to make many critical decisions concerning the planning, functioning, and evaluation of the laboratory program. In-service education is an important phase of the laboratory's role and the director's responsibility will include orienting new teachers in the selection and use of numerous new materials and techniques.

Many curriculum laboratories are open throughout the year and faculty utilization of the facilities is voluntary. At times entire faculties will wish to come to the laboratory for a workshop or study session. Off-duty teachers, on many occasions, will frequent the laboratory during vacation months. Some surveys have shown that as high as eighty to ninety percent of district faculty members will avail themselves of laboratory services and many of those teachers will use it a large number of times.

Making the Curriculum Laboratory Effective

One of the major tasks confronting status leaders in supervision is to make the curriculum laboratory or curriculum-development center into a more effective agency for the cooperative improvement of education. To accomplish this, curriculum laboratories, as well as instructional-materials centers, will be consuming greater amounts of space within the school with a corresponding decrease in the proportion of traditional administrative office arrangements. Increasing emphasis will be upon the unique needs of the individual teacher and his quest for information and materials of instruction. Thus, greater numbers of options will allow the teacher to choose the particular educational approaches to develop for his classroom use in conjunction with a personal style that he considers best adapted to his teaching situation. Greater amounts of budgetary expenditures will be made, not only on laboratory facilities and equipment, but on services, supplies, and software as well. Quick access to information and materials will be provided the teacher as well as competent advice or assistance whenever it is needed or desirable. The laboratory station will concentrate on local area concerns, provide a free exchange system with other district laboratories of ideas and materials (where possible), and cooperate in many ways with regional laboratories and publication centers (to be discussed later).

In a sense, the curriculum laboratory needs to be an educational scanning station that attempts to provide faculty personnel with a highly sophisticated level of information on educational developments and trends. If successful, the laboratory can have a stimulating effect on the creation of improved educational policies and techniques for the district.

The operation of the curriculum laboratory cannot become a finished or closed system. Status leaders will need to build a scheme that will permit the development and utilization of the laboratory to be an ongoing process. Linkage agents should be provided between the local curriculum-laboratory effort and other local agencies as well. Laboratory experiences can permit faculty members to investigate and construct together as a team whenever they wish; as part of an educational man-machine operation, these experiences can provide improved performance expectations that might not be possible if attempted individually. As a vigorous facility that fosters communication and self-growth, the laboratory should stimulate faculty to increase their study efforts, improve the chances of bringing about change, increase the opportunities for collaboration and team effort, and move the faculty towards a more significant role in strengthening the organizational climate of the local agency.

REGIONAL LABORATORIES AND PUBLICATION CENTERS

Regional Laboratories

Typical of the new regional laboratories established under Title IV of the Elementary and Secondary Education Act is the Southwest Regional Laboratory for Educational Research and Development. This laboratory has been established under a joint Powers Agreement and is concerned with the educational needs and resources of the region that it serves. The regional laboratory program was established to translate research findings into products and processes that could be utilized immediately by local school systems. Cooperation between various regional laboratories permits a coordinated attack on national education problems as well as reflecting the educational needs of local areas.

Problems considered essential for investigation by the Southwest Regional Laboratory are: pupil mobility and how it affects educational progress; identification of skills generally required in the primary grades and considered essential to success in learning; and the continuation of training and re-training of teachers, researchers, and product developers. The Laboratory uses a pragmatic approach to the solution of educational problems; it is product-oriented with the objective of producing reliably tested exportable and reproducible material and procedures applicable to the school setting; it is user-oriented so that teachers and administrators are involved in all phases of product development from planning through implementation; it employs self-correcting procedures in each of its projects, and continuous evaluation enables revisions in projects to be made at any time.

Although six or seven of the new regional laboratories are now closed for lack of federal support, the remaining laboratories appear to be having rather remarkable success in the area of curriculum development. Serious attempts are being made to have the important findings of these laboratories disseminated to the local district levels so that they can incorporate them in their own experimental programs.

State Curriculum Publication Centers

In order to make up-to-date curriculum publication materials available throughout the state, the California State Department of Education has established eighteen curriculum publication centers at strategic locations based on population density and geographical accessibility. With regional curriculum development uppermost in the plan, the State Department is attempting to reduce the amount of duplication in the state curriculum materials that are published. Local district supervisors and administrators will find curriculum materials developed throughout the state readily available and thereby save a great deal of local district and school time that might be spent in developing materials that have been developed and published elsewhere in the state.

Curriculum development leadership, for some time to come, will be in the hands of scholars and experts with local district personnel following the guidelines set up by these regional and national groups. The National Education Association's Project on Instruction, too, has recommended the desirability of such curriculum development centers. As a result, local supervisory personnel must be certain that these regional materials become adapted and implemented in ways that meet the needs of the learners in the local schools. Even with the existence of state curriculum centers, there is still much to be provided for by the local curriculum library at the district level.

A Proposal

President Nixon has proposed the creation of a National Institute of Education that would focus on educational research and experimentation in the United States. The purpose of the National Institute of Education would be to begin the serious, systematic search for new knowledge needed to make educational opportunity equal. It would take the lead in developing new measurements of educational output and would pay as much heed to the so-called "immeasurables" of schooling (largely because no one has yet learned to measure them) such as responsibility and humanity as it does to verbal and mathematical achievement. In developing these new measurements, the Institute may begin by comparing the actual educational effectiveness of schools in similar economic and geographic circumstances.

In its initial stages the Institute will offer a coherent approach to research and experimentation as a first step towards educational reform. While it would conduct basic and applied educational research itself, the Institute would direct a major portion of its research by contract with universities, non-profit institutions, and other organizations. Ultimately, related research activities of the Office of Education would be transferred to the Institute and educational research and experimentation of other Federal agencies would be linked by the Institute to national educational goals. Particular emphasis will be given to the furtherance of the Experimental Schools program.

THE PROFESSIONAL LIBRARY

Greater emphasis is being placed upon providing today's classroom teachers with the latest ideas in their various subject-matter areas. To do this, many school systems are developing professional libraries at the building or central office level so that every teacher has direct access to the intellectual resources so necessary in his work. Numerous districts are receiving strong financial assistance from federal or state agencies to make this possible.

Many in-service training programs for teachers are greatly aided by the installation of a professional library. The vast amount of written materials that attempt to assist faculty members in keeping aware of the developments in their individual fields must be organized so that they are readily available to the staff. Many other types of materials also essential to the assisting of pupils in their work should be displayed so that faculty members will be encouraged to use them.

The American Library Association has recommended several conditions that should exist for professional libraries. These should consist of: a basic book collection of two hundred to one thousand titles depending on the size and needs of the faculty; twenty-five to fifty professional magazine subscriptions; pamphlets, filmstrips, curriculum guides, resource units, and other instructional items; a minimum annual expenditure of $200 to $800 depending on the size of the faculty and the availability of other professional materials; and administrator, teacher, and librarian participation in the selection of the materials.

A basic service that the professional library should provide is coordinating many of the intellectual activities of the school. In this way there can be a strong crosscurrent of exchange of faculty ideas. Reference data must be made available and a plan made that will lead to the development of curriculum materials at both the school and the district level. As materials are selected for the library, they should be carefully reviewed by the faculty to assure them that there is an equitable distribution between the various disciplines or areas of the school.

The board of education might include in its policies statements that pertain to the perpetuation of the professional library so that it can be assured of continued support. Administrators and supervisors should recognize that the library offers one of the best avenues for the expansion and enrichment of professional reading habits of the staff. Periodically, teachers will wish to receive from the supervisor bulletin information regarding recent acquisitions and special collections of information to be found in the library.

The professional library should be financed as a special item in the district budget and sufficient moneys allocated for its support. The librarian is the person responsible for proper expenditures and should provide an annual financial statement to the district office.

Significant research journals can be purchased on microfilm which adds an important new dimension to the materials that can be housed in the professional library. Photocopying machines are extremely useful in aiding teachers who wish to have copies made of original materials that can be used or displayed in the classroom. Magafile boxes for storing journals and other materials as well as Princeton files are excellent means of housing large collections of items that teachers may wish to use in their entirety.

The professional library should be conveniently located, it should house the essential reading materials that teachers will need, and it should be organized and directed by a professional librarian who can provide the services required by teachers. In many respects the librarian will have to be a public relations expert so that persons in the community will understand the purposes and basic services that the library fulfills. His task will include planning, organizing, administering, and evaluating all phases of the professional library service so that it will meet the professional growth demands of the school and the system.

MEDIA AND DEVELOPMENT CENTERS

Curriculum reconstruction has set in motion an important flow of ideas in the field of American education. As curriculum developments are based on a spirit of inquiry, on experimentation in many fields of knowledge, and on taking a close look at both the known and the unknown, educators find greater and greater need to rely upon specialized devices that can aid them in implementing educational objectives. Covering the entire field of knowledge within the curriculum has become a sheer impossibility. Therefore, greater reliance must be placed on sharing certain pieces of knowledge that can be woven into conceptual patterns for pupils as a basis for living and further learning. The emphasis placed upon questioning as opposed to teaching illustrates the direction that education is taking toward investigation and discovery. New devices and resources are intended to supplement the teacher's effectiveness and their introduction requires the assistance of development centers and institutes to assure their use. Through these centers the supervisors must be given help in bringing people to the point where they are willing to learn new behaviors and take part in new and cooperative activities. Bridging the gap between the traditional and the new-media approach is a challenging task for development centers and regional institutes to fulfill.

Relating Content and Learning Processes to Media

The properties of the new media make possible a completely new and different approach to the study of teaching and the curriculum for professional teacher development. This conceptual framework is developed by:[1]

Extending Human Capacities. The limitations of human sight, hearing, attention, and concentration in the study of teaching are reduced by magnification, amplification, selectivity, and isolation. Deficiencies of recall and interpretation are minimized by authenticity, reproductivity, and simplification of observed phenomena.

Providing New Content. The whole of teaching experience becomes available by the removal of the limitations imposed by time, space, and distance. Replication, collation, integration, and authenticity make a new kind of relevant content available for study.

Interrelating Existing Content. The observation, demonstration, and participation activities of the teacher reach higher levels of efficiency and pertinence. Concurrent interrelated observations (simultaneity) of acts of teaching and acts of learning are better related for more effective teacher development.

Increasing Learning Potential. Perception may be expanded, tryout situations simulated, and feedback provided by a variety of new media. Automation, immediacy, and variation increase the possibilities for meeting individual differences and special interests of teachers.

Collectively, media materials are a way of bringing recent research, learning, and technology together and approaching a problem. The selective and planned use of new media for the improvement of the professional sequence of teacher education demands an analytical approach. If the new media are to be used effectively, the users must answer the "for what?" and "why?" questions. The media used must be an integral part of planning rather than an adjunct to an established operational design. The conceptual development of teacher education requires content relevance, interrelatedness, internal consistency, and potential for media utilization in the development of objectives and curriculum.

Components of the New Technology

Educational technologists frequently insist that the system approach be utilized in introducing and using the new media. There must be a close association between equipment and the school curriculum, and instructional technology is a powerful tool to bridge the gap. Basi-

---

[1] American Association of Colleges for Teacher Education, *Professional Teacher Education* (Washington, D.C.: The Association, 1968), pp. 68–69.

cally there are eight important components of a system analysis that should be considered by any school district planning to introduce new technology:[2]

1. *Capability of the hardware.* Actually such an appraisal is difficult because of the lack of independent standards for judgment. In a few instances, overzealous hardware peddlers have tried to realize a quick profit at the expense of school systems. They have thus undermined the more responsible approach taken by the majority of companies in this field.
2. *Capability of the software (program).* As Hilda Taba (1967) warned: "There is danger of harnessing million-dollar gadgets to ten-cent ideas." This problem remains critical.
3. *Nature of the community.* Communities, as indicated earlier, vary in their receptivity to new technology. Furthermore, some media may be suitable to one situation and not to another.
4. *Individual difference considerations.* Technological aids such as educational television may be designed for group presentation without contributing to a school's plan for individualization.
5. *Teacher factors.* Teachers may resist the introduction of new technology. Because of inadequate teacher education, they may not be adequately informed about technology. They may feel that the use of new media will add an extra burden of time and effort. To offset these problems, teachers must be involved in program implementation. Furthermore, teachers need retooling to use the new technology effectively.
6. *Curricular coordination.* Curriculum specialists must also be involved to insure that educational technology is geared to the continuity, scope, and sequence of the curriculum.
7. *The nature of the subject matter.* With our present state of development some subjects and some aspects of these subjects are more appropriate to the application of educational technology than others.
8. *Evaluation procedures.* As is the case with the total instructional program, plans for the evaluation of educational technology should be carefully designed so that adequate feedback is available.

Instructional media relates to many performance factors; most important among them is arousing interest and promoting the change process. Media are profitable devices for both large groups and individual use, and they do strengthen and speed up the process of adoption and acceptance of new ideas and methods.

[2]Richard I. Miller, "Educational Technology and Professional Practice," Address to the John Dewey Society, Dallas, Texas, March 11, 1967.

Staff Development Centers

Several staff development centers have been recommended for location in or near school campuses. These centers would have university or college affiliation on a contractual basis and would contain a highly diversified staff. Each center's staff would consist of supervisors and curriculum specialists, career teachers, university or college faculty personnel, psychologists, social workers, and community ombudsmen. These professionals would provide teaching services, in-service training experiences, and assistance to school faculty members and teachers, as well as being extremely visible to members of the community. Highly sophisticated materials of instruction can be developed by these centers, and, in some areas, centers such as these virtually have become the focal point for the improvement of curriculum and instruction for the entire school program. Both consultant assistance and teacher instruction is made available by specialized professionals whose function it is to stimulate inquiry and evaluation in their broadest sense.

Some experts have advocated the development of teacher-directed centers in which the local teachers' association or professional council assumes the responsibilty for providing teaching, observation, and conferencing to assist the classroom teacher. On a collegial basis, the teacher-directed centers would offer laboratory services completely devoid of any supervisory or administrative overtones.

IDEA: A Program in Action

Illustrative of the Staff Development Center concept is the Institute for the Development of Educational Activities (IDEA). Recognizing one of the greatest needs in education in the 1970's, IDEA has provided the means for the wide dissemination of cognition about the new and hopeful innovations found in education today. It considers the individual school unit as one of the most strategic elements to be found as a basis for educational change. The school has a body politic consisting of young and old from the community and it is staffed with professionals who utilize the facilities to shape an educational program that has relevance to youth. It contains, therefore, all the necessary ingredients against which plans for the future can be made.

Over twenty schools in Southern California are members of the League of Cooperating Schools, a subsidiary of IDEA. Regular conferences and work sessions, school consultations and observations, study, research, and planning bring about a climate for change within the League. Boards of education and superintendents, committed to the project through formal action and agreement, lend support to the new innovative procedures that are begun in these schools. Principals and the Research and Development staff become attuned to each other's interests and approaches as the result of summer-session meetings and bi-monthly conferences.

The schools in the League form the basis for a vast laboratory for educational research. Very different schools located in diverse school districts are tied together in a cooperative agreement designed to utilize as effectively as possible the mutual interests and collaborative resources of all the cooperating educational units. This collective effort represents a research enterprise designed to examine processes of change and to evaluate special projects. The League stimulates similar innovative activities in many schools; it provides an unusual setting for the education of teachers, for discovering more about how best to conduct the educational enterprise; and it coordinates the exchange of personnel and ideas as well as the training of research workers and educational leaders. Once an innovation has survived the League, it will be taken by IDEA's Innovation and Dissemination Division and put into practice by a consortium of demonstration schools which will perform a crucial function in the innovation process because they will attempt to carry on where most efforts stop. These demonstration schools will attempt to bridge the gap that has traditionally separated research and innovation from actual practice in the school.

A Materials Dissemination Center has been operative to serve educators participating in IDEA's demonstration schools. It gives direct support to the demonstration schools and is available to serve schools which need assistance in the building of curricula specifically designed for continuous progress. IDEA's Information and Services Division operates a variety of programs designed to generate and spread new developments in school improvement. It has spearheaded several projects such as: (1) summer institutes for school administrators; (2) institutes for professors of education; (3) seminars designed to establish priorities in the elementary school; (4) seminars to explore the impact of new technology on education; (5) seminars for the purpose of investigating the progress and impact of the new chemistry of learning; (6) educational newsletters; (7) international conferences on education; (8) educational surveys conducted by George Gallup; (9) youth conferences on education; and (10) production of films dealing with educational improvement. The Educational Grants Division, through the medium of grants, supports research beyond the scope of internally organized and operated programs. This Division constantly taps the vast reservoir of ever increasing knowledge and it is especially designed to generate new ideas outside of the organization; but through its close relationship with other line divisions these ideas are incorporated into action programs.

The typical public institution often considers that it must insulate itself against the possibility of becoming involved in a high risk operation. It does not wish to sanction the right to become involved in an operation that might fail. The structure of IDEA forthrightly encounters the high risk and failure factors and exerts every effort to make new ideas become operable through the existence and acknowledgment of an experimental design for the continuance of the trial and error process. Even a new organization such as IDEA may become involved in redesigning itself through its innovative programs. The linkage system is a powerful agent for change and its full use may release the conceptual thrust that is necessary to mount an effective educational program that is change oriented.

SUMMARY

In viewing any instructional practice that holds much promise, the area of curricular aids and facilities should be thought of as an approach that is barely in its infancy. With the vast expansion of new instructional media, the teacher will feel the need for ever-increasing assistance from resource centers to keep abreast of new educational developments. In addition, there will be a feeling of personal satisfaction as a result of keeping up-to-date on the latest developments and techniques in one's professional field. Only through such resource centers can the supervisory staff hope to replenish continually the many "idea" needs of the teaching force.

SELECTED REFERENCES

Association for Educational Communications and Technology. *Basic Guide for Media and Technology in Teacher Education.* Washington, D.C.: National Education Association, 1970.

Association for Educational Communications and Technology. *Technology and The Management of Instruction.* Washington, D.C.: National Education Association, 1970.

Davis, H. S. *Instructional Media Center.* Bloomington: Indiana University Press, 1971.

Evan, William M. *Organizational Experiments: Laboratory and Field Research.* New York: Harper and Row, 1970.

Fuchs, W. R. *New Learning: Technology in the Service of Education.* New York: Herder and Herder, 1971.

Jacobs, Paul I., Milton A. Maier, and Lawrence M. Stolurow. *A Guide to Evaluating Self-Instructional Programs.* New York: Holt, Rinehart and Winston, 1966.

Lindsey, Margaret, and Associates. *Inquiry Into Teaching Behavior of Supervi-*

sors in Teacher Education Laboratories. New York: Teachers College Press, 1969.

Martin, W. T., and Dan C. Peck. *Curriculum Improvement and Innovation: A Partnership of Students, School Teachers, and Research Scholars.* Cambridge, Mass.: Robert Bentley, 1966.

Rossi, Peter H., and Bruce J. Biddle. *The New Media and Education: Their Impact on Society.* Chicago: Aldine, 1967.

Smith, B. O. *Research in Teacher Education: A Symposium.* Englewood Cliffs: Prentice-Hall, 1971.

Smith, Karl U., and Margaret F. Smith. *Cybernetic Principles of Learning and Educational Design.* New York: Holt, Rinehart and Winston, 1966.

Evaluation and the Future

Part Four concerns itself with a forward-looking view on the cooperative evaluation of the effectiveness of teaching, on the continued evaluation of the total educational program of the community and the supervisory task, and on the great movements in education in America that will enlighten the status leader as to the future of supervision and the new functions that it will fulfill.

Inasmuch as the teacher's position today is one of status and high preparation within the organization, evaluation of teaching will be a shared experience. In essence, the entire instructional staff of the school should be involved in a thoroughgoing and penetrating evaluation of the excellence of the teaching-learning environment being promoted within the school. Beyond this the total educational program of the community should be evaluated through the offices of authorized accrediting agencies as a means of increasing the strategy of planning future school programs. This is best done by introducing the use of these outside experts in the critical process of assessing educational excellence. To be certain that status leaders who provide instructional services also are evaluated as a means of self-improvement, various procedures may be used that will assist them in learning how to change their behavior as a concomitant to improving their performance.

It has been noted by those involved in the cooperative venture of instructional leadership that "supervisors need an inordinate vision of what the schools should be doing in the years ahead." There are many significant and important developments under way in education and these provide an uncommon insight into what lies in the future for those engaged in instructional leadership. As supervisors offer leadership in the educational planning and development process, they must be in a position to make highly significant contributions to the furtherance of the efforts of all professional educators as they work together in the years that lie ahead. As a change agent, the status leader should be able to define clearly the organizational pattern that will lead to the development of cooperative procedures for bringing about change and improvement in the educational program. His is a role in which there will be the formulation and joining together of a program that is based on new research, the dynamics of change, and a sense of accomplishing the "impossible" on occasion. With the proper establishment of goals and objectives, the inspirational supervisor can assist the professional staff in the cooperative improvement of the entire instructional program as a sound base for designing adequate and valid programs for the future.

CHAPTER 10

Cooperative Evaluation of the Effectiveness of Teaching

In recent years there has been a growing concern about the progress being made relative to the teacher evaluation process in the American public school. With new developments in curricular organization, with rapid advances in the entire field of cultural knowledge, and with notable change in the area of teaching-learning values as perceived by the public, practical educators and professional scholars everywhere are attempting to devise a working model that will serve to objectify the evaluation process. At present such groups as the NEA Department of Classroom Teachers and the American Association of School Administrators have indicated that the profession is a long way from identifying objective criteria that can be successfully utilized in detecting the "teaching acts that permit optimum pupil growth." On the other hand, there are many scholars who maintain that pupil development that is progressing in both the cognitive and affective domains can be readily measured objectively as a means of ascertaining the quality of teaching and learning being observed in any classroom.

More and more the public is recognizing that highly competent teachers are essential in every classroom in the nation whether it be elementary, secondary, or collegiate level. In determining teaching quality, the accumulation of reliable evidence rather than that based on assumptions must be found and used by school administrators and supervisors alike as they make basic decisions as to teaching effectiveness. Because the sole use of abstract measurement of the effectiveness of teaching defeats the purpose of total, reliable measurement, the search for a series of universally effective teacher models as an evaluation base needs to continue. Regardless of the fact that progress toward the measurement of teacher effectiveness has been slow, the profession must continue to seek out ways in which effective teaching can be isolated and identified so that it can be measured quantitatively as well as qualitatively. Continued refinement of the observation tools and a discovery of the relationship between the classroom behavior of teachers and the corresponding behavioral patterns found in pupil change should be anatomized and then reconstructed. The types, sequence, and organization of teaching activities that result from teacher-made decisions must be charted so that they are observable on a tangible basis in the evaluation process.

It appears likely that any future attack on a tangible observation technique will include the process of teacher self-evaluation. By this means, the threat of contractual loss must be minimized with a heavy emphasis on teacher development based on individual initiative and a professional sharing for the responsibility found in the evaluative process. Undoubtedly students in tomorrow's schools will be much more highly regarded as partners and supporters in the evaluative act. That little support for traditional evaluation procedures can be expected by the teaching profession is indicated by a recent NEA report from a national survey that showed that more than one-half of the teachers surveyed failed to express even limited confidence in the evaluation system administered by their districts. Better assessment of the setting for learning, the processes fostered to engender vigorous learning experiences in the classroom, and the significance of teacher-student rapport must be thoroughly investigated as a basis for profound and significant advancement in the teacher evaluation process in the years to come. Some significant developments in the entire field of teacher evaluation as it affects the supervisor and administrator will be discussed in the remainder of this chapter.

BASIC CONCERNS

A Behavioral Approach

To assure an evaluation process that has a rational and uniform basis, several factors must be considered that are related to a behavioral analysis. It is important that behavioral characteristics be defined as they relate to the expectations of the teaching position. A detailed description should be designed that adequately describes the mental, physical, professional, social, and personal characteristics that are to be appraised. Both the responsibility for and the procedures to be followed must be clearly enunciated in the appraisal. The appropriate questions to be asked, the kinds of information that are to be compiled, and the appraisal devices to be employed should be made available to each of the administrators or supervisors who will be involved in the evaluation process. Appropriate data can then be compiled that is relevant to the behavioral characteristics that are collected and recorded. Behavioral descriptions should be based on such factors as the teacher's knowledge of his subject matter, how his pupils will achieve, the amount of cooperative effort that he puts forth as a member of the faculty, the kind of person he is on a professional basis, and the excellence of his instructional program in the classroom. Such data should be verified by more than one person. In addition, for each teacher undergoing evaluation, a profile chart can be constructed and an appraisal report made.

To make certain that a systematic approach is used in the appraisal process, a uniform basis for evaluating all candidates should be established. The factors concerning teacher effectiveness that the administration considers essential might be identified by them and published for faculty referral. In each instance there should be a strong link between the appraisal instruments and evaluation procedures to the factors that have a behavioral base. A detailed record of the judgments of the evaluators who participated in the analysis of the teacher's effectiveness need to be kept for further review and appraisal.

Board of education policy should prescribe the responsibility for appraisal. Each person being evaluated should understand the how, what, and why of the evaluation process and be in a position to behave accordingly in a fashion that will lead to a successful evaluation rating.

Contemporary Research

Because no one really knows how to select, train for, encourage, or evaluate teacher effectiveness, three national associations—the Department of Classroom Teachers of NEA, the National School Boards Association, and the American Association of School Administrators—convened a seminar of educational researchers whose work might provide new insight into the teacher-effectiveness problem.[1] The central problem in understanding teacher effectiveness has been one of establishing relationships between teacher behavior and teacher effects. The interaction that takes place in the classroom is within a social context that includes such variables as physical equipment, cast of characters, laws and customs, and needs and ideas of community members. The formative experiences of teachers (training, socialization, ascribed positions, etc.) affect teacher properties (skills, motives, habits, knowledge,

[1]Bruce J. Biddle and William J. Ellena, Editors, *Contemporary Research on Teacher Effectiveness* (New York: Holt, Rinehart and Winston, 1964), 352 pp. See also Selma Greenberg, *Selected Studies of Classroom Teaching: A Comparative Analysis* (Scranton: Intext, 1970).

etc.) which in turn affect teacher behaviors (traits, responses to environment, etc.) and bring about immediate effects (overt and covert pupil responses). These then affect long-term consequences, such as achievement of pupils, new ideas in education, aggrandizement of the profession, understanding of education in the community, and new roles and functions for education. As a rule, measurements by a priori classification, behavioral observation, and objective instruments are to be advocated over measurements made by existing records, self-reports, and rating. Electronic recordings of classroom interaction should be used, rating forms should be eliminated until an understanding of their biases is available, greater utilization should be made of existing records (census, expenditures, etc.) and extended development should be undertaken of school record keeping to include behavioral observation and objective instrument records in depth and over a period of decades.

Although researchers have long been concerned with whether evaluation should be of the teacher or of teaching, practice indicates that it is the teacher (as a counselor, person, and member of the school staff) who is evaluated. Fortunately there is a growing participation in evaluation by classroom teachers, although a noticeable diversity in evaluation standards within school systems is found. The Ryan study published by the American Council on Education on teacher characteristics postulated three dimensions of teacher behavior identified as warmth, organization, and stimulation. Seven basic teacher characteristics identified were: favorable opinion of pupils, favorable opinion of classroom procedures, favorable opinion of personnel, traditional versus child-centered approach, verbal understanding, emotional stability, and validity of response. Another study (Turner) focused upon the assumption that teaching may be viewed as a series of problem-solving or coping behaviors. Objective instruments were developed to measure the potential of teachers for doing coping tasks. Scores on these tests are related to the teacher's formative experiences, intelligence, and attitudes or values and to such variables in the context as subject matter and the age of pupils.

Tape recordings of classroom interaction have been an important step. Such recordings indicate that students of teachers whose behavior measures high in logical operations should show higher scores on critical-thinking tests than those (all other factors being equal) with teachers having low ratings in logical operations.

Interactions and Transactions in School Learning

What are the interactions and behavioral transactions between human beings in the school learning situation? Historically, research on social interaction has been shaped by influences from three sources:

educational, clinical, and social psychology. The first influence from education concerned the conditions under which effective classroom teaching could take place. The second influence from clinical people saw the public schools as a proclaimer of mental health. The third and most recent influence from professional social workers has been to study groups like those in a classroom.[2]

Good teacher characteristics must be identified by either identifying permanent human qualities or by assuming they can be learned, and thence provide more good teachers and fewer poor ones. The education of children is dominated by two themes: (1) individual development, and (2) the relationship of development and readiness. Thus, educators assume effective learning experiences will result from adapting the curriculum to the level of the individual learner. Attempts to relate relationships of variables to a good learning process have produced concepts that seem to have little relevance to classroom learning.

Clinical concepts of educational experiences seem not to be consistent, for example: (1) a child must be reasonably adjusted in order to learn well, and (2) a child continually readjusts to various stimuli. The influence of mental hygiene workers has been to raise new questions about learning rather than to answer old ones. To students of "group life" the influences streaming from the group itself bring about changes in individuals' beliefs and behaviors. They believe classroom learning is the result of mutual influences in a dynamic process.

Judging teacher effectiveness proved to be inconclusive on all tests and rating scales tried so far. For teachers who were not rehired, highest on the list of factors contributing to dismissal was "poor discipline." Today, observational methods for teacher ratings are being tried. Use of positive language in verbal control showed greater success with groups than where negative verbalizations were used. Children with more integrative teachers showed significantly "better" behavior both mental and social. Jersild *et al.* found that children's behaviors in activity programs differed from those in traditional programs, and were not satisfactorily measured by paper and pencil tests.

Are teachers more effective after they have studied child behavior? Yes; the experimental group did much better all around. Conclusions reached concerning the teacher's understanding of child development show that teachers are more effective guides of children's learning when they know about the youngster's abilities, home environment, emotional problems, and attitudes. Variables such as sex, marital status,

---

[2]J. Withall and W. W. Lewis, "Social Interaction in the Classroom," *Handbook of Research on Teaching*, edited by N. L. Gage (Chicago: Rand McNally and Company, 1963), Chapter 13, pp. 683–714.

or parental status of the teacher and such matters as size of school and subjects taught had little or no relationship to the teachers' inventory scores or to ratings by pupils of their teachers in a study by Leeds and Cook.

The social climate in the classroom varies with the type of leadership the teacher provides. Learner-centered study groups revealed a greater objectivity and warmth in their attitudes toward children, whereas leader-centered groups were more conventional and cold. All of the findings favored the learner-centered groups. Correlations between pupils and teachers liking each other and amount of learning taking place are inconclusive. Gage states that using the "understanding of pupils" as a basic objective of teacher-education curricula is hard to defend. Teachers in "good climate" classrooms support the group status system by a satisfactory margin, but teachers in "poor climates" did not.

A student's emotional and intellectual needs should be taken into consideration in determining the kind of instruction he is to receive. For fast learners, Wispe found SAT scores did not differ with either type of teaching (teacher-centered or learner-centered), but the less able students did benefit in the directive-type learning sessions. Maier and Maier placed groups of college students together in problem-solving situations. Differences were significant. Forty per cent of the "developmental" discussion groups reached high-quality decisions as against nineteen per cent of the "free" or "permissive" groups.

The search for a single, easy measure of teacher effectiveness is being slowly abandoned in favor of a complex construct-making approach. Our current concepts are less abstract, and tend to point more directly to relating physical movements and intents of teachers in the room to an organized concept, like classroom control or climate. The current concern may be seen as giving increasing attention to careful development of theories of the classroom interaction as a dynamic process in which the teacher plays an important part but does not alone determine the outcomes of learning.

Feedback, Learning, and Evaluation

A great breakthrough in technology—automation and cybernation —has resulted from the feedback principle. Schools have now organized a special variety of feedback networks which are called evaluation. Thus, says the Association for Supervision and Curriculum Development (ASCD), the process of evaluation, when it has been blended into the background system of purposes, values, and policies, *controls the next step.*[3]

[3]Association for Supervision and Curriculum Development, *Evaluation as Feedback*

If any system of evaluation is to exert proper feedback, it must satisfy these criteria: (1) evaluation must facilitate self-evaluation; (2) evaluation must encompass every object valued by the school; (3) evaluation must facilitate learning and teaching; (4) evaluation must produce records appropriate to the purposes for which records are essential; and (5) evaluation must provide continuing feedback into the larger questions of curriculum development and educational policy. ASCD urges school districts to regain control of their own evaluation programs by employing consultants who are knowledgeable in both measurement and instruction, and by undertaking in-service education activities to improve the evaluation practices of local educators. Instructional leaders should study the whole problem of interaction between evaluation and curriculum development and should plan ways to insure adequate feedback of evaluation into the program. The effect of evaluation on students, teachers, administrators, and curriculum workers should be studied, and continuing attention should be given to all major objectives of the educational program.

Teachers should recognize that they are in the process of becoming effective primarily by their own definition. Teachers generally have chosen teaching as a strategy for the patterning of sequences of activities for moving the perceived self toward expanding effectiveness. Instructional leaders should attempt to gain insight into what the individual teacher considers self-adequacy and help him expedite the process of becoming, as well as clarify the teaching relationship within these goals.

Communication Channels

Assessing the effectiveness of teaching on a cooperative basis requires that the communication linkage between the teacher and "others" is a two-way process. As the teacher views any evaluation procedure, he must be permitted to be a sender as well as a receiver. As the sender forwards his message, a transmission channel must be directed toward the receiver. Effective cooperation between the sender and the receiver requires that two individual transmission channels must be established and each of these should provide feedback information for the sender.

As the supervisor, in fulfilling his function as a service agent to the teacher, establishes communication with the teacher, he must provide the teacher with feedback channels that are open whenever he needs them. Privileged communication, in particular, should be afforded protection in that it should be routed through the transmission channels

---

and Guide (Washington, D.C.: The Association, 1967). Refer to Chapters 1, 2, and 3.

with little opportunity for leakage to a third party. In each instance, the supervisor should make certain that the teacher understands the performance requirements expected of him as cooperatively derived by faculty and instructional leader groups.

Effect of Negotiations on Evaluation

In a recent survey by the Educational Research Service (ERS), it was learned that future negotiation will give more attention to objectives and methods in teacher appraisal.[4] In terms of reactions to supervisory practice, the successful educational leader must: (1) take great care in conducting and recording evaluations; (2) bring greater teacher involvement to the evaluation process; (3) encourage teacher organizations to start policing their own ranks; and (4) recognize that teachers are demanding the right to evaluate their instructional leaders. Teachers and administrators should view evaluation as a cooperative process wherein the individual being evaluated (supervisor or teacher) and the one responsible for making the assessment feel a joint responsibility to focus upon performance areas needing improvement as well as those showing strength, to work together to achieve the best results, and to evaluate the result.

EVALUATION: THEORY AND PRACTICE

The improvement of teaching must be a project that is both teacher oriented and teacher involved. Teachers must willingly accept the rationale that underlies any upgrading movement and voluntarily move towards its realization. Any overt or undue administrative pressure will cause only a negative type of participation and a resentment toward the very goals that are to be accomplished. In fact, teachers' groups or associations should be active in assisting the school system to develop evaluation procedures that are tailored for a particular district or situation.

In the past insufficient time has been given to the observation of teachers and the scheduling of formal conferences with them afterwards. Further, too little of a constructive nature has come from both of these areas of concern. As a result, a good deal needs to be done to strengthen the procedures utilized in observing classroom procedures as well as the designing of effective supervisor-teacher conferences.

One of the factors that supervisors and administrators must continuously guard against is the tendency to rate teachers high who have

---

[4]"Evaluation of Teaching Competence," *NEA Research Bulletin*, vol. 47 No. 3 (October 1969), pp. 67–75

similar personality characteristics as the evaluator and to rate those teachers low who have ones dissimilar to those of the person doing the rating. There is no evidence that this is the case in any significant number of situations, but there is no assurance that this could not happen. In situations where the supervisor and administrator are very close in their working relationship with those being rated, this could be a real danger. It is highly important that the person doing the rating be as objective as possible. Any similar or different personality characteristics must be overlooked by the rater as he attempts to rate these characteristics only as they apply objectively to the over-all effectiveness of the teacher in the classroom. This may, at times, result in an almost complete personal detachment from the individual being rated so that the rating itself will not be unreliable due to the similarity-dissimilarity factor.

Any evaluation procedure must view closely the behavior characteristics of the teacher in terms of his objective strides to become the best professional person possible. This individual should be one who communicates well with his fellow workers, students, and others in the community. He will need to be able to express himself so succinctly that he is not only clearly understood by those with whom he associates, but that he is respected for his articulateness and polish in all avenues of expression. His ideas should readily convey the impression of an alert, intelligent mind that is forever seeking new knowledge and better means of solving problems. He should be known as a person who places great value in the educational task in which he is engaged. His perception of education should be that it can accomplish much good in the world and that he has been assigned an important task in exciting and challenging the minds of young people. He should strive for excellence in all walks of life: personal, social and psychological. His deliberations are such that he seeks to ever improve the conditions that surround his classroom and his teaching. He works long hours with his professional colleagues and others in the school-community situation to improve the instructional program and he gives freely of his time to better the stance of the profession as a whole. Above all, he is a scholarly individual who is well versed in his field of specialization and he is concerned that he keeps abreast of new trends and developments. To evaluate this person is a rewarding task as he exemplifies so many fine attributes that aptly describe an outstanding teacher.

Evaluating Teachers: Methods and Procedures

A nationwide research project by the National Education Association delved into programs for evaluating classroom teachers and opinions on evaluation.[5] Initial findings were that: (1) about half of the school systems follow formal procedures in evaluating teachers; (2) written ratings or evaluations are required in three-fourths of the schools for probationary teachers and in two-thirds for continuing teachers; (3) the principal is nearly always responsible for evaluation, but often shares that responsibility with other officials; and (4) although more than three out of four superintendents and principals expressed confidence in their school system's program of evaluation, over half of the teachers did not.

In terms of the *number of evaluations*, most probationary teachers were evaluated once or twice a year, but seldom more than three times a year. Continuing teachers usually were evaluated once a year. In relation to the *preliminary steps taken before making an evaluation*, more than 90 percent observed teachers teaching in the classroom first, while three-fourths held conferences with teachers. Less direct steps were: gathering impressions of the teacher from seeing him outside the classroom, listening to impressions from pupils, studying pupil achievement records, studying office records, noting what parents said about the teacher, and noting what other teachers said about the teacher. *Observation of teaching* found only 27.1 percent of the principals observing probationary teachers on a regular schedule, while 18.3 percent observed continuing teachers on such a schedule. During the first term of the study 33.9 percent of the secondary school teachers were not observed while teaching and 17 percent were observed four or more times. For elementary school teachers, 20.8 percent received no observations while 33.7 received four or more observations. The median number of observations were: elementary school teachers—two; secondary school teachers—one. The *most recent observation* was made by the principal for about two-thirds of the teachers who reported, while 20.3 percent of elementary school teachers and 13.0 percent of secondary school teachers were observed by the supervisor. 7.8 percent were observed most recently by department heads. The median length of the most recent observation was 22 minutes, the observation was requested by 10.8 percent of the teachers, one-fourth were notified a day in advance, and with frequent observations teachers were less likely to object to a visit without notification. Only 9.7 percent of the probationary teachers and 5.4 percent of the continuing teachers felt an adverse effect on teaching. Half of the teachers reported a conference following the observation and nearly half reported that this most recent observation was helpful to them. The *conferences* that were scheduled in-

[5] *NEA Research Bulletin*, "Methods of Evaluating Teachers," vol. 43, no. 1 (February 1965), pp. 12–18.

dicated that preliminary ones were held by 80.5 percent of the principals with probationary teachers. Over 50 percent of the principals frequently, but not always, held conferences after observing teachers. The median number of conferences was two for probationary and elementary school teachers and one for continuing and secondary school teachers. 21.5 percent of the teachers reported having four or more conferences during the term, while 35.0 percent reported none at all. *Self-evaluation by teachers* was found to be good preparation for an evaluation by the principal. However, the teacher may be reluctant to do a written self-evaluation; may be reluctant to note other than his good points; or may tend to exaggerate good points. It was found that 19.2 percent of the teachers reported making written self-evaluations. Self-evaluations were found more often in large systems, and in elementary schools more than in secondary schools. Finally, in terms of *professional help and guidance,* 21.2 percent of the teachers said that they did not receive such help from their evaluations. Teachers who received written evaluations were more likely to have received the necessary help than those who did not receive such evaluations. 12.4 percent of the teachers felt that help received was either too little or too late. Some help was received only through impersonal means such as faculty meetings, printed materials, and fellow teachers. Some teachers thought that many professional needs which could be taken care of through evaluation had not been met. In order to meet the many demands placed on a strong evaluation program, many school systems are in the process of revising their approach to evaluation in this area.

Evaluation and Teaching Growth

It has been stated that we can evaluate teaching and teachers better if we can identify the basic and important features of the teaching task. What are these basic features that we must recognize in teaching?[6]

Teaching is complex, but not infinitely so. It is a knowledgeable art and it can be studied objectively, but it needs structure for the classification of its elements. There are at least three good examples of studies of group interaction that have provided such classifications. The California statement of teaching competence in the late 1940's was the result of a five-year study by teachers, administrators, college professors, and teacher association representatives. The California statement

[6]Gale W. Rose, "Performance Evaluation and Growth in Teaching," *Phi Delta Kappan,* vol. XLV, no. 1 (October 1963), pp. 48–53. See also James E. Heald, *Selected Readings on General Supervision* (New York: Macmillan, 1970), pp. 279–291.

yielded six major factors, twenty-seven sub-factors, and 205 particular factors that were considered significant. The Provo (Utah) School District project in 1956–1957 investigated the classroom teacher-pupil interaction situation. The Provo program classified six major teaching functions, twenty-five secondary functions and forty-two sub-functions. Most recently, the Weber (Utah) School District developed a teacher observation code that specified ten major aspects and eighty-six particular aspects. *Teaching is a set of forms of habitualized human behavior* that is observable and measurable, analyzable, and modifiable. As observable and measurable, teaching covers a range of situations with the typical teacher covering his complete repertoire in 120 minutes. Six 20-minute observation periods are adequate, allowing for time-of-day and day-of-week variations. As analyzable, there is a recognizable repetition of teaching pattern with the range varying from narrow (static) to flexible (fluid). As modifiable, teaching should be learned, modified, and relearned. Teacher-training institutions are responsible for developing this set of behavior, but teachers must recognize that teaching habits may be changed. Analysis provides an adequate and efficient basis for such a change. *Teaching behavior in role theory terms* began during World War II. The ultimate criterion is the teacher's work and its effect upon pupils. Two levels of criteria are identifiable: (1) The teacher as a person with all his attributes; and (2) the teaching process as a series of complex acts performed by the teacher. The effects achieved and the fulfillment of the teacher role are important aspects of this. Studies in this area show a need to rate adequately and accurately and a need to better define the teaching function. In terms of the concept of role, the natural basis from which to view teaching behavior is its orientation: task, function, and behavior. To be practical, predictive studies must tie down actual teaching performance. *Teaching has immediate, measurable meaning and effects* as all the important results of teaching are not postponed to the remote future. Some immediate, important teaching effects are interest, pursuit of learning goals, respect for the teacher, respect for each other, functioning independently, learning content material, and learning skills. The learning situation may be organized into one large group or many small groups; it may be applied to individual differences and it may be creative or stifling. *Teachers are not good observers of their own performance* since valid, adequate self-perception is rare. Feedback procedures are necessary to reflect the teacher-pupil situation, to curtail unsuccessful procedures and to evaluate the total situation. Errors, unperceived by many, can become repeated and ingrained unless cooperative evaluation takes place. *Teachers have anxieties about their teaching* that need to be resolved constructively. Anxiety is normal and will increase if problems go unresolved or through worrying about the wrong things. Anxiety is reduced through doing a good job and knowing it. Anxiety reduction can be achieved through observation, analysis, and evaluation wherein problems are faced and cooperatively worked on for solution with supervisors and administrators. *School administrators have the central responsibility for the evaluation and improvement of teaching,* but they are seldom adequately prepared to do it. There are two basic reasons for supervisors and administrators accepting this responsibility: (1) it is within the context of school evaluation which requires professionally trained personnel, accounting to the public, and determining educational goals and how they are being reached; and (2) teaching must be improved through quality analysis, correction of errors, and the "upgrading" of certification and selection. Why this lack of administrative preparation in evaluation? There are several reasons: college programs generally do not offer this, on-the-job training programs are seldom available, little help is given in how to analyze evaluations, and evaluation procedures are often twenty years behind the development of new educational theory and techniques. The future demands that the administrator be given opportunities to retool himself in perfecting his ability in this critical professional area.

Administrative Evaluation and Its Effects

Recently five school districts embarked on an attempt to develop better programs of teacher evaluation. In a study of forty-five elementary school principals in these districts, all of them responded to these areas of evaluation: requisite for teacher acceptance; importance of the principal's skill; need to involve teachers; values, hazards, and problems; supervision vs administration; and the importance of evaluation.[7] In each of the district programs an attempt was being made to incorporate into a consistent whole a series of basic components as follows: (1) the purposes of evaluation; (2) operational criteria for the description and classification of data on teachers and their work; (3) instrumentation which embodies the criteria; (4) data collection procedures relevant to the criteria with particular emphasis on classroom observation; (5) evaluation frameworks for determining what the data mean; (6) feedback techniques with particular emphasis on conferencing; and (7) uses, supervisory and administrative, of the evaluated data.

[7]Gale W. Rose, "The Effects of Administrative Evaluation," *National Elementary Principal*, vol. 43, no. 2 (November 1963), pp. 50–53. See also C.M. Lindvall and Richard C. Cox, *Evaluation as a Tool in Curriculum Development* (Chicago: Rand McNally, 1970), 115 pp.

Requisites for teacher acceptance. Nearly every principal stated or implied that teachers, in general, are not accustomed to being involved in a process of evaluation based on fairly extensive criteria and a considerable amount of classroom observation. Many teachers were found to be somewhat nervous or tense when the evaluation process is intiated. The principals reported that many teachers, after the first few contacts, will accept and welcome the experience if three other conditions are obtained: (1) if the major focus is really on improving the teacher rather than on inspectorial fault-finding; (2) if the information produced is meaningful and useful to the teacher; and (3) if the principal takes the necessary time to collect adequate information and to discuss it with the teacher. *Importance of the principal's skill.* The principals observed that teachers do not respond alike and pointed out that one of the important skills of administration is to be able to deal with each teacher in the way most helpful for him. This was particularly true of the feedback process. Teachers are very interested in knowing what has been recorded about their teaching, and a principal can damage, rather then improve, his relationship with teachers if he is inept at this point. It was the principals' consensus that no matter how well selected the criteria or how adequate the procedures, if the persons fulfilling the evaluative role are not professionally competent, the whole structure will come tumbling down. *The need to involve teachers.* It was indicated that teachers can become tense and frustrated and rapport can deteriorate if the total conditions of the evaluation program are not established properly. Teachers should have prior and continuing involvement in the designing and testing of the evaluative criteria. *Values, hazards, and problems.* The values of the evaluation program were cited as: (1) the improvement and professionalization of teaching; (2) the clarifications and insights teachers gained about their own work; (3) the understanding and insights the principal gained about teaching and the school operation; and (4) the rise in morale, esprit, and feeling of professional security among the staff as their sense of common purpose and teamwork developed. The hazards listed were: (1) the possible breakdown in rapport and communication if appropriate conditions were not established; (2) a program too narrowly conceived or too specifically oriented to purposes remote from the improvement of teaching; and (3) inadequacies of procedure or skill on the part of the principal and insufficient time devoted to the program. The problems were: (1) finding time to do an adequate job, which was considered to be a most frustrating element; (2) developing skills in communication and consistent follow-through with teachers; and (3) the problem of varying value systems and interpreting criteria in assessment of data about teaching. *Can administrators also supervise?* There is an argument that a principal cannot at the same time have administrative authority over teachers and also be accepted as their confidant and advisor. Some observe that individuals tend to withdraw from and avoid those who have some power over them; others note that many individuals are drawn to those they see as having power over them and feel most comfortable in a dependent relationship. *Is evaluation important?* There does not seem to be any controversy over this issue. It is clear that adequate programs are difficult to develop and operate. If school administrators and faculties were willing to devote the time and energy necessary to professional competence in this area, there might be some real breakthroughs in evaluation.

Achievement of Local Objectives

A new evaluation instrument in use in the Midwest, Canada, Arizona, California, Nevada, and Hawaii has been designed to facilitate the evaluation of teacher competence by professionally qualified observers trained in its use. This is the Instrument for the Observation of Teaching Activities (IOTA) and it seeks to answer the question, "What can the good teacher *do?*"[8]

Using a wide sampling of definitions of good teaching, descriptions are used under the six roles of: Director of Learning, Counselor and Guidance Worker, Mediator of the Culture, Liaison with the Community, Member of the School Staff, and Member of the Profession. In assessing teacher competence, independently-made interrater judgments correlating at .90 or higher have repeatedly been obtained with IOTA. With careful evaluator training, this shows that educators can agree on what they have observed in a wide variety of classrooms. Teacher participation in an IOTA Teaching Effectiveness Workshop significantly improves teaching ability as shown by: 1) higher scores on the indirect/direct ratio on the Flanders Analysis; 2) more student than subject matter emphasis entered on the Minnesota Teacher Attitude Inventory; and 3) more positive attitudes towards administrators on the Leadership Behavior Description Questionnaire.

At present exploration is being made of the use of IOTA as a self-appraisal technique by teachers. With virtually immediate audio and video feedback systems, teachers trained to use IOTA for self-appraisal would not have to rely on the appraisals of others as to their teaching ability.

It is evident that a school district could benefit from developing a teacher evaluation program that is built around local definition along

[8]Warren Kallenbach, "Who Gives an IOTA?" *The California School Administrator,* vol. XXIV, no. 3 (June 1969), pp. 8 and 19.

with a reliable and valid measuring instrument designed to accompany it. Further, a well-structured evaluator training program would provide the means of achieving high levels of agreement among evaluators who are trained in their application. Meeting these two requirements—local definition and agreement—will do much to assist in the prediction of the consequences of how certain acts of classroom management will affect pupils' knowledge and insights.

METHODS AND EFFECTIVENESS

Much needs to be done to overcome the rather uncomplimentary image that the community has of the teacher if evaluation is to be successful in allowing only outstanding individuals to stay in the profession. Too often the role of the teacher is misunderstood and too narrowly interpreted, which does not permit him to become a truly effective community leader. This, in turn, makes it more difficult to attract outstanding persons into the profession as they view the teaching role as one of secondary appeal in the eyes of the community. Frequently the teacher perceives his role with apprehension as he recognizes the vast chasm that exists between what is expected of him privately as compared to the inordinate expectations for his behavior in the community. To be governed by one set of rules for his private life and another for his public appearances seems somewhat unreasonable to many potential aspirants to the teaching profession.

What are some of the teaching practices that should be considered as the administrator or supervisor evaluates the effectiveness of the teacher? Certainly the teacher should use a reasonable number of different learning situations in the classroom. He will provide challenging materials for each child in his class, from the slow learner to the superior student. He should give evidence that he has provided interest and ability grouping in his class and that he has attempted to bring instructional materials into the classroom to meet those needs. He will have carefully developed unit and lesson plans for each of the areas that he plans to cover. Field and other community experiences should be arranged so that the child has an opportunity to relate his classroom experiences with those outside the classroom. Supplemental materials, audio-visual aids, and outside speakers can serve to enrich the classroom experience. In many ways the teacher demonstrates that he is an important participant in the total teaching force and does everything possible to relate the learning experiences in his classroom to that of the entire school.

Each faculty should determine for itself the kind of evaluation that will best meet its individual needs. It must be ready to assure the system, however, of a continuance of a perceptive evaluative plan that conforms to district standards, yet will make teachers feel that it is a part of the professional growth process.

Analysis and Investigation of Teaching Methods

Research on teaching methods has been a study of consistencies in the behavior of teachers and the effect of these consistencies on the learning process. At present teaching methods cannot be considered to be the product of scientific research. Only in the last few years has scientific knowledge begun to reach the point which might permit the systematic design of a pattern of behavior for teachers that would maximize the achievement of the pupil with respect to specific objectives.[9]

Wallens and Travers found the origins of teacher behavior patterns classified as patterns: (1) derived from teaching traditions; (2) derived from social learnings in the teacher's background; (3) derived from philosophical traditions; (4) generated by the teacher's own needs; (5) generated by conditions existing in the school and community; and (6) derived from teaching traditions. Beyond this a number of general teaching methods have evolved from teaching traditions such as the recitation method, the lecture method, the discussion method, the laboratory method, the project method, and the critical thinking method. Research has shown that it does not seem to make much difference which teaching method is used as no method seems to be any better than any other method. This is to be expected as none of the teaching methods were designed systematically in terms of what is known about the learning process. Therefore, the time has come for teaching methods to be based on a learning model stemming from psychological research. Such a systematic design for a method of teaching must have two steps: (1) a set of identifiable conditions related to learning must be specified; and (2) teacher behavior must be designed so that it generates the necessary learning conditions.

A learning model for analyzing teaching methods would contain the preceding two steps and take into consideration the response variables (derived from any publicly observable behavior) and the independent variables (related to the learning process and manipulated by the teacher). The teacher would exercise certain controls over the efficiency of the learning process through manipulation of situation characteristics (external stimuli affecting the learner), motivation, reinforcement, readiness, and mediating response. The variables in

[9]Norman E. Wallens and Robert M. W. Travers, *Handbook of Research on Teaching,* edited by N. L. Gage, (Chicago: Rand McNally and Company, 1963), Chapter 10, pp. 448–505.

each of these categories will have to be defined in the actual design of a teaching method. A large part of the ultimate product of teaching model development would be a set of laws of teacher behavior that would follow the general form, $T = f(r_g + R_i)$, in which T represents the behavior of the teacher and is a function, f, of the goals to be achieved, R_g, and the present behavior of the pupil, R_i. The design of the teaching method may have to assume that a response system of the teacher T can be developed which is appropriate and efficient for achieving R_g.

There is a great need at present for an attempt to design a teaching method that makes use of a wide range of learning principles. Supervisors and administrators must be willing to give practical assistance to the implementation of such basic research whenever possible.

Teacher-Pupil Interaction

An objective way of reviewing and analyzing teacher-pupil behavior in the classroom is through a feedback technique. Through the use of trained observers or by teacher self-analysis, the behavior that occurs in the classroom can be objectively determined. By using the Flanders technique, the verbal behavior that occurs in the classroom can be carefully categorized: teacher talk, student talk, and silence or confusion. Such teacher factors as these are considered: acceptance of feelings, praise or encouragement, acceptance or use of student ideas, asking questions, lectures, giving directions, and criticizing or justifying authority. Student related factors include: student talk by response and student talk by initiation. Silence or confusion is the last reaction type. Through the use of observers or by using a tape recorder, the kind of teaching that goes on in the classroom can be categorized. The behavior that is observed every three seconds is placed on a chart. From an analysis of this chart, the observer can readily determine the kinds of verbal initiations and responses that took place on the part of both the teacher and the students.

Teachers have a great deal to gain by this method of self-analysis. In addition, another method of receiving feedback from teaching is possible through microteaching. By using this technique, teachers have an opportunity to present a short segment of a lesson before a small group of students. Immediately afterwards the lesson can be reviewed and evaluated by another teacher, a supervisor, or any other combination of professional persons that a teacher might desire. At a later time the same lesson is presented on a revised basis and the two are then compared. An excellent opportunity avails itself to visually demonstrate how new techniques used by the teacher can materially aid in the development and refinement of new learning objectives and teaching behaviors. Comparisons can later be made with model teaching situations in which the ideal teaching situation has been demonstrated by teacher experts using laboratory facilities. Teachers, through the use of the microteaching plan, can develop much better insight into the intricacies of their own classroom behavior as balanced with student action, reaction, and response.

Students Evaluate Teaching

A program directed toward exchange evaluation has been inaugurated to enlist the aid of both students and colleagues in evaluating the effectiveness of instruction. The SET (Students Evaluate Teaching) program is based primarily on the fundamental concept that most students, when stimulated properly, will comment fairly and surprisingly accurately on matters of a curricular and methodological nature that occur in the classroom if they are convinced that the instructor is genuinely interested in obtaining their opinions.[10] Such opinions can be a valuable source of information for self-evaluation of the teacher.

To maintain anonymity, the SET program provides that a resident teacher's class shall be led in discussion by a visiting instructor in the same discipline on the quality of instruction that has taken place during the school term. Pupils will have been prepared for this evaluation visit by the resident teacher who makes certain that they understand that he approves thoroughly of the visiting evaluation accomplished during his absence. He assures the class that they probably will not know the visiting instructor, that he will not know them, and that they will not be introduced. The basis for discussion with the pupils (probably one class period) will be an agenda agreed upon or developed with the resident teacher. If possible, a secretary should be present who will take notes and make a transcription which, together with the conference between the two teachers after the visit, would constitute the total evaluation. Special precautions should be taken to assure the teacher that this evaluation information does not come into the hands of anyone responsible for the supervision of the resident teacher. The basis of the visiting teachers—class conference could be such questions as these: (1) What were the materials of instruction? (2) What was the function of the subject matter used? (3) What and how many methods of instruction were employed? (4) How effective were the methods and materials employed? (5) How did the instructor help students with their own personal problems? (6) What was done to promote better institution-community relations? (7) How were democratic attitudes and relation-

---

[10]Alden W. Smith, Project Director, SET (Students Evaluate Teaching) Programs. Unpublished papers, California State College, Fulllerton, 1970.

ships fostered? and (8) How were good human relationships furthered?

The SET approach should help the instructor help himself. If he cares to submit the findings of his evaluation to his superior or his peers for discussion or for any other reason, the decision would be his and his alone. The evaluation itself provides an excellent opportunity for dignified and effective student expression and involvement in the most important aspect of the institution, the classroom experience. In a sense cooperative and responsible evaluation is at its best with tripartite dimensions: teacher—students—colleague.

It is apparent that student evaluation of the learning process and the teaching procedures promoted in the classroom will continue to increase. School faculties, in an age of student activism, are beginning to show less fear of student evaluation. They are more willing to recognize that this is another avenue of evaluation that can assist them in reaching worthwhile instructional goals.

Excellence in Performance

In spite of the fact that evaluation of the teaching process is seldom a popular task, nevertheless each teacher in the faculty is undergoing a continuous evaluation of his teaching as long as he remains in the classroom. Students, fellow faculty members, faculty committees charged with evaluation, heads of departments, the supervisory and administrative staff, and even lay persons in the community are often making judgments as to the effectiveness of teaching, although this is based, at times, on hearsay and impressions. Because today there is a greater insistence by many students and faculty on teaching of good quality, the teacher must depend upon evaluation that should be discerning, thorough, accurate and fair.[11]

A first step in the direction of improved teaching is to establish between the teacher and his colleagues the basic qualities of instruction that are important and will be evaluated. In addition, the necessary channels of communication should be developed that will provide for forthright discussion of what is expected of any teacher within a given discipline or grade level. In some institutions it has been found helpful to organize seminars for new teachers, usually under the direction of an experienced faculty member, in which an opportunity is available to review and evaluate one another's work. In other situations, seminar groups have listened to class sessions of members of the staff who are not identified, and these have been made the basis for critical examination. As the merits and demerits of the tape presentation become obvi-

[11]C. Easton Rothwell, *The Importance of Teaching*, (New Haven, Connecticut: Hazen Foundation, 1969), pp. 56–66.

ous, these ideas can be transposed to the teaching performance of the seminar members. Videotapes, too, can be extremely helpful as a basis for seminar discussion or for self-evaluation of one's own teaching.

"Paired" teaching with the assignment of an experienced and established teacher to a new teacher offers early counseling and evaluation opportunities to the inexperienced professional. Lately, some serious efforts have been made to evaluate the specific tasks that the teacher accomplishes to assist learning and how successfully he does them. This should include the kinds of changes in the student the program attempts to promote and the development of the work of the class so that pupils are aware of the direction in which the progress is moving and its beneficial effects on them.

Teacher-made tests can make available information that will assist the instructor in recognizing the ability of the students to comprehend the materials that are placed before them and their ability to solve the problems that arise from the application of these materials. Even the application of good scholarship on both a theoretical as well as a practical basis serves as a means of assessing the teacher as exemplary or not.

Interaction Analysis and Videotaping

Interaction analysis has recently come to be viewed as a possible panacea for some of the difficulties encountered in designing a teacher-evaluation program. This concept is particularly true when interaction analysis is coupled with the videotaping of teacher performance. These two forces can become a powerful device for modifying teacher behavior and their potential for making a difference in teacher effectiveness requires serious consideration as a viable supervisory technique.

Most interaction analysis systems require the classroom observer to record information, utilize a simplified and accurate coding technique, and, finally, analyze the data that identifies the patterns of interaction that have taken place between the teacher and students in the classroom situation. Interaction analysis often can reveal patterns of teacher behavior that the teacher was not aware were occurring. The Flanders technique (described earlier) is a pioneer effort in the area of observing teacher-pupil interactions. Several new studies have been completed in this field and their implications are described in the paragraphs that follow.

The Southeastern Education Laboratory (Atlanta) assessed the effects of three types of feedback-evaluation procedures (two of which involved the use of videotape) in changing the question-asking behavior of in-service teachers.[12] Three groups of sixth grade teachers par-

[12]Charles H. Adair and Allan R. Kyle, "Effects of Feedback on Teacher Behavior," ERIC *Research in Education*, May 1970, p. 95.

ticipated in the three-stage study with each group using one of the following feed-back procedures: (1) standard observation practice (teacher-supervisor conference following classroom observation by the supervisor); (2) self-analysis of videotaped teaching session; and (3) directed self-analysis (supervisor-assisted) of a videotaped teaching session. The findings of the study were; (1) that the two video-based procedures appeared equally effective and were more effective than standard observation procedures in reducing the percentage of rhetorical questions asked by teachers; and (2) that each of the three procedures was effective in increasing the percentage of probing questions asked.

The Educational and Cultural Center (Syracuse) has developed and field-tested an instrument to describe teacher behavior during classroom teaching, planning, evaluation, and diagnosis.[13] It is designed for use by a team of clinicians, the number depending on the purpose for which the instrument is to be used. The instrument contains specific items for behavior under each category and sub-category: (1) Teaching (General techniques, Cognitive, Affective); (2) Planning (Scope and Sequence of the Curriculum, Curriculum Materials in Subject Area, Learning Process and Child Development, Innovative Programs and Practices); and (3) Evaluation-Diagnosis. On each item teachers may be observed to operate at one of four levels: (1) knowledge of (the environment for); (2) ability to establish (the environment for); (3) ability to analyze (the existing environment for); and (4) ability to evaluate (the existing environment for). Teacher questionnaires and interviews supplement classroom observation records in the description-writing process. A program is being developed to prepare clinicians to use this behavioral analysis instrument on a widespread basis.

Arizona University (Tucson), through its Tucson Early Education Model, surveyed forty-two TEEM-trained teachers (EP) and 75 non-TEEM teachers (NP) in Iowa, Texas, Georgia, and Louisiana to determine if teachers ask questions which elicit intellectual operations in children.[14] Teachers were audiotaped for forty minutes in classrooms. Their questions were classified according to an Intellectual Operation model based on Guilford's Structure of the Intellect. The six classifications were: (1) perception, (2) cognition, (3) memory, (4) divergent production, (5) convergent production, and (6) evaluation. Analysis of data revealed that EP and NP teachers differed in teaching style. Although both groups placed inordinate stress on knowledge and memory ques-

[13]"Behavioral Analysis Instrument for Teachers," Educational and Cultural Center, Syracuse, N.Y., ERIC *Research in Education,* May 1970, p. 94.

[14]Barry J. Zimmerman and John R. Bergan, "Intellectual Operations in Teacher-Child Interaction," ERIC *Research in Education,* September 1970, p. 65.

tions that precluded the opportunity to teach other intellectual operations, EP teachers exhibited a significant shift away from this practice. The TEEM process approach attempts to prevent the teacher's imposition of intellectual demands for skills not present in the child's repertoire and captializes on the motivation inherent in his success. This new emphasis will have great impact on teacher-child interaction, especially when employed with disadvantaged children.

In Monmouth the Oregon College of Education has geared itself to a program entitled "A Competency Based, Field Centered, Personalized and Systematic Model for Elementary Teacher Education" (Com-Field). Although the competency-oriented program concerns itself with the assessment of competence based upon the products that derive from a teacher's behavior rather than the behavior per se, it does not deny the significance of what a teacher does as a means to an end. A portion of the experiences focus on an understanding of *self as teacher.* In this instance self-confrontation experiences take the form of videotape playback of actual teaching experience, clinical supervision interviews, and small-group discussions that focus around peer reaction to performance. A central thrust of self-confrontation experiences at this level is their focus upon the definition of a teaching style that is consistent with perception of self or individual and self in context.

Feedback by teacher comment, by television playback, and by self-analysis, singly or together, has reduced anxiety in subsequent performance as measured by nonfluencies in speech.[15] Nonfluencies were counted in eight categories: sounds such as "ah"; correction; sentence incompletion; repetition; stutter; intruding incoherent sound; tongue slip; and omission. Performance ranged from a low of 10.4 nonfluencies when there was videotape recording, teacher comment, and playback to a high of 37.1 nonfluencies when there was no video tape recording, no comment, and no playback. Since videotape playback without teacher comment resulted in almost double the nonfluencies (21.3) of those resulting from videotape playback with teacher comment, the conclusion was reached that a positive interaction between the two practices is to be desired. It was interesting that the mere presence of a television camera and recorder reduced student anxiety somewhat, perhaps because of a "Hawthorne" effect.

Greenberg, in a study of a number of classroom researchers who have embarked on large-scale observational studies of classroom teaching and behavior, has analyzed the studies of Bellack, Flanders, Hughes,

---

[15]Myler P. Breen and Roderick Diehl, "Effect of Videotape Playback and Teacher Comment on Anxiety During Subsequent Task Performance," ERIC *Research in Education,* January 1971, p. 40.

Smith, and Taba.[16] Bellack's study, "The Language of the Classroom," investigated teachers' and students' linguistic behavior; Flanders' study, "Teacher Influence, Pupil Attitudes, and Achievement," analyzed spontaneous interaction between teacher and student; Hughes' study, "Development of the Means for the Assessment of the Quality of Teaching," dealt with teacher-pupil interaction in the classroom; Smith's studies on the logic and strategies of teaching viewed teaching as a system of social action, involving an end-in-view, an agent, and a situation; and Taba's study, "Thinking in Elementary School Children," examined the development of thought under optimum training conditions. Greenberg found that there were advantages in each of these studies to taped observations, the ability to code after observations, the ability to code from a different perspective, and the ability to use different systems of analysis. There is reason to think that a system of recording these behaviors on tape and/or film and then analyzing them into several different category systems (as the five above) will be found to be as useful and efficient as the use of one general classification system. Multianalysis may be more appropriate where many different kinds of information are needed.

In conclusion, interaction analysis and videotaping has provided the status leaders with a method of revealing, in a tactful way, the teacher behavior patterns that need strengthening or may require correction. In essence, this procedure is a means of making teachers aware of their own effectiveness in the classroom and, in turn, of becoming accountable for their efforts to improve on the progress of pupils assigned to them. This analytical process will make teachers sensitive to the need for self-inquiry and self-evaluation as they review, with the observer, the results of class interaction coding and videotaping. Training procedures are helpful that include group discussions of appropriate behavior, demonstrations by supervisors, and immediate corrective feedback by the status leader. Evaluation by means of videotapes, behavior rating scales, a behavioral task, and attitude tasks have shown a change in teachers. As a result of interaction analysis and videotape training programs, there has been a notable improvement in teacher-pupil interaction and reinforcement of acceptable learning techniques. Interaction analysis and videotape projects like the one on "Teacher Self-Appraisal" being conducted by the University of Arizona in cooperation with the public schools of Tucson will offer new and exciting ways of constructively aiding the teacher in self-improvement and evaluation.

[16]Selma B. Greenberg, *Selected Studies of Classroom Teaching: A Comprehensive Analysis* (Scranton: Intext, 1970), 160 pp.

CLINICAL EVALUATION

Early in the 1970's investigations in the field of teacher evaluation have turned the main focus of their attention on two concerns: (1) that the primary goal for the evaluation of teachers should be the improvement of instruction; and (2) that the members of any school organization should cooperatively establish educational objectives that will serve as a guide for the evaluation of teacher performance. Evidence of this trend has been shown by the demand of the Association for Supervision and Curriculum Development (ASCD) and other leading educational organizations that supervision has an inherent responsibility to focus on the improvement of classroom performances in a personalized way through observation, conference, and assistance in a completely open and cooperative manner.

These procedures require the encouragement and direction of a self-activated professional improvement plan by individual faculty members as well as a basic concern by the staff for the improvement of the total instructional program of the school. The establishment of a supervisory model appears to be essential to the success of any such improvement plan and the emphasis here should be based on the ability of the status leader to cooperate with, serve, and assist teachers in meeting new and self-generated instructional goals. Closely allied to the service concept is that of challenge and reward and any supervisory model has a basic requirement to demonstrate that from its evolvement will come an appreciation of, as well as a satisfaction with, the evaluative process. Included in this approach is the glaring need for faculty to concern itself with the development of appropriate educational objectives and the attainment of those objectives. This emphasis is opposed to an utter concentration on superficial teaching techniques and methods in isolation from basic goals and objectives. Teachers should be given vigorous assistance and encouragement in evaluating the way in which their classroom objectives are being attained. This would involve giving far less attention to the evaluation of routine methods utilized by the teacher in conducting classroom instruction. In each instance the teacher has the right to expect that the evaluation process will be cooperative, fair, and objective in relation to the latest known scientific methods.

Observation

Both the verbal and nonverbal behavior of the teacher in the classroom are elements of concern to the status leader as he attempts to analyze teacher-pupil interaction. To be effective, the status leader can be of most help to the teacher through observation by assisting him in identifying areas of strength and weakness and relating these to the specific educational objectives that the teacher has developed for his own use. If the teacher needs technical assistance in solving his problems, the supervisor can provide this assistance later on a one-to-one basis or involve two or three other teachers concerned with the same problems so that they may be supportive of one another in solving a mutual problem. The latest research, however, indicates that observation of classroom instruction should have more reference to the behavior of students than to the verbal or nonverbal behavior of teachers, thus focusing on how receptive students were to teaching procedures rather than the skill with which the teacher demonstrated his repertoire.

The essence of any good classroom observation technique is the development of a mutually satisfying approach that assists both the teacher and the status leader to reach commonly subscribed goals. The teacher should be consulted prior to the observation as to the kind of evaluation procedures that will take place. Instructional objectives, in turn, should specify teaching responsibilities. The excellence of the classroom observation process must far outweigh the mere frequency with which the observations are held.

Greater attention needs to be given to the attitude of teachers toward observation than often has been the case in the past. Teaching performance can benefit from the observation and the teacher will wish to feel that he has profited from the experience. Some teachers, however, may view their experience negatively, while others will consider that it affords them the kind of insight that will upgrade their teaching performance. Each type of teacher requires a different approach and the status leader has the responsibility of dispelling the idea that a threat to the security of the teacher exists rather than a challenge. Some system of rewards acceptable to both teachers and supervisors can be established that will make all facets of evaluation (observation, conference, and assistance) palatable and advantageous to the participant.

Planning for observation will give teachers an ample opportunity to confer amongst themselves and to evaluate their present methods and materials. Following that, students should be consulted as to their aspirations and concerns in relation to the teaching situation as it exists in the school. The last planning stage requires that teachers and status leaders become involved in reviewing the over-all objectives that are so important to the faculty and, on the basis of this review, construct suitable ways of measuring the skill of the faculty members in meeting their objectives.

Observation can be made by peers as readily as it can by status leaders. For years teachers have been active in supervising interns in teacher training programs. Colleges and universities have long relied on the skill of experienced teachers in working with internees and there is little reason why the same skills of observation and evaluation cannot be used among their faculty colleagues. Peer evaluation, of course, requires that careful in-service measures be taken to insure that the teachers involved have the proper skills necessary for a fair and objective observation experience.

The basis for satisfactory observation techniques appears to reflect these qualifications: the observation is a learning experience for both the status leader (or peer) and the teacher; it requires that both observer and teacher understand and mutually agree on acceptable goals of instruction; observation should be a continuous process, but also related to the need; the number of observations (whether several or few) should be sufficient to permit an accurate professional judgment; and several status leaders and/or peers are essential to the observation process in the event there is any question as to the ultimate success of the faculty member. The appraisee, then, should know exactly what is expected of him, how his position is defined, the exact nature of his major job targets, and the procedures that will be followed in observing his performance.

Conference

Most teachers agree that they can profit by a suitable exchange of ideas concerning their teaching and its effectiveness. As the result of such an interchange, numerous opportunities arise that lead to the development of new ideas and behavior patterns related to improved classroom instruction. Such a conference should allow for a complete, open sharing of thoughts on the part of both participants as to the various suggestions that should be capitalized upon.

The supervisory conference should include a thorough discussion of the teaching situation that was observed, the ability of the teacher to meet the situation as it developed, and the overriding factors related to the larger school and community as they affect classroom teaching. In many of its aspects, the conference should provide the teacher ample opportunity for self-appraisal so that he will, at a later time, continue to judge his performance in the light of the suggestions made. It is important that the basic understandings related to good teaching already will have been described at the district level as a matter of written policy. This previous commitment will permit an early agreement as to those good teaching techniques that will be required for improvement in a specific situation.

The teacher should be assisted in the conference to reflect on the behavior and various attitudes that arose during the visit. Only when he can understand and evaluate properly the many classroom experiences that have occurred will he be able to draw conclusions and formulate hypotheses that will permit his own changed behavior.

Throughout the conference the atmosphere should be an informal one. The teacher should be made to feel at ease and he should know that his ideas and opinions are being respectfully heard. The teacher should have ample opportunity to state his problems as he views them, and he should be given every opportunity to indicate ways in which he considers that he could improve his own teaching. All matters discussed in the conference, of course, should be treated in confidence. At the end of the conference the supervisor or administrator should review and summarize the major items that have been discussed. A plan of action should be agreed upon so that there will be an opportunity for professional growth before the next conference is held. A record of the conference should be maintained in the teacher's file to provide a basis for future discussions.

Recent research indicates that the behavioral style of supervisors in supervisory conferences appears to be closely related to the perceptions of teachers as they view certain dimensions of the conference, such as communicative freedom, amount of learning, and over-all productivity.[17] Generally *positive* evaluations by teachers of the quality of their supervisory interpersonal relationships appear to develop: (a) when a teacher perceives his supervisor's behavior as consisting of a heavy emphasis on both telling, suggesting, and criticizing, *and* on reflecting, asking for information and opinions, etc. (high-direct, high-indirect); or (b) when a teacher perceives his supervisor as putting little emphasis on the telling dimension and much on the asking-reflecting dimension (low-direct, high-indirect). Generally *less positive* or even negative evaluations by teachers of the quality of their supervisory interpersonal relationships appear to develop: (a) when a teacher perceives his supervisor as predominantly emphasizing the telling dimension and not doing much in the way of asking or reflecting (high-direct, low-direct); or (b) when a teacher sees his supervisor's behavioral stance as relatively passive (low-direct, low-indirect). If supervisors are able, via their behavior with teachers, to create supportive relationships, the chances are good that the contacts with the supervisor will be seen by the teacher as productive and helpful and that, ultimately, this will be transferred into more productive classroom behavior on the part of the teacher.

[17]Arthur Blumberg, "Supervisory Behavior and Interpersonal Relations," *Educational Administration Quarterly*, Spring 1968, pp. 34–45.

Assistance

Following the observation and conference sessions, the teacher should be prepared to work on the improvement of his own instructional program. The gains that he has made during the past can now be consolidated and he will be in a position to begin making corrections in the areas of work that have not proven successful. In several instances the status leader may have given him some ideas about the establishment of new targets and together they may have come forth with several options or alternatives. Each time the status leader may wish to aid the teacher in appraising the situational choices and reviewing the feasibility of each possible course of action. The importance of assisting the teacher in knowing how to proceed through independent action in improving his own skills and techniques cannot be overemphasized. The status leader will have the responsibility of determining what further contacts need to be made with the faculty members during the course of the year and it is possible that contact situations may be advisable and agreed upon during the summer months while under contract.

There are many examples of assistance in the evaluation process that can be provided by status leaders. At times the teachers may not recognize the lack of *relevance* of a course to the lives of the young people in class. In some fashion the teacher must be assisted in discovering that his teaching must be related to the background, drives, and interests of pupils if they are to be motivated to learn. It may mean that the content of the courses will require changing and the task of the supervisor will be to assist him in seeking new content and relating the subject better to the pupil as well as to the community. Some teachers may lack the means of receiving proper *feedback* as a basis for changing behavior. The status leader's function is to help the teacher view a reflection of what is happening in his classroom and to be of assistance in locating ways in which he can find out for himself what needs to be done. Such studies as those reported by Flanders on verbal behavior, Ryans on verbal and nonverbal behavior, and Hughes on the functions of verbal and nonverbal factors can assist the teacher in gaining insight into his personal role as a teacher. The provision of *Learning Activity Packages (LAP)* may aid certain teachers in approaching better and more effective ways of individualizing their instructional program. The LAP technique is meant to provide help for teachers in identifying objectives and to assist students in selecting the proper route by which they may reach those objectives. Cognitive, educational environmental, affective, and social activities are all related to the improvement of student performance and the design of an organizational system for the classroom that can improve student-teacher interaction. For a few, the development of acceptable *behavioral objectives* may prove burdensome. Group assistance may be necessary in devising objectives that can capture the interaction of the learner, the course, and the teacher all in a unified manner. In a meaningful way, behavioral objectives should aid the teacher in self-evaluating his teaching techniques in relation to the progress being made by pupils. The teacher and the status leader will discover that through mutual planning, effort, and dialog the development of behavioral objectives can provide a valuable learning experience for both parties.

The status leader, in any situation, will wish to identify the learning that is taking place and to develop cooperatively with the teacher criteria that will be used to judge the efficiency of the teaching performance. In an attempt to do just this, the Cincinnati Public School System has devised the *evaluative cycle process*. The evaluative cycle begins when the appraiser and the principal meet with the appraisee to agree on specific job targets for the year. Before the beginning of the spring vacation the appraisee copies his job targets from his work sheet on an appraisal report form on which the appraiser records his evaluation. An appraisal conference is scheduled by the appraiser with the appraisee and the principal to review the year's progress and what needs to be accomplished in the future. During the intervening time faculty members have been encouraged to go to their status leaders for any assistance that they might need. Elimination of the fear of being evaluated by a highly unsophisticated·"check-off" system has caused teachers to work harder, show more concern, and have fewer problems.

SUMMARY

The responsibility of the supervisory staff for the cooperative evaluation of the effectiveness of teaching is great indeed. Regardless of the type of evaluation procedure or instrument utilized, there must be evident maximum opportunities for encouraging, assisting, and rewarding professional growth. There must be a manifestation of the concept that the attainment of quality education is possible only through the vehicle of quality teaching and that no efforts are being spared to make it possible for the teacher to attain such a high level of teaching behavior.

Underlying much of value for teacher evaluation is the whole matter of teacher retention. Evaluation is not and never should be largely a separation device. In a practical vein, the main purpose of evaluation is to prevent, if possible, the occurrence of failure—to discover the early warning symptoms of the onslaught of probable teaching difficulties, to diagnose these early, and to give professional assistance to the teacher before the effects are too devastating for the teacher to overcome. Along with the concept of retention is the matter of building the professional image of the teacher in the eyes of the community. No concept of teacher evaluation will long stand the test of time if there is insufficient opportunity to include the determination of competency on a peer as well as an administrative basis, and the profession must take long, responsible strides in this area to achieve such a level of achievement.

Cooperative evaluation must reflect the existence of the teacher's role in the identification of instructional problems, curriculum development, and many similar educational tasks that have given him an increasing awareness of the vitality and importance of his position. Teacher growth, as measured through evaluation, must have been fostered through many avenues so that his own sophisticated abilities will be evident at the precise time that evaluation occurs. Teacher dissatisfactions and frustrations should not be permitted first to become evident at an evaluation conference; these matters should be solved long before formal evaluation procedures are initiated.

Within its total context, cooperative evaluation of the effectiveness of teaching should reflect a climate of operation in which the teacher can make optimum use of his unique capabilities as they relate to excellence in the area of classroom instruction. Evaluation techniques should be based on the premise of maintaining high faculty morale, good teacher-administrator rapport, high standards of personnel performance, a high level of respect for the teacher, and freedom from non-professional tasks that reduce teacher effectiveness. In essence, professional loyalties should be heightened, not lessened, by the conceptualization of a philosophy of evaluation that encourages teacher growth and dedication.

SELECTED REFERENCES

Adams, Raymond S., and Bruce J. Biddle. *Realities of Teaching: Explorations with Videotape.* New York: Holt, Rinehart and Winston, 1970.

Anderson, O. Roger. *Structure in Teaching: Theory and Analysis.* New York: Teachers College Press, 1969.

Association of Teacher Educators. *Supervisory Conference as Individualized Teaching.* Washington, D.C.: National Education Association, 1969.

DuBois, Phillip H., and G. Douglas Mayo, editors. *Research Strategies for Evaluating Training.* Chicago: Rand McNally, 1970.

Educational Research Service. *Evaluating Teaching Performance*. Washington, D.C.: National Education Association, 1969.

Flanders, Ned A. *Analyzing Teacher Behavior*. Reading, Mass.: Addison-Wesley, 1970.

Fryklund, Verne C. *Analysis Technique for Instructors*. New York: Macmillan, 1970.

Gallagher, James, Graham Nuthall, and Barak Rosenshine. *Classroom Observation*. Chicago: Rand McNally, 1970.

Johnson, David. *Classroom Analysis: The Social Psychology of Education*. New York: Holt, Rinehart and Winston, 1970.

Mayer, Robert F., and Peter Piper. *Analyzing Performance Problems*. Belmont, California: Fearon, 1971.

NTL Institute for Applied Behavioral Science. *Ten Interaction Exercises for Classroom Teachers*. Washington, D.C.: National Education Association, 1970.

Wittrock, Merle. *The Evaluation of Instruction*. New York: Holt, Rinehart and Winston, 1970.

CHAPTER 11

Evaluating Schools and Supervision

In any organization the fundamental purpose of evaluation is to identify those behaviors that tend to enhance or inhibit the progress of the organization toward achievement of its objectives. Often a major weakness in evaluation programs is a lack of predetermined objectives. A good evaluation program does have subordinate purposes that further delineate the mandatory nature of such a program. These purposes are: provision of a continuous process in which the completeness and validity of objectives can be confirmed; establishment of a medium through which the effects of changes in technique or resource allocations on achievement of objectives can be determined; refinement of information collection and analysis procedures leading to the identification of elements which make a critical difference in the learning program; and provision of the only legitimate basis for the systematic integration of resource utilization.[1] In essence, the central core around which evaluation must revolve is the measurement of changes in pupil behavior and the effectiveness of those who are responsible for the degree of success that is attained in making those changes possible.

One phase of the great forward movement in evaluation that has been attained in the 1970's is the national assessment of educational progress. The Committee on Assessing the Progress of Education (CAPE) has utilized the services of the American Institute for Research, Educational Testing Service, the Psychological Corporation, and Science Research Associates in submitting objectives that would serve as bases for developing assessment questions. Three criteria were used: the objectives had to be ones that scholars in the field consider worthwhile, that the schools are currently seeking to attain, and that thought-

---

[1]Donald E. Davis and Neal C. Nickerson, *Critical Issues in School Personnel Administration* (Chicago: Rand McNally, 1968), pp. 64–65.

ful laymen consider important for youth to learn.[2] The results reported will use these subdivisions: male and female; four geographic regions— Northeast, Southeast, Central, and West; four age groups—9, 13, 17, and 26 to 35; different types of communities (large city, urban fringe, middle-sized city, and rural-small town); race; and two socioeconomic levels. Data will be published only in terms of large groups of individuals located within the four major geographic regions. Such data will help taxpayer action that must be guided by sound information as a basis for improving the schools which, in turn, will improve the quality of all aspects of society.

Evaluation tactics for the school and supervision must result in the development of an end product in learning that challenges the learner to respond to such stimuli as simulation, games, problems, and other classroom techniques. One of the prime movers in all evaluation maneuvers is the teacher, but even this stance is undergoing rapid change and evolvement. Any modern evaluation process must include greater reliance on the judgment of students and parents as they develop an increasing awareness of the need for effective teaching and learning. Furthermore, self-renewal of successful educational practices cannot be expected unless evaluation provides keen insights into. the nature of knowledge and how the learning process can capture for the learner a spirit of inquiry and a desire to succeed.

EVALUATION OF SCHOOLS

Evaluation should be considered an essential segment in any planning procedure related to the development of the curriculum. Planning not only looks to the future; it also reverts to the process of review and measurement as to where the instructional program is, as well as where it should be. Evaluation is a means of appraising the situation to determine the facts and their relationship as the organization looks to the future. No evaluation can be accomplished, of course, without the development of an appropriate set of criteria that are based on the aims and objectives that the school is attempting to reach. Evaluation, in fact, continues constantly and is crucial to careful planning and effective supervision.

The tack that evaluation takes is largely determined by the systematic structure that is forged by the staff. The Planning-Programming-Budgeting-System (PPBS), a structural procedure for the decisions to be

[2] *The Shape of Education for 1969–70* (Washington, D.C.: National School Public Relations Association), vol. 11, pp. 29–33.

reached in making policy, is one conceptual approach to this process which includes evaluation and feedback. Its basic function, in the area of instruction, is to analyze the learning process. After a feasibility study or pilot project, the district utilizing PPBS should have a better notion of how to improve the implementation process. Performance measure, criteria of accomplishments, work-load measures, and system renewal devices can be developed.[3] Planning calendars should be designed that will assist those concerned with decisions and evaluation at all levels within the system. The program budget, therefore, provides a system for the evaluation of school output and school costs over time and provides a comprehensive framework for rational planning. Although the best way to control the quality of output is to control the quality of input, the schools do not have this choice and this fact should be made clear to the public.

Although the schools are becoming increasingly more interested in the concept of self-study, the school is enmeshed in a cloud of shifting public opinions and demands.

Several important forces at work have serious implications for education. The rapid accumulation of knowledge is demanding greater selectivity and discretion for the learner in determining what is to him valuable information and what is not. Increasing expectations and selectivity of personnel by business and industry require extended educational preparation and training. Mass-media communication is breaking down the barriers of community isolation and provincialism and awakening an almost universal demand for a quality education for all who can profit from it. The accent on greater productivity for everyone has challenged the school to provide for individual differences in myriad ways. The shortened workweek has resulted in a widespread recognition of the need for education for profitable, wholesome leisure time activities. The "population explosion" has increased the population of the United States by nearly 30 million in ten years and has annually added more than 1 million children to the school rolls.[4]

In many respects, schools need assistance from the educational profession and the public in attaining a sense of direction through evaluation and self-study. This will necessitate a total approach to evaluation involving faculty, students, parents, community, accrediting associations, and many other contributing agencies.

[3]Harry J. Hartley, *Educational Planning-Programming-Budgeting: A Systems Approach* (Englewood Cliffs, N.J.: Prentice-Hall, 1968), pp.98 and 250–252.
[4]Stanley W. Williams, *Educational Administration in Secondary Schools: Task and Challenge* (New York: Holt, Rinehart and Winston, 1964), p. 481.

Evaluation of End Products

An important concern in the area of educational evaluation is the establishment of a statement of worth concerning the product that has been or should be attained. In the past, there was a tendency to make judgments of the worth or value of various phases of the educational programs by merely observing the activities as though the attainment of objectives was being measured. Learner behavior was considered less important than teacher behavior because the behavioral objectives for learners had not been prescribed prior to the teaching act in the classroom. Today this approach is not acceptable and the behavior of learners is the basic criterion by which evaluative judgments about the educational program need to be made. Creating such measures for the assessment of learner achievement is time consuming, but this can be accomplished with vigorous faculty-supervisor effort in the development of individual pupil attainment measures. Evaluation can become an exceptionally valuable tool when it is conceived on a systematic basis and the predetermined behavioral objectives are explicit and measurable. In this way faculty and status leaders make accurate decisions about instructional activities based on the effectiveness of their product and the resources required to maintain or increase their value.

Educational Performance Indicators

Evaluation of many kinds constitutes an important aspect of school program assessment. Educators recognize the need for systematic evaluation not only of the direction in which they are attempting to move, but also of how successful they are in terms of the progress they are able to make as they move toward those objectives. Evaluation implies an audit function in that it becomes the process of assembling and analyzing processes and systems.[5] It usually involves measurement and can take place in any educational setting. The classroom teacher, the department head, the school principal, the supervisor, and many other groups become involved in evaluation activities at various times. *Evaluation as Feedback and Guide,* a yearbook of the Association for Supervision and Curriculum Development, is an excellent source in this critical performance area.

The New York evaluation study for the development of a new type of comprehensive, statewide evaluation program represents a pioneering attempt to develop for educators a set of reliable indicators of the success an educational program is enjoying. Educational Testing Service has found that the indicators must provide estimates of the amount

[5] *Educational Testing Service Annual Report* (Princeton, N.J.: Educational Testing Service, 1968), pp. 44–50.

of change in students as they go through any phase of an educational system. This necessitates repeated assessment of the same students over a period of time. It also has discovered that all elements of the total educational process must be taken into account; this requires some system for including adequate measures of all the major factors that affect a student's educational progress.

Out of the New York evaluation study it is hoped that educational performance indicators can be developed to serve three purposes. First, to provide a series of measures to indicate how well a school system is meeting the needs of its students, taking cognizance of the conditions in which the system operates. Second, to identify the areas in which a school system needs help, such as more professional services, specific educational improvements, and the like. Third, to clarify in concrete ways what schools are doing for different kinds of children, thus enabling policy makers and the public to come to grips with the specific goals they want for their schools.

Instructional Objectives Exchange

Never before the decade of the 1970's have so many educators been committed to the idea that instruction should be evaluated primarily by the results it produces in its learners. The Center for the Study of Evaluation at the University of California, Los Angeles operates: (1) as a depository bank for instructional objectives and related evaluation measures on which educators can draw for purposes of local instruction and evaluation; (2) as a dissemination center which keeps educators informed about projects involving the development of instructional objectives and evaluation measures; and (3) as a development agency committed to development objectives and measures in fields where satisfactory pools do not exist. All objectives made available by the Instructional Objectives Exchange are stated operationally, that is, in terms of measurable learner behavior. All evaluation measures (not only test items, but also diverse types of learner performance measures) are based on these operationally stated objectives. Status leaders in a variety of subject fields may draw on a bank like this to make available alternative objectives and measuring devices to assist school personnel in their instructional and evaluation activities.

Role of the Parent in Evaluation

Should parents have a voice (preferential if not determinative) regarding the school curriculum? Should parents have a decision in the kind of teacher they feel their children need? Although many would give a negative reply, there are many options within the basic standards and goals of the school. Often the professional choice is only one of several objectively useful choices, and the professional's word is final because he has a monopoly of authority. If community involvement is to be real, if parent-teacher partnership is to have any meaning beyond lip service, some experts would say that the proper role of the profes- sional would be to outline the educationally sound alternatives and to afford the parents and the community a choice among them.[6]

A serious defect is the assumption that parent participation is so special that it requires special attention and designated periods, like Brotherhood Week. Participatory democracy in education, on the other hand, gives parents and community a tangible respect for the intimacy and complexity of the professional problems of education. As parents begin to become more or less equal partners in the process, their con- cerns soon broaden and they begin to ask for help. Continuity of sociali- zation among the homes, the child's peer group, and the schools could be restored if parents participated in the formal education process. In effect, the realignment of the participants in public education could produce: (1) for parents, a tangible grasp on the destiny of their chil- dren; (2) for professionals, a surcease from an increasingly negative community climate and an addition of new allies; and (3) for children, a school system responsive to their needs, resonant with their personal style, and affirmative in its expectations of their efforts. Educational reconstruction of this order would signal significant changes in the processes of evaluation and accreditation as educators now know them.

Accrediting Associations

There are regional accrediting agencies that provide services to every state in the nation. Although these associations evaluate schools on the basis of preset standards, they advocate the use of self-evaluation techniques as a part of the accreditation process.[7] Factors such as teacher assignment, staff morale, class loads, student-teacher-com- munity involvement, plant and equipment, and innovative practices are carefully reviewed to ascertain whether or not the school is meeting acceptable regional standards. The *Evaluative Criteria* devised by the Cooperative Study of Secondary School Standards has provided basic assistance to regional associations in the development of their own accreditation instruments.

The six regional accrediting associations, with their goals, are these: (1) the Middle States Association of Colleges and Secondary Schools (to raise the educational standards of schools and colleges within its area);

---

[6]Mario D. Fantini, "Alternatives for Urban School Reform," *Harvard Educational Review*, vol. 38, no. 1 (Winter 1968), pp. 12—16 (reprint).
[7]Williams, *op. cit.* pp. 484–495.

(2) the New England Association of Colleges and Secondary schools (to determine that schools meet definite standards in a variety of areas); (3) the North Central Association of Colleges and Secondary schools (to encourage the maintenance of excellence in all its member educational institutions); (4) the Northwest Association of Secondary and Higher Schools (to foster continuous self-evaluation and self-improvement through the systematic use of the *Evaluative Criteria*); (5) the Southern Association of Colleges and Secondary Schools (to identify and recognize good schools and encourage their continuous improvement); and (6) the Western Association of Schools and Colleges (to help school staff and students determine how well the school program is fulfilling locally-established educational objectives). The approval or accreditation of schools by these associations does much to assure the public that these institutions are meeting recognized and reliable standards of accreditation and that they are in possession of new guidelines to consider as they proceed toward a new accreditation period. Each and every accrediting association makes a careful assessment of the instructional and in-service program of the school; which offers much assistance to the supervisory staff in evaluating the total educational program.

Accrediting agencies are constantly permitting more experimentation in various fields of educational concern. Exceptions are being made to preset standards when it can be demonstrated that the institution is making certain strides toward the development of important new concepts. As much flexibility as possible is being permitted to assure that data used on a comparative basis and preconceived standards do not interfere with the potential impact of new ideas and new directions.

Other Agencies

State departments of education often assume responsibility for the assessment of the quality of education in the various schools within the state. Personnel within the state department of education typically are assigned the function of passing judgment on these schools by deciding whether or not they meet the standards considered minimal by the state. Often this assessment is made through the filing of annual reports and visits made to schools where it is deemed necessary. In states where there is a strong central state education agency, there appears to be tighter control by the state on the accreditation process.

Educational consultants are often found at colleges and universities. These persons, with the prestigious backing of the university's good name, are generally well qualified to render the services required by the district. When an outside voice is needed in the evaluation process, the university consultants and/or teams are in an excellent position to speak with authority in regard to their findings. The public is likely to consider their review to be quite objective inasmuch as they are "outside" the educational establishment. Some universities maintain bureaus of research and field studies that have services available on a contractual basis. These agencies generally are committed to the upgrading of education within their area of influence and strive diligently to provide real help to many schools in their region. In addition, many colleges and universities have competent professors who value the opportunity to work closely with educational leaders at the district and school level on problems of practical significance.

The civil rights movement has been closely allied with the evaluation of education. In fostering parent control of large numbers of community schools within the ghetto areas, these groups frequently have been quite critical of how the schools have responded to the moods of the minority communities. Through the use of demonstrations and threatened or actual boycotts, the extremists have attempted to influence the decision-making authority of school boards as well as the structural arrangements of school operation.[8]

The art of measurement, as provided by a private agency such as the Educational Testing Service, can be of great assistance in the definition of goals and the evaluation of educational progress. More and more, educators are asking for measurement and advisory services as they need help in knowing how to go about defining educational goals.[9] They seek assistance in evaluating new curricular materials, and they want help in developing measures for judging the effectiveness of alternative curricular programs. New ways of recognizing and describing nonacademic qualities and characteristics that affect educational progress are being sought. In a broad sense, educators are seeking a blend of curriculum studies, developmental research, and consultation. Educational Testing Service, in participating in a study in depth on a partnership basis, must be ready to draw upon all elements of its current resources and upon its extensive background of experience in research, development, programs of measurement, and advisory and instructional programs.

The Educational Opportunities Survey has demonstrated that education must be viewed as a vehicle that has broader implications than just the school itself. Community improvements are as necessary as improvements in the classroom if equal opportunities are to be made available to *all* youth in America. Evaluation, in this sense, must measure not only what is happening in the formalized classroom environ-

---

[8]Stephen J. Knezevich, *Administration of Public Education* (New York: Harper and Row, 1969), p. 208.

[9]Educational Testing Service, *op. cit.*, pp. 19–20.

ment of the school, but the totality of the community's informal educational climate as well. The comprehensive demands of our culture must be brought into focus and translated into the kinds of products that require diagnosis, prediction, and evaluation.

In effect, many agencies have had an influence on the evaluation of educational programs. Some of these not previously mentioned are:

1. The National Congress of Parents and Teachers with its publication *Looking in on Your School.*
2. The Los Angeles Cooperative Council on In-Service Education has advanced the entire continuum of research by reducing the time lag in making education research as practical as possible through classroom experimentations.
3. Regional assessment projects that utilize the systems approach in analyzing what tasks pupils are able to accomplish as they complete certain phases of their education.
4. The multitude of federal programs that are under contract with the U.S. Office of Education, and the Research and Evaluation Division of the U.S. Office of Economic Opportunity; both link theory with practice and are concerned with the evaluation of innovation concepts.
5. The National Citizens Council for Better Schools with its publication *Yardsticks for Better Schools.*
6. The Research and Development Centers that are sponsored by the U.S. Office of Education and have impeccable reputations in the field of educational research.
7. The regional educational laboratories under the Elementary and Secondary Education Act of 1965 that take research findings in the educational field and translate these into practice at the school level.
8. The James B. Conant studies on secondary schools that had great public impact in determining how these institutions were meeting his standards.

Organizational efforts and reports such as those listed above give ample evidence of some of the new trends in self-evaluation and accreditation. The idealities of research and the realities of the situation make, on occasion, wide gaps and difficulties confronting objective-styled evaluation. Both formal and informal measures must be used in evaluation procedures. At the risk of not having any evaluation at all of educational programs, every institutional agency must program itself so that it can facilitate the evolvement of a variety of measuring instruments that adequately measure the product as it relates to relevant and intelligent goals.

New Developments

The Martha Holden Jennings Foundation has financed a new measurement program called the Yardstick Project. This project has been devised to assist status leaders in measuring how well their schools are performing and to aid them in testing the effectiveness of the decisions that they have made. Project Yardstick has developed growth measurements for school districts to determine the programs of students in relation to their social setting, economic backgrounds, and IQ. Also, it has devised a planning model that, through computerized assists, can simulate mathematical responses to a variety of hypothetical situations. The growth-gauge concept measures the contribution of the school district to the development of students and qualifies what students bring to their performances apart from what the school contributes. This gauges what the school begins with and what it is able to accomplish in terms of the progress of its pupils. Also, the planning model can devise a wide range of options to the solution of a particular problem. It has the ability to present figures and costs that aid status leaders in making decisions that are accurate and based on facts. By 1971 Project Yardstick had expanded to encompass twenty-four school districts.

The Western Association of Schools and Colleges has proposed that a new "quality assurance" program be developed as a new dimension in school evaluation. The new instrument would include five aspects for assessing how well a school purports to do: (1) quality assurance—assessing both the product and the process of education; (2) behavioral objectives—utilizing specific, measurable goals for every facet of education for grades 1–12; (3) program budgeting—using long-range planning and cost analysis to help determine educational effectiveness; (4) self-evaluation—using modern techniques of the social sciences in assessing instructional programs; and (5) innovation—adapting to education the improved management techniques of business, industry, and government. The primary purpose of the mission would be to formulate an accurate basis from which a school may design ways of increasing and improving learning by its students. Unmistakable evidence exists that ways need to be formulated for a school to measure itself so that it will have an objective basis on which to develop an effective program of instructional improvement. Utilizing specific, measurable, behavioral objectives as a basis for evaluating the effectiveness of instruction is important as well.

ES 70 (Educational Systems for the 1970's) is a new network of twelve creative school districts across the nation, including Nova High School in Florida. ES 70 has just launched a long-range project to design and activate the instructional programs of this decade. An important phase of the project is evaluation of the product, and assessing its impact upon the student population.

In 1970 the American Association of School Administrators Commission on Administration Technology called for the creation of a research, planning, information, and development division (RPID) in any school district in a city of 30,000 or more. One facet of this operation would be to set goals, examine and describe existing programs, and, with operations research, determine the strategies to accomplish the goals, and the means of feedback to various personnel to monitor how well the system works. With rising expectations as to what the public schools can and should do, teachers and status leaders have a joint responsibility to expand their accountability in the areas of long-range planning, decision-making, and problem solving.

EVALUATING THE SUPERVISORY PROGRAM

Perhaps one of the most valid commitments for any supervisory program is the emphasis that it places upon the entire process of evaluation. Few supervisors would contend that such evaluation confine itself alone to teachers, programs, and practices. It is readily apparent that a total program of evaluation by a supervisory staff must include, among other measures, evaluation of the effectiveness of the role of the supervisor and the adequacy of the supervisory services offered. No justification can be made for any program of supervision that does not provide services that lead to dynamic and readily identifiable programs of instructional improvement. A constant flow of data concerning professional and lay judgments of many kinds must be an integral part of the evaluation process. Objective evidence for this should be gathered based upon a thorough study of the purposes and processes of supervision. Many kinds of evaluation instruments may be used, such as judgments by the administrative staff, teachers' opinion polls, self-evaluation instruments, case studies, supervisory activity logs, and total program appraisals.

In many respects the evaluation of a program of supervision reflects three aspects of analysis: philosophy, preparation, and evaluation. To be effective philosophically, the supervisor needs a basic understanding of the guiding principles and purposes related to the programs under his supervision. His warmth of understanding of personnel and his ability to contribute to the growth of these individuals should be paramount. In the area of preparation, the supervisor must have had a rigorous background of training and experience in educational preparation, classroom teaching, and curriculum work. Relative to evaluation, he should be an expert in the field of total program evaluation. His attitude should be one that promotes unfettered communication between himself and the certificated staff, his services should be highly oriented to the whole realm of instructional improvement, his emphasis should be on a balance between the use of the group process and individual attention to teachers, his concern for orderly pupil growth and progress must be evident, and his ability to invoke and encourage stringent evaluation of the total program of instructional services must be noteworthy.

In recent years a modest attempt has been engendered by the education profession to derive valid methods of evaluating supervisory programs. Some noteworthy research in this field, however, has been accomplished and this is discussed in the remaining pages of this chapter.

Basic Concepts

Educational leaders, much like teachers, are in need of evaluative techniques that can assist them in gauging the effectiveness of their work. Good evaluative procedures can be as effective in rating the excellence of the supervisory program as they are in determining the skill with which the classroom teacher is manipulating the teaching-learning situation. Evaluation procedures should determine what steps are being taken in the supervisory program, the manner in which those steps are meeting the basic goals or objectives of the program, and what action must be initiated to improve the total program of improvement of instruction. Every opportunity must be given the teacher to be an active participant in the evaluative process if it is to reflect the thinking of the entire professional staff.

What are some of the areas that should be considered in the evaluation of the supervisory program? Initially, the supervisor or administrator should be evaluated in terms of how well he is functioning. In relation to giving the teacher support, he should: be of assistance in solving the many problems that confront the teacher, provide the kinds of information that are required by the teacher to improve his work, consistently suggest concepts and ideas that will improve the learning situation in the classroom, and act as a confidant in matters that the teacher wishes not to discuss with the administration, but that still calls for professional help on a problem-solving basis. On a personal basis the supervisor or administrator should be extremely sensitive to the relations that exist among faculty members and do whatever he can to solidify them. His reputation in the school or district should be such that he is known for his positive attitude in helping teachers to become successful, permanent members of the teaching force. He should have a real respect for individual faculty members and do all in his power to promote an atmosphere of professional and personal independence that encourages them to grow professionally as career teachers. Even his criticism of a teacher's work should be proposed in such a manner that the teacher recognizes that the supervisor or administrator is doing his utmost to assist him in solving his problems so that he can become a better classroom teacher.

The human aspect as it is related to the improvement of teaching has proven to be a large factor in motivating teachers. All those in the classroom, both students and teacher, must be given an opportunity to assist in the improvement of instruction. Their contributions can do much to assure a greater interest in accomplishing a real gain in the betterment of learning activities in a particular room situation. The supervisor or administrator, in all instances, should show a real concern for the success of each of the teachers with whom he works and recognize that this represents one of the most important expectations of his role as educational leader.

To make possible a high level of supervisory leadership, those assigned to supervisory tasks must be given a commensurate amount of time to permit them to perform satisfactorily. Administrators, in particular, have to be freed from many routine administrative functions if they are to be permitted to concentrate on their many instructional responsibilities. The development of the curriculum program cannot be expected to move ahead as it should until the proper amount of staff time for instructional leadership is provided.

Improving Supervisory Services

What changes are desirable in the typical allocation of responsibility for providing instructional services? To find some answers to this question, a research project was inaugurated to ascertain desirable changes in services for the improvement of instruction as identified by more than 400 superintendents, principals, and supervisors from a random, stratified sample of California school districts.[10] The most striking finding was that all respondents wished to see teacher groups have more responsibility in providing supervisory services.

In response to the question as to the most desirable improvement in providing supervisory services at the district level, 31 percent said that more supervisory personnel was the most desirable improvement; an additional 9 percent indicated the need for more supervisory personnel in specialized curriculum areas. Approximately 9 percent of the

[10]Helen C. Wood, "How Can Supervisory Services Be Improved?" *California Journal for Instructional Improvement*, vol. 4, no. 4 (December 1962), pp. 24–26. See also Gerald Ellis, "Teacher Accountability: A Supervisory Lever for Pupil Progress and Success," *Croft's Elementary Principal's Service*, November 1969.

respondents asked for more supervisory services, without specifically mentioning personnel. A total of 49 percent of the responses to the question pointed to a need for more personnel or more services from the supervisory staff. In addition, 15 percent of the responses indicated the desirability of more and better supervision by principals. These responses often included suggestions as to various ways in which principals might be provided assistance with noninstructional responsibilities to free them for more instructional leadership. Better facilities and conditions for teaching were considered the most desirable change for improving instruction by 14 percent of the respondents; the need pointed out most frequently was for smaller classes. The greatest need for improvement was identified by 12 percent of the responses in the area of district organization and coordination. Other responses included more involvement of teachers, more research and experimentation, and improved supervision, with frequent suggestions that more in-service education be provided for supervisors and administrators. Among the major changes, not already identified, that were suggested for the improvement of instruction were: that more use should be made of college consultants; that in-service programs should include opportunities for continued professional growth of supervisors and principals; that improvement of the conditions for teaching should be a major concern of the instructional improvement program; and that districts should be reorganized where necessary so that they are large enough to provide their own supervisory staffs.

Teachers Evaluate Supervisory Performance

By 1971 two school systems (Aurora, Colorado, and Fayette County, Kentucky) were encouraging the evaluation of supervisory personnel by certificated staff members. In Fayette County, the purposes of evaluating supervisory personnel were as follows: 1) to improve the quality of supervisory services through a systematic appraisal of performance; 2) to provide a source of information relative to supervisory practices; and 3) to provide each supervisor with information as to how he is perceived by others. The appraisal results are used exclusively by the person being appraised and each status leader is requested to review and analyze carefully the appraisal results that are submitted to him by the staff. The areas that are covered in the appraisal form with a rating of "Highest Ranking Qualities" or "Lowest Ranking Qualities" are: organization, administration, planning, communications, relationship with staff, relationship with community, professional growth and ethics, instructional leadership, personal characteristics, and relationship with pupils.

In Aurora, teachers evaluate their supervisory leaders once annually in February. Teachers use the same forms as those completed by the supervisor's district administrators and the evaluations are signed by the teachers, with the original being given to the person being evaluated. The areas covered are: curriculum improvement, relationship with staff, relationship with community, personal characteristics, professional growth, and management ability. Discussion of the evaluation by the teacher with the status leader is optional, although this is encouraged. Aurora is in the process of revising the evaluation criteria so that the ranking is better understood by both the certificated person and the supervisor.

Coordination and Accountability

Research in upgrading supervisory services in the 1970's has shown that the behavior of status leaders ranked highest when they had a firm and tangible belief in the worth of people and respected the individual differences among faculty members. Many indications exist that status leader-teacher groups that work together are far more productive than single teachers attacking their problems individually. Teachers do wish to have status leaders share their knowledge with them and willingly give them assistance whenever it is needed. Faculty personnel consider that many good ideas have come from attendance at conferences by status leaders who have later shared this information with them. Status leaders are highly thought of when they recognize the professional growth of teachers and take a personal interest in them by giving words of encouragement as well as commendation. Teachers feel that the district has the responsibility for establishing basic premises for evaluation of supervisory services, and that faculty personnel need to be involved in the assessment of those services to the district and to the staff.

Quality supervisory performance requires that status leaders be held accountable for creating an overall educational development plan and insuring its success. The plan should be systematically devised with a timetable of program expectations over a period of one, two, or even five years. A strong research base can do much to aid with the close evolvement of productivity as it relates to the goal structure. As community expectations for education continue to rise, the responsibility level for supervisors will grow accordingly. The accomplishments of students will be more closely correlated with the professional growth of both teachers and status leaders. It is likely that in the near future school systems will have their instructional programs subjected to an educational audit by an outside agency. The Texarkana contract award in mathematics and reading to Dorsett Educational Systems, Inc. is a good example of this trend.

Evaluation Studies

The Educational Research Service in a new survey, Evaluating Administrative Performance, has discovered from a sample group of 157 school systems that a little over one-third have specific procedures for evaluating administrative and supervisory personnel. ERS considers that a trend is developing in the evaluation of status leaders in the schools, that annual evaluations are the most common, and that the immediate superior is the person who most frequently evaluates the administrator or supervisor.

Role expectations of the status leader by the faculty as he fulfills his supervisory tasks are important measures of the quality of supervision. Teacher-supervision specialists at times may consider the teacher a disembodied abstraction and tend to plan supervisory activities with the presumption that all teachers need the same kind of assistance, e.g., help, sympathy, model lessons, and the like.[11] Therefore, it behooves the status leader to consider the needs of individualized supervision if he wishes to be rated highly by his teaching colleagues. In large measure this means that the status leader should increase the emphasis on teacher help in his supervisory program so that it relates closely to the needs and personalities of individual faculty members.

Several research projects have demonstrated that effective evaluation of supervisory personnel is based on the contribution of the supervisor to the goals of the school system as well as a keen insight into the support required by teaching personnel to carry forth their instructional duties. As teachers work more in teams, status leaders are expected to give them more autonomy and a greater role in decision-making as they strive to improve the instructional program. Teachers are taking a greater interest in sharing in the evaluation of supervisory programs and it will be imperative to develop a set of appraisal techniques that are acceptable to the appraisers (teachers) and the appraisees (status leaders). Teachers, as well as supervisors, must understand the nature of the supervisory task in order to make accurate judgments concerning its accomplishments. Appraisal questions like these need to be asked: What are the cooperative instructional targets? What is the commitment to the faculty, students, and community? What is the relation of the appraisal procedure to the total program of supervision? What coordinate working relationships are essential to involve all faculty in program improvement? What provisions have been made for written school district policies governing

[11]Joseph Satin, "The Principal and Individualized Teacher Supervision," *Education Age*, vol. 5, no. 4 (March-April 1970), pp. 8–10.

evaluation procedures? What data have been gathered to gauge the effectiveness of the supervisory program in meeting its goals? What official records are available that will signify the scope, depth, and intensity of supervisory services at the appropriate level?

Bath Studies Its Instructional Services Program

The city of Bath recently hired a consultant to identify the strengths and weaknesses of its supervisory program, to identify points of issue relative to the program, and to develop recommendations for the improvement of the program. Although the study was focused largely on the services of the district supervisory staff, it was concerned also with instructional services provided by administrators, department heads, and counselors in the various district schools.

To acquire background for the study, the consultant held several conferences with the superintendent and assistant superintendent of schools. Questions were raised and many issues identified in these conferences. Following this much background information was gained from reports, handbooks, course-of-study descriptions, bulletins, and other printed materials developed by the district supervisory staff. When this was completed, many interviews of an hour or more in length were held with many of the aforementioned personnel, including teachers, in the Bath city school system. These persons were chosen for interview purposes by their school or group as representative of their total personnel. The interviews included a discussion of the outstanding characteristics of the supervisorial services program, problem areas found in the program, and recommendations for improvement. In addition all district personnel were invited to write their particular points of view and submit these directly to the consultant.

Two months later the consultant presented his findings and recommendations to the superintendent and board of education. The major recommendations concerned themselves with clarification of supervisory roles, better organizational balance, better utilization of principals and assistant principals, increased emphasis on instructional improvement activity within individual schools, improvement of classroom visitation techniques, increased use of demonstrations by supervisors, added para-professional assistants for the teacher, improved salary incentives for outstanding teachers, greater reliance on teacher evaluation of the instructional services that they receive, and organization of a district council whose primary interest is in the development of the instructional program.

The comprehensive recommendations were well received by Bath educators and an immediate improvement program was put into effect.

Six months later the district supervisory staff made a formal report to the board of education as to the implementations made for each recommendation.

SUMMARY

The force that makes possible the development of any good supervisory program is the result of the coordinated efforts of both administrators and teachers. This coordination demands not only the willingness of both groups to listen to suggestions, to carry on experimentation, and to propose new ways of approaching instructional problems, but also the willingness to analyze cooperatively the effectiveness of the supervisory activity. Further, it means a readiness to take a searching look at the effectiveness of the entire educational program in terms of the elements of cooperative planning, instructional inspiration, and the professional insight that is demonstrated as the local organization plans for the future. Such an evaluation demands the development of a suitable model, as the check list indicated previously.

In many respects there must be certain concepts that are essential to the development of any supervisory program evaluation model. These are: the involvement of teachers in the establishment of the evaluation criteria; the recognition of how well the program is meeting the requirements of local policy and needs; the fulfillment of democratic principles that respect the personality and intelligence of teachers; the concern for evolving basic purposes through group decision; the knowledge that the program must work toward behavioral change among staff members; that a high regard is shown for objective and comprehensive methods of teacher evaluation; that the program encourages teacher initiative and innovation; that communication flow is facilitated; that in-service opportunities of the highest order are provided; and that appraisal of the program is a continuous process. The supervisory program should be evaluated from the point of view that supervision, after all, is a method for improving the teaching-learning situation and not merely an inspectional instrument that violates the dignity and aspirations of the teaching force.

SELECTED REFERENCES

Association for Supervision and Curriculum Development. *Improving Educational Assessment and An Inventory of Measures of Affective Behavior.* Washington, D.C.: National Education Association, 1969.
Association for Supervision and Curriculum Development. *The International*

Dimensions of Education. Washington, D.C.: National Education Association, 1970.

Educational Research Services. *Evaluating Administrative Performance.* Washington, D.C.: National Education Association, 1968.

Gross, N., *et al. Implementing Organizational Innovation: A Sociological Analysis of Planned Change in Schools.* New York: Basic Books, 1971.

Hudgins, Bryce. *The Instructional Process.* Chicago: Rand McNally, 1971.

Leacock, Eleanor B. *Teaching and Learning in City Schools: A Comparative Study.* New York: Basic Books, 1969.

McGrath, J. H. *Planning System for School Executives: The Unity of Theory-Practice.* Scranton: Intext, 1971.

Ranniger, Bill J., E. Wailand Bessent, and John T. Greer. *Elementary School Administration: A Casebook.* Scranton: Intext, 1969.

Snyder, B. R. *Hidden Curriculum.* New York: Alfred A. Knopf, 1971.

CHAPTER 12

The New Dynamics of Supervision

The new status leader attempts to broaden, deepen, and invigorate teaching performance in all of its many aspects. Recognizing that competent leadership must be viewed as a demonstration of individual ability and understanding, he provides effectively for the development of outstanding teachers who are embarked on a program that leads to the attainment of quality education. To do this, the modern status leader liberally educates himself in the context of modern world thought and culture, becomes knowledgeable in a variety of subject-matter fields and disciplines, and is prepared to lead the way cooperatively with the faculty in numerous areas associated with experimentation and research. His image as an instructional leader is one that is impeccable as perceived by teachers. His personal integrity, his understanding of human growth and the development of learning, his unquestioned role as a contributor to educational progress, his ability in the area of coordinate decision-making, and his rich perception of the worth and talent of individuals in the educational hierarchy are characteristics that are readily viewed by teachers as an indication of his talent to play a joint leadership role with the faculty in the area of instruction. He demonstrates a genuine concern for the many needs of teachers who require professional growth opportunities and he recognizes that release from the tensions of academic freedom and the encouragement of scholarly pursuit and attainment are among the many characteristics that identify the effectiveness of helpful supervision to teacher performance.

The remainder of this chapter will attempt to give people in status positions a vision of some concepts and ideas that relate to the tasks of the schools and supervision in the years that lie ahead. It also will discuss some of the new educational developments and concerns that are be-

ginning to unfold in the decade of the seventies. A few of these new concepts that are examined are: national assessment, performance contracting systems, private operation of public schools, automated instructional monitoring systems, educational systems automated programs, educational audit systems, citizens' school-community committees for educational excellence, the POINT plan, the Initial Teaching Alphabet system, middle schools, district-wide accreditation plans, synergistic environmental climate, cybernetics, and the Delphi projection technique.

SIGNIFICANT DEVELOPMENTS

What lies ahead in education? It would be quite naive to undertake the awesome task of describing all the movements, events, and innovations of significance in education at a period fast approaching the decade of the eighties. At this time, however, there is rather strong evidence that education is ending one era and beginning another. Concepts, ideas, and dreams that were beginning to be formulated during the period immediately following World War II are now entering the stage of trial and error. The quickened pace of our culture and our times has projected educational plans and commitments into a new era that defies the imagination and resourcefulness of even the most experienced educator. Little wonder, then, that the explosion of knowledge accompanied by the advances of sociological sophistication of the American public has triggered many new educational innovations that were little beyond the fantasy stage twenty years ago.

Perhaps the most difficult challenge for today's supervisor or administrator is to project his thoughts concerning the knowledge that he must command in order to: (1) relate his efforts to notable, changing teacher behavior in the modern school; and (2) ascertain the changes that accrue in the fulfillment of the role of the supervisory leader as education steers a stellar and somewhat unknown course in the next two or three decades. In response to the needs of education, supervisors and administrators will become both observers of and participants in the innovations that are making newspaper headlines in the decade of the seventies. Some of the more notable developments and commmitments in education are discussed here.

A rather startling proposal has evolved through the initiation of the National Assessment Project. For years little attempt has been made to ascertain the progress of education on a national basis. Not until Ralph Tyler, Director of the Center for Advanced Study of the Behavioral Sciences, launched a program under the auspices of the Carnegie Corporation was such a massive evaluation of American education attempted. The project, as stated earlier, will attempt to provide the United States with information about the strengths and weaknesses of its educational system, to identify educational problems that need the attention of resesearch-oriented programs, to arouse the interest of American citizens in their educational program and its needs, and to make comparisons of American education with that of foreign countries. Supervisory staffs most likely will be involved in studying the results of this national project and utilizing its findings as a basis for corroborating new developments in their own local programs. Directly in conjunction with this project is the Pennsylvania Study of Quality Education. In an effort to determine the adequacy and efficiency of education in the state, the Pennsylvania study has aroused the interest of educators everywhere in observing the ability of a state to determine the present status of education and how it may be improved in the future. This massive and ongoing program of evaluation is both focused and cumulative and it is expected that it will lead to greatly improved educational opportunities for young people in the state. Also in line with this is the Educational Opportunities Survey under the sponsorship of the U.S. Office of Education. Five percent of the country's public elementary and secondary schools have been sampled with the intent of identifying the academic abilities of children, student-home characteristics, the effectiveness of the school's educational program, and facts and attitudes of teachers, administrators, and supervisors as related to the various schools in which they serve.

No reference to significant educational movements could overlook Compact for Education, the new interstate alliance of education and politics aimed at upgrading public education. As an outgrowth of James Conant's suggestion that there be a mechanism for a better interchange of information and for a clear, nationwide educational policy adequate to meet public demands, the interstate Compact, as an information center for the states, will recommend ways for the states to solve specific problems and to act from a position of strength in educational matters. The Compact, too, will act to strengthen state and local control of educational affairs. Supervisory leaders may well expect the Compact's educational commission to recognize some of the hitherto unnoticed or unsolved probems unique to certain states or regions and to provide political as well as educational support to the solution of these probems. Lastly, in this context, the new Three-State Program which is federally financed in Arizona, California, and Nevada will try to unravel the mysteries of the human thinking process. This experimental plan will provide specific teaching aids for instructors of the more than 13 million grade-school children in the Southwestern United States along with school management and planning advice. Under the new Southwest Regional Laboratory for Educational Research and Development, experimentation will be carried out with cooperating school districts. Early projects may include communication skills at primary and pre-school levels, problems related to children from bilingual homes, administrative planning, and management systems. Such a project will do much to assist the states in applying the results from significant educational research to classroom experience.

A new aspect of accountability in education has arrived with the advent of the performance contracting system in the city of Texarkana. The Texarkana project brings another emphasis in using performance contracting with private industry as a basis for reducing the dropout problem. Dorsett Educational Systems has opened four operational Rapid Learning Centers to prevent dropouts by raising the achievement levels of students through improved reading and mathematics instruction. The cost is $80 per pupil per grade level in these subjects covering eighty hours of instruction. Dorsett Educational Systems, then, will be paid $80 for every pupil whose proficiency it raises by one grade level using eighty hours of mechanized instruction. For any student who does not succeed, the firm will be paid nothing. A wide range of educational technology will be used, including programmed machines, tapes, records, tests, and television. Motivation is promoted through the issuance of green stamps, radios, and television sets. The teacher programs students on an individual basis, and students are selected on the basis of being two grade levels or more behind in achievement. Early test results show that, with the eighty hours of instruction, average students have increased one grade level in mathematics and one and one-half grade levels in reading. Many school systems nationally are watching this experiment in accountability with much interest as a possible means of locating educational program areas that fit a pattern of precise definition and can be assessed accordingly.

The Behavioral Research Laboratories (BRL), 1970–71, became the first private company to operate a public school in its entirety. Gary, Indiana, public school system has contracted with BRL to operate an elementary school at a cost of $800 per student annually under an agreement that BRL will bring students' achievement scores up to or above the national grade-level norms in all essential areas of the curriculum. For those students who do not reach those levels, BRL will refund the fees paid by the city. An independent agency will make an evaluation of the plan after three years and in the fourth year the school will revert to the control of the Gary public school system. This agreement is another of an increasing number of educational performance contracting systems in which private companies are held accountable for the academic growth of pupils as a basis for determining whether or not fees will be paid for each pupil. In Gary the control of the school will be under a manager and a learning director will serve under him.

Teachers in the future may find great difficulty in making the student record-keeping task manageable without some systematic method for accumulating, organizing, and filing information about each individual's progress. To accomplish this purpose, a real-time information storage and retrieval system is needed with information being fed into the data bank daily or weekly. In exploring this concept, Educational Testing Service (ETS) is developing an Automated Instructional Monitoring System (AIMS) that is based on a model that is keyed to a few specific teaching systems.[1] A diagnostic capability has been added wherein the system can recognize certain conditions in the information about a student that would suggest certain kinds of remedial work and training. The first step in such a system is to develop a model keyed to the curricula and to automate the school records as a basis for more widespread individualized instruction.

Closely related to the teacher's need to monitor individual students' progress is the status leader's need for information about the entire school system. ETS is exploring the feasibility of developing a system that would provide for efficient collection of educational information and presentation of that information to status leaders as an aid in identifying problems, weighing alternatives, and making decisions. This information system will give school administrators and supervisors the facts they need about the resources that affect the management and results of their educational programs. Thus, Educational Systems Information Program (ESIP) will assist status leaders in answering such deceptively simple questions as: What is being taught? How is it being taught? How well is it being taught? What do people think about it? A preliminary study is taking place in Cincinnati where an audit of achievement in several academic areas in senior high schools is taking place. The audit is aimed at determining how a broad range of information about the achievement of students, as a group, can be obtained more efficiently with less time and cost than is required for individual assessment.

The Education Audit Institute in Washington, D. C. has been established to provide assistance to schools and educational agencies in the rapidly developing new field of educational accountability. The Institute will assist operating school systems in accounting for the results of their educational programs and in training and preparing the profes-

---

[1] *Twenty-One Years Later: ETS Today* (Princeton, N.J.: Educational Testing Service, 1970), pp. 11–14.

sional staff for a self-appraisal role. The drive to achieve more effective individualized education has given impetus to the need to devise a series of competent practices that will enable any educational agency to determine its progress in relation to self-established goals and to pinpoint its successes, as well as locate the program gaps that require attention.

CURRICULUM AND TEACHING

Curriculum Change

The whole area of the curriculum is undergoing rapid and exciting change. Much new knowledge and authority in curriculum development is beginning to formulate from the interdisciplinary areas of sociology, political science, economics, psychology, and philosophy. The basic discipline of supervision and educational administration now is providing new knowledge concerning the management and facilitation of educational systems. Even the pattern of the traditional curriculum is undergoing remarkable change as the result of new concepts, such as the nongraded curriculum and the modular schedule. New, predictive systems of education are being exploited as the search for new arrangements and categories of accumulated information is systematized into a more meaningful pattern of learning for children. Social and economic forces, demographic pressures, technological advances, and the explosion of knowledge are all making vital impressions in the realm of curriculum change. Both political and administrative forces are fostering rather sizable appendages to the curriculum program: programs for culturally disadvantaged youth and de facto integration, congressional programs devoted to the needs of special-interest groups, and other similar plans, are recognizable characteristics of the revisions taking place in the curriculum. Even the opposition to many facets of public education by the extremist groups has taken its toll on the type of modification found in current programs. Court decisions, religious dissension, and racial strife have brought widespread adaptations to the curriculum that are sometimes based more on expediency than on long-range, professional judgment. The supervisor and administrator, however, must not overlook the fact that the center of energy for curricular revision and innovation ultimately should be in the school. As indicated by King and Brownell in *The Curriculum and the Disciplines of Knowledge,* the school is an epitome of the world of knowledge and the well springs for change lie in the communities of discourse which characterize this world. The nucleus for change must be established in the school with a commitment from faculty members. It is with this school-centered group that the supervisory staff of the future undoubtedly will have its greatest impact.

Teacher Training

New developments in the teaching-learning field could hardly take place without a strong assist from improved teacher training techniques. As modern technological devices such as television, programmed learning, and the computerized classroom are developed there must be corresponding changes in the teacher behavior characteristics that can accommodate the new requirements. Realizing that in-service training procedures must be developed to accommodate teachers currently on the job, intriguing possibilities are presented to teacher training institutions as to ways in which they can prepare their graduates to face a new world of instructional methodology and technology. As J. Lloyd Trump has so aptly indicated in the area of improved staff utilization, there is a pressing need to change the nature of teacher presentations, to change the character of independent study, to provide for more student discussion, and to change the process of evaluation of students if we are to improve the quality of learning in tomorrow's school. These and other changes must be accommodated by a vigorous appraisal and revitalization of teacher training programs. The Teacher Education Experimental Project represents a unique effort to provide career teachers with a professional curriculum that becomes an integral part of the total program in higher education for a minimum period of six years. A strong liberal educationl overtone is advanced for the first three years, the fourth year is largely laboratory-centered, and the fifth year is an intensive internship period. The sixth year represents the beginning of professional employment coupled with a return to the campus to attend research seminars as a basis for a systematic review of their new teaching experiences. The project, in time, will provide liberally educated and technically competent teachers who will soon become the educational leaders of tomorrow.

An interesting experiment is being conducted by the New York City Schools through their School-Community Committee for Educational Excellence in a search for ways of producing more effective teachers and inducing experienced teachers to move into areas of cultural disadvantage. The New York experiment would place teacher trainees as assistant teachers during their senior year in college. Their first postgraduate year would include training as a beginning teacher; the second postgraduate year would result in their placement as a full-time teacher under supervision. Such a proposal will be extremely helpful in providing a program of training articulation as the teacher trainee moves from the college to a teaching position. Utilization of such a technique as the Flanders system of interaction analysis also shows good potential for teacher training as well as teacher evaluation. The observer recording a teacher trainee's class session would make a rating of 20 to 25 observations per minute according to the teacher's activities under categories which would include teacher talk, direct and indirect influence, and student talk. Such an analysis of teaching acts as they occur through spontaneous classroom interaction provides a good basis for the analysis of the teaching-learning situation. Tomorrow's supervisory staff undoubtedly will be more intimately involved in both planning and facilitation of teacher training programs so that the professional products of these institutions of higher learning will have less difficulty in adapting themselves to the realities of the everyday teaching situation.

Teacher Retention

Recognizing that the early years of a teacher's career are exceedingly important in terms of that teacher's later contributions, Washington educators have initiated a state-wide project to assist this individual in making a successful beginning. The Project for the Orientation and Induction of New Teachers (POINT) is a joint effort of the Washington State Department of Education, the Washington Association of Education, and NEA's National Commission on Teacher Education and Professional Standards (NCTEPS). The POINT project recognizes that teacher-education institutions must assume responsibility for assisting beginning teachers, that new teachers should be assigned light, favorable teaching loads, that expert supervision must be made available to them, and that effective guidance must be provided to help them assess their teaching potential. In one experiment, teacher trainees are interviewed and accepted for employment at the end of their junior year in college; in their senior year they continue their studies while receiving their first induction into teaching. The internship or residency requirement will continue into their graduate year as they pursue their academic and professional program in conjuction with the same school system where they began teaching earlier. The use of videotape recordings, summer camp programs, student teacher induction programs, and other extensive orientation techniques will be utilized during the first three or four years to assist the new teacher toward becoming a competent, professional educator. New strategies in interviewing will assist further in the development of techniques to make possible the selection of the "right person" for the "right position." This critical and sensitive task can best be accomplished on the basis of a "structured" interview situation in which the events and impressions of any interview can be based upon information that follows a reasonably precise pattern of development that represents adherence to the basic, required knowledge as agreed upon earlier by district educators.

A recent survey of the Special Committee on the Assignment of Teachers appointed by the National Commission on Teacher Education and Professional Standards (NCTEPS) has shown that much attention must be given to teacher assignment by supervisors and administrators. Concerning those who were misassigned, 59 per cent did not have subject matter competence appropriate to the grade level and/or subject taught, and 25 per cent lacked training in teaching methods appropriate to those areas. What must be done to correct this situation? The NEA Commission made these recommendations: (1) experienced teachers should be designated to work with beginning teachers; (2) multiple-interview techniques should be used in hiring; (3) experienced teachers should be moved from one school to another to teach courses for which they are specifically prepared; and (4) the use of a team-teaching arrangement to assist in the gradual introduction of beginning teachers to their role and responsibility should be accomplished.

What can be learned from teachers who resign their positions? A New York experiment has adopted procedures for conducting formal terminal interviews with teachers who leave as a method of district evaluation. A four-page terminal questionnaire is used in conjunction with an oral interview with a district administrator. Such an approach provides the district with another means of determining the success or lack of success of its personnel and instructional programs, even though some of the reasons may be strictly nonprofessional. Such an appraisal can lead to improved induction programs, better teacher evaluation procedures, and improved supervisory practices by the school and district staff. In conjunction with the teacher drop-out problem, a study by Sorenson, Schaefer, and Nyman (1965) of teachers who expressed the intention of remaining in teaching, as compared with those who said that they intended to leave teaching, found that those teachers who planned to remain reflected an improving attitude toward the school and its curriculum, that most students were interested in school and would learn, that the teacher must have a positive mentally healthy point of view, that the teacher must work diligently to see that students do not fail, and that close classroom control must be maintained. Leavers were critical of the school and its students, would not define the responsibilities of teachers, and would not recommend strong controls for student behavior. Such results indicate that each district must work diligently to improve its program of induction of new teachers, that teacher placement services must give greater assistance to the rightful placement of new teachers, and that the supervisory staff must set the tone of two-way communication to and from the teacher.

TASKS AND EXPERIMENTATION

Earlier discussions have considered such innovations as independent study and research, educational television, teaching machines and programmed learning, testing, team teaching, and the nongraded classroom. In each of these areas remarkable progress is being made to adapt these innovations to the classroom. In the future, individualized instruction through the use of computers and other methods of self-study will require new skills on the part of the supervisory leader as he works with professional educators in this highly technical field. Supervisors and administrators will necessarily spend much time in assisting teachers in learning how to diagnose individual learning problems, using tutorial techniques to assist them with their learning difficulties, and interweaving the use of computerized equipment within the whole fabric of the classroom instructional program. Major changes must become effective in the development of the instructional program of the school in terms of its basic organization and its lock-step procedure. Its traditional graded system of assigning students must be replaced and a nongraded plan of assignment must be made with individualized plans being designed for each student within the school. Supervisors and administrators must assist faculty members in the proper assignment of space and facilities as they move toward a new world of instructional promise and possibility.

As students progress at a much faster or slower pace according to their individualized instructional experiences, the supervisory staff must work even more closely with teachers in assisting them with the development of new ideas and guidelines that can give challenge to students in terms of highly flexible rates of progress. Guidance personnel, librarians, and para-professional assistants will all be involved intimately in the plans of the supervisory staff as they give an assist to teacher progress. Precise job descriptions, availability of computerized equipment and document-retrieval systems, and the acquisition of highly specialized resource personnel will represent new emphases in the fulfillment of the supervisory task. Research demands, pilot experimental programs, and greater awareness in the whole area of human sensitivity and response to the computerized system will call forth from supervisors and administrators a comprehensive understanding of the new task and challenge of the automated-system learning approach. Trial and error will be an accepted technique for exploring and widening the horizon of the automated classroom world. In fact, computer-oriented instruments are affecting a large number of classroom teachers in the decade of the seventies and supervisory leaders must be prepared to make major decisions within the confines of this new technological world. Explaining, understanding, and implementing these teaching aids will soon become a routine task for administrators and supervisory personnel. Good public relations will include the orientation of pupils and the lay public as to the input and output expectations of the computerized classroom as it relates to the overall instructional program of the school.

Independent study, of course, presents new frontiers to the supervisory staff to overcome. Assistance must be given to teachers as to ways to help students budget their time, to prepare reports about the progress of students under the independent study plan, and to become extensively familiar with the current literature and research beginning to accrue in this challenging, new educational approach. Independent study plans such as those found at Abington, Pennsylvania, and Anaheim, California, must be carefully observed as classic projects in the areas of flexibility of scheduling and individualization of instruction. How to help a capable student spend a maximum amount of time in independent study, how to prevent potential drop-outs from leaving school, how to assist each student in adjusting his schedule to match both progress and ability, and how to utilize successful team-teaching techniques in conjunction with the modular plan are representative of new tasks confronting the supervisory staff.

The development of reading centers shows great promise in assisting teachers to diagnose reading difficulties, and in aiding them in the development of a planned program once the diagnosis has been made. The success of the new reading center approach is largely due to the in-service training of teachers who learned diagnostic techniques, the remedial method, and the availability of significant professional aids. Supervisors and administrators must encourage teachers to utilize in-service training opportunities in remedial reading, to continually explore for better methods of remedial instruction, to recognize the advantages to be gained from the reading center's clinical services, to utilize the latest instructional media as a means of strengthening and reinforcing the child's reading skills, and to develop techniques for greater inclusion and cooperation of the home in furthering the acquisition of reading skills.

The recent development of the Initial Teaching Alphabet system (I.T.A.) offers a new challenge in reading instructions as opposed to the traditional orthographic methods. In the event that the I.T.A. system takes on national significance, supervisors and administrators will be involved in reacting to another form of curriculum innovation, the major impact of which will be felt on classrooms of succeeding grade-levels. Changes in the attitudes of teachers, reading progress expectations, and even reading goals will be affected. The advent of unusual student activity in an early grade level, such as the use of card catalogs and encyclopedias, reference materials from the library, and newspapers and periodicals could bring drastic changes to the learning expectations of children in the lower-grade levels. Schools in lower socio-economic areas may be in a position to accelerate their programs in culturally deprived areas in the event that the movement is a success. It should be noted, however, that the program is in its exploratory stages and further research and experimentation will be necessary before decisions are made on wide-spread adaptations. This new writing medium offers a further illustration of continued scientific exploration in the exciting field of reading.

Another dimension in the area of reading progress is found in the implementation of programmed reading instruction. Supervisors and administrators will need to demonstrate to teachers how this new technique can be used. Reduction of board work, increased vocabulary, improved comprehension, and spelling proficiency through repetition may be outgrowths of this new media. The most notable example of the success of this program is found in the Brookfield, Illinois school system. Lastly, the stirring possibility of grading essays by computer is fast becoming a reality. Programming computers for this task must begin with human evaluation and involve human judgment that will permit a high reliability coefficient in testing. With highly reliable computer-program discrimination, English teachers and other persons who require literary materials from their students will be able to spend their time making critical idea judgments and suggestions regarding essays as opposed to the routinized, time-devouring task of grading essay papers.

The middle school offers a uniquely new concept that is largely free of the image of the senior high school and is at the same time, free to serve as an educational laboratory for the early adolescent. Devised as a plan to serve the transitional phase between the paternalism of the neighborhood elementary school and the highly departmentalized environment of the senior high school, the middle school departs yet further from the elements of the present junior high school in its early sophistication and its high-school-oriented program. The most common organizational structure of the middle school is found in the 4-4-4 plan which attempts to provide for a maximum flexibility of scheduling that will accommodate the varying rates, interests, and abilities of adolescent pupils. Another organizational plan is described as the 5-3-4 system. If the gradual replacement of the traditional junior high school program occurs, the middle school will offer interesting possibilities to supervisors and administrators as they attack the problem of curriculum improvement within the structure of a new educational plan.

The introduction of fifth and sixth graders to some areas of specialization, the encouragement of additional group activities among middle-school children, the rearrangement of grades to assist in de facto integration and better racial balance within communities, the inclusion of stronger guidance programs for middle-school children, the possibilities for complete nongradedness, and the adaptation of the school to individualists who appear to have more in common with each other than with any other grade level, are organizational problems and challenges that will demand the skill of the supervisory staff in readjusting school faculties to the new middle school programs wherever they occur. The middle school system is most notable in such places as New York City, New Haven, Connecticut, Pittsburgh, Pennsylvania, and Little Rock, Arkansas.

Two interesting developments that require the attention of supervisory personnel are the proposals for district-wide accreditation and the departmentalization of elementary schools. There is real logic in the idea that accreditation should be more than just school-wide. The lay public is not only interested in the quality of the program administered in the various schools in the district, but also in the total educational program provided for the district. If district accreditation, in addition to school accreditation, becomes an important phase of the task of the various regional accreditation commissions, supervisors and administrators will be highly involved in a new and important aspect of evaluation procedures. Far greater efforts must necessarily be expended by supervisory staffs in terms of unifying, articulating, and coordinating the various elements of the district's educational program. Disjointed educational plans and efforts have resulted in some districts because of the lack of a total evaluation system. Total district accreditation should help correct this. The movement toward the departmentalization in elementary schools should not be viewed by supervisors and administrators as totally improbable and unrealistic. The NEA's Educational Research Service recently identified 97 large school systems which were using departmentalization in one or more elementary schools. In an age of increasing specialization there appears to be a need for more than one teacher to teach certain academic subjects such as English, social studies, mathematics, and science.

As indicated by Steinnett, Kleinmann, and Ware, *Professional Negotiation in Public Education,* since 1960 there have been concerted drives "to gain for public school teachers the right to collective action in negotiating with school boards regarding salaries, conditions of work, and other matters." Although supervisors and principals are seldom directly involved in professional negotiations, there is evidence that the results of their professional acts may become matters of discussion at the negotiating table. Such items as teacher load, class size, teacher assignment, sabbatical leaves, discipline of teachers, supplies and equipment, and a host of other items that relate to the instructional program are matters of direct concern to supervisory leaders as they work with the professional faculty. As teachers continue to show increased aggressiveness and even militancy in terms of their rights and obligations to contribute to the development of educational programs and policies, supervisors and administrators must become exceedingly well informed in the whole area of professional negotiation and collective bargaining. These individuals must be able to discern the difference between what is considered negotiable and what is not, to recognize areas of teacher concern and tension, and to be able to establish continuing, harmonious relations with faculty members as they seek to expand their professional role as affluent members of the educational hierarchy.

SOLVING MAJOR ISSUES AND PROBLEMS

As leaders in status positions in the school system, supervisors face a difficult task as they attempt to identify the major issues and problems that must be solved by all professional educators in the years that lie ahead. Some problems that confront the instructional leader, such as sit-ins, boycotts, or walk-outs (actual or threatened), are highly visible actions that are both abrasive and abrupt in their effect on the educational program. Other problems, like the existence of inert teachers who operate under a different philosophic pattern in regard to change than the creative planners, represent a subtle yet effective challenge to the programmed operational scheme that is designed to move the organization forward. Some of these issues and problems are discussed as a basis for projection into the future as it relates to supervisory leadership.

Supervisory personnel, now and in the future, have a single, basic purpose which is to improve the *teaching-learning situation.* There is nothing more important in a school than that which happens when a teacher relates to a pupil.[2] The supervisor must strive to develop new programs of education, but in the light of each development there must be a corresponding change in the teaching role if the implementation is to be successful. His task is to make certain that change is a balanced affair and that as new programs in education become effective there will be new descriptions of the roles of teachers and new definitions as to the manner in which teachers and pupils will relate to one another.

[2]William Georgiades, "New Dimensions of the Teaching Art," unpublished paper presented at the CASA Conference, December 7, 1969.

More and more emphasis will be placed on establishing new and improved learning environments in which the roles of guidance, direction, and encouragement will be substantial. As individualization of instruction is promoted, the role of the teacher will change correspondingly through the development of such cooperative teaching techniques as team teaching, varied group instruction, and the advancement of independent study. Much discretion must be used as innovations are selected and each choice should reflect the type of community involved, the concerns of the faculty, the extent of support available in terms of funding and leadership, and other similar factors. Each change agent, such as supervisor or principal, must reflect carefully on how the teaching-learning act will be affected by each innovation and be certain that pupils, teachers, and the community are aware of its implications.

The constant challenge to improve the teaching-learning situation often is the result of a united dissatisfaction with the status quo. For those who govern our schools, there is a corresponding demand for *accountability*. Because there exists a basic, legal responsibility for school governance vested in the hands of the administrative staff (hence in the area of supervision), there need to be three bases for honest sharing in the study and decision-making essential to the resolution of any situations or problems that may arise in the instructional program. This basis for working together is openness, independence, and the ability to live with ambiguity.[3] First, openness refers to being open to new experiences, new ways of knowing, new options, and new perceptions about the school, its educational program, and the direction in which it is moving. Second, there should be independence in the matter of critical analysis and evaluation before reaching a decision, rather than acquiescence to a decision based primarily on a popular-vote count. The supervisor must weigh the options for himself, whether it refers to a school boycott, a "professional day," or the threat of lodging a complaint with the board of education if certain instructional demands are not met. Emotional peer-group unreasonableness is a difficult force to stand up against, but it must be opposed if the group assumptions are patently false. Supervisors must encourage group members to do their own individual thinking as essential to any and all cooperative problem solving. Third, living with ambiguity is representative of living with the unknown and suspending judgment until all the evidence is in. Supervisors must provide an emotional climate that accepts questioning while tolerating the frustrations of unsolved problems. Teachers and students must be given a reasonable opportunity to

---

[3]Editorial, NASSP Spotlight, no. 89, September-October 1969, pp. 7–8.

experiment in areas that have been studied and on which there is agreement, recognizing that stability alone is not the mark of a good school. The public must be given assurance that the schools are responsive and responsible to them while the staff is attempting to develop more precise ways of accounting for their actions.

Few *in-service programs* for educational leaders have been successful unless they have had a strong regional or national base. Constant attention to issues that are important to practicing instructional leaders must be given on a broad base. Typical of these are the 1970 career-development programs sponsored by the AASA National Academy for School Executives (NASE). The academy represents a unique concept in career development which links meaningful recognition with in-service study by educational leaders. The seminars and clinics of the Academy focus on the emerging and complex problems whose resolution demands new skills and insights. Supervisors and administrators who demonstrate great concern for their own professional development should attempt to enroll in this or similar types of in-service training experiences that will enhance their own supervisory skills and techniques.

Organizations require concentrated effort in the development of common operational goals that are guided by a common ethics structure. The purpose of the supervisory, and thus, the planning function, is to build a *synergistic environment* within which the institution can cultivate synergistic policies and programs to improve teaching and learning.[4] A climate such as this will permit a variety of differing philosophies and personalities to work harmoniously together as well as provide opportunities for them to grow in stature and responsibility. The purpose of the synergistic relationship is to maintain balance in the institution, allow for reform measures to take place due to the variance in personnel represented, and eliminate manipulation as a tool for gaining ends. This system will permit the emergence of new leadership and foster interaction among leaders already established in the organization. The entire process of self-renewal will be aided as this process continues.

Earlier discussions have revealed the concern by educational leaders for *projection methods* that would enable them to look into the future, recognizing that the image becomes more and more uncertain the further the projections are made. Where rigorous analysis is not possible because hard data are unavailable, because theory is inadequate, or for other reasons, the judgment of experts must be relied

---

[4]L. Craig Wilson, *et al.*, *Sociology of Supervision* (Boston: Allyn and Bacon, 1969), pp. 351 and 361.

upon. The Delphi Technique is one method of using judgments systematically by serving two functions in solving a given problem, or in choosing among innovations, by: (1) generating ideas and judgments; and (2) combining the judgments of panel members into a single position.[5] Delphi structures a carefully designed program of sequential, individual interrogations (usually conducted by questionnaires) interspersed with information feed-in and opinion feedback. The Delphi technique can be applied to situations involving factual judgment (*this* may be the case), conditionally factual judgment (*if this* is done, then this may be the case), and value-judgment estimation in conjunction with preference selection. Through several rounds (perhaps three or four) of individual contacts with members of a panel, a revision of earlier projection estimates occurs and a convergence of ideas and opinions takes place, thus leading to a true consensus as a basis for projection on an issue that needs clarification. Utilizing this technique permits supervisors to project on issues and problems through the crystallization of the reasoning process and to discover and pinpoint controversies that may be at the base of these same issues and problems.

One of the root causes for the insecurity teachers feel in instruction and pupils reflect as learners is the earlier failure on the part of educators to answer the question, "What observable or measurable performance does the school want learners to be able to accomplish as a result of twelve years of formal education?" Much of previous discussions have hinged on methods that can be used by supervisors to help teachers attain desired *learning systems* in pupils of all ages and stages of development. In explicit terms, there are several basic steps that the supervisor can assist the teacher in taking that will make it possible to develop a hierarchy of learner performances. The concrete steps are these:[6] (1) development of gross learning objectives (behavior and content) in inquiry and communications skills; (2) development of explicit learning objectives stated in behavioral terms; (3) development of evaluation instruments from precise learning objectives stated in behavioral terms; (4) development of learning systems based on evaluation instruments; (5) during the development of the learning systems, the individual components are tried out with representative samples of learners and teachers; (6) following experimental production of the learning systems, full-scale tryouts are conducted with representative samples of learners and teachers; and (7) dissemination of the new learning systems based primarily on demonstration workshops and in-service train-

[5]Werner Z. Hirsch, Editor, *Inventing Education for the Future* (San Francisco: Chandler, 1967), pp. 14–15. For a summary by Olaf Helmer, see Chapter 4.

[6]James N. Keeline, "Rationale for the Development of Learning Systems," unpublished paper for *Instructional Innovations*, 1970, p. 6.

ing sessions for teachers. School districts must possess the capability of producing learning systems based on objectives within parameters set by the local school population, community representatives, teachers, and supervisory personnel. A learning system based on specific, local determinations can achieve the desired learning outcomes best suited for that locality. Supervisors should seek for ways to develop learning systems that exist within the personnel base of operations in their own school system.

A new educational function that is appearing on the horizon is instruction of staff members by supervisors and administrators as to the structure of the organization and how it relates to the rationality of *shared educational leadership.* Increasing numbers of professionals are receiving far more extensive training and preparation than their earlier counterparts. This, in turn, heavily loads the teaching profession with professionals who hold extremely high credentials. Basic skills in organizational activity can provide an opportunity for many of these professionals to reach personal as well as organizational goals. Differing rationales as to the requirements of local organization and instructional help are aspects that need the utmost attention and analysis if the supervisor is to enjoy the goodwill and cooperation of his fellow workers. In view of hostility by staff members to the superior-inferior tactics of past autocratic approaches to administration, today's supervisor must base his actions primarily on the premise that he is responsible for the education of staff members so that they can function successfully within the organization. This requires that faculty play an integral part in the designing of organizational goals and promoting the development of controls and structure that permit the organization to engage itself in a process of self-renewal and re-direction.

Strong evidence exists that today's school should be closer to the community. The factors involved in greater parent participation in school-community affairs has been discussed earlier. A vibrant movement in this direction has been the *community-school program* with its major focus directed toward relating the instructional programs in the day-time classes to life and its activities in the community.[7] Coordinating classroom activity with family life, with peer-group associations, and with institutional influence requires new and different experiences in both the preparation programs and in-service programs for professional personnel. Classroom teaching in a community operation will change radically as teachers become the directors of learning as opposed to

---

[7]Clyde M. Campbell, "The Community School: Its Past—Its Present—Its Future," *The Community School and Its Administration* (The Mott Program), vol. VIII, no. 1 (September 1969.)

dispensers of knowledge. Supervisors must learn to work with star teachers who will: direct the learning experiences of children for whom they are responsible; assign children to beginning teachers, interns, para-professionals, other students, or to teaching machines; and assist neighbors, friends, and citizens at large to motivate youth to learn. In fact, successful cooperation between the home, the neighborhood, and the school will be a significant breakthrough in learning within the next five years. Citizens will become active in influencing decision-making to be assured that the interests of their children come ahead of other interests. In the future they will indeed be involved in policy development, program evolvement, and the evaluation of achievement. Supervisors must make the community school a laboratory and proving ground as a basis for forming a unity of intent on the part of the community toward taking a giant step to make school-community cooperation possible under a new and different system of reference.

The systems approach in education has brought about a greater interest in *cybernetics*. Cybernetics is representative of a new discipline that focuses on the investigation of communication and control—two areas that are of prime concern to the supervisory task. Communication and control, through cybernetics, suggest a concern for component elements of a system and for how they might function together to produce the most effective integrated system.[8] An example of feedback theory in the area of control would suggest that when an error between the expectations of what parents want their children to learn in school and what the children actually learn becomes too great, the force of public opinion (communication) makes itself felt upon the board of education who in turn will make changes in policy (control) to reduce the error. To fully understand the applications of cybernetics, the supervisor needs to take a pragmatic view of the communications and control system as it operates in almost any sociological, political, or economic system. A planned systems approach does provide for the constant monitoring of the internal activities of the system so that necessary adjustments can be made to reduce error in expectations or achievements. Inasmuch as many supervisory decisions are made under conditions that are not certain, supervisors must seek to develop systems that will be both predictive and rational in the handling of errors that infiltrate any decision-making procedure.

As youth in the community become more and more active in the mainstream of American thought and action, supervisors must seek

[8]Frank W. Banghart, *Educational Systems Analysis* (London: Macmillan, 1969), pp. 27 and 30.

ways in which they can help youth find *social involvement,* work to-gether, learn from other youth, learn from citizens in the community, and confront the problems that are found in the locality. The current stresses in today's society indicate that youth and adult groups do need to work together on new programs that will allow for differences of opinion and expectations to arise and for these to be resolved through positive interaction. Through released time or some other means, youth in school must become more actively involved in social service work in the community as a means of affecting behavioral change and permit-ting extensive participation in solving the problems the community faces—an avowed demand of many youth. It is imperative that teachers be given help in assisting students to become actively involved in the social process, to learn how to make dialog fruitful and meaningful, to develop new attitudes and beliefs concerning others, and to feel that they are engaged in projects that will improve the conditions that beset society. Schools should promote programs of community service in many areas of the curriculum in which youth would be able to take a more active role in solving problems that take on local and regional significance.

For too long a period of time the *minority problem* has been devoid of meaningful action at the local level in many communities. If the school is to retain its validity and virility in this crucial area, educators everywhere in America must begin to make inroads in devising a cur-riculum program that solves one of the most demanding problems—minority opportunities—confronting our society. In a time of awesome social readjustment, particularly with Negroes, the school must make several decisive moves and supervisory leaders should be prepared to help teachers become more effective in working with ethnic minority groups. Supervisors should establish several bases from which teachers can function: (1) communicate in a socially responsible way by inform-ing laymen about the knowledge and learning function that the school is fulfilling; (2) provide listening posts in the school so that minority wants and grievances can be heard; (3) re-examine the traditional cur-ricula objectives and translate them into concrete statements that em-phasize both long-range and short-range needs; (4) attempt to give youth from deprived homes the kinds of experiences that they are likely to read about so that they can correlate content with real-life experi-ences; (5) form genuine neighborhood partnerships between the com-munity and the school; (6) stimulate motivation on the part of the home and neighborhood to raise the level of learning that takes place in the community; (7) utilize greater amounts and higher levels of instruc-tional materials regarding the heritage and contributions of ethnic minority groups; (8) recruit well-qualified, mature teachers to teach in the ghetto, utilizing minority staff wherever possible; and (9) open more formal channels for the flow of communications between the minority public and the instructional staff.

THE SUPERVISORY LEADER'S ROLE IN THE FUTURE

The central concern for any supervisory task force will turn eventually toward the future dimensions of the role and function of supervisory leadership. Is the role one, as some experts predict, that will fade in importance in the next decade or two because of the rapid upsurgence of the professional preparation of the teacher coupled with his increasing tendency to move toward a power-position at the policy-making level? Or does the increased sophistication and specialization of educational matters appear as a symbolic augury that argues favorably for the increase of supervisory leadership at ever higher levels of operational creativity and decision-making? In ten or twenty years the vestiges of time will supply objective evidence as to the ascendency or decline of supervisory services. In the meantime, careful investigation of the developments and trends that appear on the horizon shows there is good evidence that instructional supervision and its related functions will continue to be in increased demand in the decades of the seventies and eighties. What, then, is the rationale behind such a claim?

There is ample confirmation that those persons who assume positions of supervisory leadership, along with concurrent teacher growth and development, are readily keeping pace in terms of the profession's demands relative to increased preparation. Supervisors and administrators, as they relate to their instructional role, are being given opportunities to become involved in decision-making at increasingly higher levels as the problems that they face are less and less insignificant and isolated. Perhaps this is best demonstrated by the fact that the supervisory role has changed from an inspectorial function in years past to increasingly new heights related to creative instructional leadership. In ever greater numbers supervisory staff members are working more closely with faculty personnel, involving these people in the highly important task of formulating basic decision, and helping them seek new and innovative ways in which to solve instructional problems. The art of supervision, in fact, is becoming more closely related to teaching behavior and the teaching acts in terms of professional diagnosis, program design, and instructional implementation. Only the most highly skilled professional leaders would ever pretend to diagnose professional problems in the area of instruction and then to provide guidance and the means of instituting alternative solutions and activities that could insure instructional progress. As a facilitator of instructional improvement within the complex framework of the educational milieu, he has increasingly grave responsibilities to free latent and inert professional talents of teaching faculties so that they may perceive the result of their own progress as related to the essential services provided by supervisory personnel.

Recent developments in demonstrating the increasing skill of supervisors and administrators include involving faculty members in an integral role in the development of teacher behavior and teacher performance, utilizing faculty talents in developing many instructional experiences, and in moving towards a more permissive approach to the solution of faculty-administrative problems related to instruction. Positive efforts are being made to widen the perception of faculty personnel as they concern themselves with the nature of the problems that confront them, and to recognize workable methods of coordinating faculty-administrator cooperative efforts in arriving at their solution. The current focus on curriculum innovation and change has permitted greater recognition of the need for trial and error techniques. Such knowledge makes allowance for what may appear initially to be rather crude efforts toward operational improvement followed by objective evaluative procedures. Increased attention is being given to the relationship of teacher behavior to the effectiveness of classroom learning by supervisors and administrators as they strive to assist in the modification and improvement of the teaching act.

In a time when professional requirements are increasing generally, those who fulfill a supervisory role in one capacity or another are no exception. Graduate schools of education throughout the nation are closely examining their selection procedures to be certain that only the most qualified students are admitted to the preparation program. Both theoretical and practical experiences are being refined as a means of assuring the competent preparation of young people who assume a supervisory role. Most noteworthy of these experiences are the new emphases toward an interdisciplinary approach, internship opportunities, simulation training, and sensitivity training. Student evaluation is often correlated with "specialist" programs and degree-program requirements further assuring graduate school faculties that the persons who complete their program represent students of high caliber. Periodic follow-ups of graduate students who are now in the field are used to solicit suggestions and recommendations as to needed changes for preparation programs as reviewed in the light of early, practical on-the-job experiences. Viewed in future terms, the major preoccupation of graduate faculties will include the present problem of selecting the right persons for training in instructional leadership. Ratings of effectiveness, advancement potential, innovative tendencies, and upward occupational potential are data items that are being collected as criteria to assist in the development of objective-type predictor factors. Recognition of the fact that supervisors and administrators, as they develop more skill in diagnosing human relations problems within their organizations, can become more effective change agents represents a new facet for increased sensitivity training for supervisory trainees. In addition, the whole problem area of developing techniques for acquiring knowledge about community expectations for school programs and related activities, overcoming the inability to make realistic interpretations of educational needs while in a supervisory or administrative post, and developing mechanisms for maintaining the adaptability of any educational organization so that it can respond to social needs, are important aspects for cognitive and sensitivity training for supervisors in preparation. An added mode of instructional simulation has been found in gamed instructional simulation. A functional simulation technique, it presents decision units in terms of points requiring action and is accompanied by feedback techniques as a result of the action consequences. The input-output factors can be related to simulation of social institutions at the subcomputer level and are able to provide ready-made exposure for persons who wish to learn more about the many facets of organizational activity. This new technique offers an interesting practice procedure in terms of simulating administrative and supervisory experiences.

New major commitments are found in the areas of communication and instructional media. For years major impediments to good communication as a result of a highly structured and formalized line type of administrative organization has made it exceedingly difficult for instructional leaders to communicate well with teachers and other staff members. Both verbal and nonverbal communication must be facilitated by a three-way approach as communication of this type employs upward, downward, and horizonal forces as representative of the many types of communication that must be maintained by the supervisory staff. As disruptive, separatist forces continue the exploitation of public education, greater skills will be demanded of supervisory personnel in maintaining and promoting a strong communication system that understands the needs of individuals and groups that comprise the educational organization. Further, the introduction of new instructional media to the classroom will make it imperative that greater efforts be made to seek creative teachers who are interested in experimenting with such media. With technological machinery providing increased educational effort toward achievement in the classroom, supervisors and administrators must continue to assist teachers to understand the rapid developments that are taking place in the programming and utilization of imaginative new equipment arriving on the market.

In the final analysis, the views of the sociologist in terms of influence or leadership are representative of a unique form of social participation that gives rise to the increasingly important position of the instructional leader in the social system. The sociologist considers such basic factors as orderliness, uniformity, and patterning as essential elements in the development of basic principles that will lead to the control and the prediction of the behavior of human beings. It is through the development of such a viable set of principles that the supervisory leader will in the future become an increasingly effective agent of change. As he assists in the definition and redefinition of school objectives, performs diagnostic services as a skilled practitioner, strengthens the organizational climate in the school system, and clarifies the relationships that educators have to one another, he truly becomes an agent for sustaining the creative efforts of professional personnel that result in change and innovation. As he functions in relation to both institutional and individual dimensions of the school's social system, he is in a unique position to create an atmosphere for change in which teachers and others will be able to identify with and pursue the objectives of the larger group. The development of a strong leadership style, provision of opportunities for teachers to use their skills in areas leading to satisfaction, and the development of communication patterns that are both connective and accurate, will lead to organizational satisfactions that will promote a readiness for institutional change.

In view of the fact that change and innovation concern people, any new behavior that leads toward change, if it is to be successful, must be congruent to the value system of the person involved in the change process. Such internalization of values must first be accomplished by assisting the individual in the redefinition of what may be outmoded and even fallacious value concepts. Once new values or value systems have been established, existing behaviors can be modified to the extent that significant change can be both rewarding and satisfying to the individual involved. More and more adherence will be given to a complete understanding of the principles of learning as a basis of instituting change in organizational and classroom patterns. Greater reliance will be placed on faculty involvement and continuing research as a method of insuring continued commitment to the idea of change and innovation. In a very real sense, the future for supervisory leadership lies in the development of professional relations between individuals and between groups of individuals. The consequences of the supervisory function will be magnified by the development of new social phenomena in the world of the classroom and the school that will have salutary effects upon the learning process and teacher performance. In view of this, the future bodes well indeed for the continued prominence of the supervisory role as an instrument for change and innovation.

SUMMARY

The challenges to the dedicated supervisory leader in the years ahead likely will lie in the continued refinement and sophistication of procedures in terms of goal definition, socialization, planning, resolving conflicts, and evaluation. One of his more difficult tasks, in an era of high teacher preparation and militancy, will be the definition of the educational mission of the supervisory task force as it relates to specific behavioral objectives. The education profession in the decade of the seventies will demand assurance that the risk capital that is invested in supervision can be justified in terms of relevant research, development, and service as a means of helping the academic community to reach its goals. Evidence must be shown that a clinical approach to learning does benefit from having in key leadership positions in instruction persons who can assume responsibility to fashion and support educational programs of excellence for all youth. Both students and teachers will demand the development of new educational experiences that will remove the school from its cloistered atmosphere to one in which it will deal with the harsh realities, as well as the promise, of the outside world. Today's teachers, in general, are not ready for this difficult and acrimonious surge into a higher level of educational involvement with the community and it will take extraordinary supervisory leadership to make this transition possible for the benefit of students, teachers, and the public alike.

Education in the future no longer will be solely a reflector of "what society is," but it will also contribute to the conceptualization of "what society should be." Supervisors will be in a key position not only to assist the faculties in finding ways to educate young people to deal with short-range and long-range social problems, but also to help guide the school in an attack upon viable societal perplexities in the role of an institution ready to challenge the rejectors of cultural advancement and improvement. In short, educators will find themselves working with multipower bases that include not only the internal organizational structure of the school, but the external bases of the home, the church, and the community. The supervisor's task will be to weld the individual strands of power together in a unified support pattern for the development and extension of the curriculum framework. The enterprise must be geared to a dominant, dynamic pace wherein resolute interaction can take place and the stress of negativism and inertia can be overcome.

Much emphasis will be placed upon the development of models that illustrate the manner in which teacher in-service education programs can be created. Analyzing coping behavior, utilizing simulated game situations, and selecting videotape descriptions of teaching strategies will represent some of the methods used to improve faculty perception and skill. The models will designate a configuration of the school's antecedent conditions, training programs, and desired outcomes as the planned program is put into effect. Value systems and attitudinal structures will be examined closely to determine the kinds of decisions to be made in reference to implementing the modular plan. The new capabilities of the model system will enable institutions to concentrate on much longer range plans by incorporating computer components that will revolutionize the storage and retrieval of information that can be commandeered by the educational leadership force when required.

In effect, the supervisory leader in tomorrow's world will be highly engaged in the process of change as it is reflected in an organizational scheme that reacts readily to the expectations placed upon it. With group goals representing the focal point of the institution's thrust to satisfy a large spectrum of societal demands, the organization's structure will be much more flexible. As a result, the proliferation of personnel hierarchical pegs in the organization will gradually be replaced by a closer, more equal relationship between faculty and supervisory staff. Group solidarity will characterize the activities of the professional staff as they dedicate their efforts to the improvement of educational programs through the processes of change, innovation, cooperation, and perceptive insight into the demands of tomorrow's world of educational opportunity and challenge.

SELECTED REFERENCES

Association for Supervision and Curriculum Development. *Ethnic Modification of the Curriculum.* Washington, D.C.: National Education Association, 1970.

Association for Supervision and Curriculum Development. *Supervision: Emerging Profession.* Washington, D.C.: National Education Association, 1969.

Association for Supervision and Curriculum Development. *The Unstudied Curriculum: Its Impact on Children.* Washington, D.C.: National Education Association, 1970.

Bolt, William J. *An Educational System for the Seventies: A Plan for Action.* Palo Alto, California: Monographs for the Seventies, 1971.

Clark, Kenneth B., and Alex C. Sherriffs. *How Relevant Is Education in America Today?* Washington, D.C.: American Enterprise Institute, 1971.

Haddan, Eugene E. *Evolving Instruction.* New York: Macmillan, 1970.

Inlow, Gail M. *Education: Mirror and Agent of Change.* New York: Holt, Rinehart and Winston, 1970.

Joyce, William, *et al.*, editors. *Elementary Education in the Seventies: Implications for Theory and Practice.* New York: Holt, Rinehart and Winston, 1970.

Miller, Richard I., editor. *Perspectives on Educational Change.* New York: Appleton-Century-Crofts, 1967.

Pratte, Richard. *Contemporary Theories of Education.* Scranton: Intext, 1971.

Thomas, J. Alan. *The Productive School: A Systems Analysis Approach to Educational Administration.* New York: John Wiley, 1971.

Index

279